THE
ASTON
VILLA
STORY

THE ASTON VILLA STORY

Anton Rippon

The Breedon Books
Publishing Company
Derby

First published in Great Britain by
The Breedon Books Publishing Company Limited
44 Friar Gate, Derby DE1 1DA
1993

© Breedon Books Publishing Co Ltd 1993

ISBN 1 873626 49 5

Printed and bound by Hillmans Printers, Frome, Somerset.
Covers printed by BDC Printing Services Ltd of Derby.

Contents

Introduction

THESE are great days for Aston Villa, who are now back at the very top and in 1993 pushed all the way for the first FA Premier League title before finishing runners-up. Indeed, with their fine stadium at Villa Park and the anticipation of still greater days to come, Villa supporters have much to look forward to in the months ahead.

Of course, Villa have long been assured of their place in football's rich history as one of the truly great clubs with a pedigree which stretches back to the last century. League champions and FA Cup winners when Queen Victoria still ruled, Villa continued their mighty progress into the 20th century and even in their, albeit brief, darker days, there has always been a talking point or two for the Villa faithful.

This book *The Story of Aston Villa* attempts to chart this fascinating football tale from its beginnings in 1874 right up to the end of the exciting 1992-93 season. It uses as its base a book by the same author first published in 1980 and has been subsequently updated to take into account all that has happened since, including, of course, another League championship and the crowning glory of the European Cup.

This book also differs greatly in the number and quality of photographs included in it, and for that must go thanks to Terry Weir, who has long been recording the events of Aston Villa through his camera, and Neil Simpson and Kevin Alcock of EMPICs of Nottingham, both for their agency photographs and their research at the Hulton-Deutsch Library in London.

Acknowledgements must also be made to the pioneering work of Peter Morris in his *Aston Villa: The First 100 Years* and Tony Matthews and David Goodyear for their painstaking efforts which resulted in *Aston Villa: A Complete Record*. Without the aforementioned, this book would have been so very much more difficult to produce.

So please sit back and take a journey through a magnificent football story, beginning in the gaslit days of Victorian England.

ASTON VILLA

Honours

Football League Champions
1893-94, 1895-96, 1896-97, 1898-99,
1899-1900, 1909-10, 1980-81
Runners-up
1888-89, 1902-03, 1907-08, 1910-11,
1912-13, 1913-14, 1930-31, 1932-33

Second Division Champions
1937-38, 1959-60
Runners-up
1974-75, 1987-88

Third Division Champions
1971-72

FA Cup Winners
1886-87, 1894-95, 1896-97, 1904-05,
1912-13, 1919-20, 1956-57
Runners-up
1891-92, 1923-24

Football League Cup Winners
1960-61, 1974-75, 1976-77
Runners-up
1962-63, 1970-71

European Cup Winners
1981-82

European Super Cup Winners
1982-83

A Golden Beginning

ACCORDING to legend, flickering Victorian gaslights were a favourite spawning ground for football clubs and the embryo of Aston Villa — one of the greatest names in the history of soccer — was no exception. It was under just such a lamp, so legend has it, in the misty cold of a winter's evening early in 1874, that members of the local Villa Cross Wesleyan Chapel lingered on their way home along Heathfield Road, Birchfield, and decided to take up soccer. Some 120 years later, Heathfield Road has disappeared in a merger with Trinity Road. But the football team which those young lads founded is now the proud owner of one of the best football grounds in the world, and also one of the finest pedigrees in the game. From that humble beginning grew the mighty Aston Villa.

The boys from Aston Cross already played cricket and, in this era of 'muscular Christianity', they now looked for a winter sport to keep them together. Strangely, Birmingham was not noted at that time for its soccer, although the game held sway in neighbouring towns like West Bromwich and Walsall. A few of the young men from the chapel had seen an impromptu game being played on wasteland near Heathfield Road and this gave them their idea. Soon, Birmingham would be as big a hotbed of soccer as anywhere.

Once the club was formed, it needed a captain, a ground on which to play and some opponents. The three requirements posed varying problems. A skipper was soon elected — a young man called Walter Price — but a ground and opposition were less easily come by. For a start there were very few pure soccer clubs in the city and something which comprised a curious mixture of association football and rugby was by far the most popular winter game.

The one big soccer power in Birmingham at that time was a club called Birmingham Clerks FC, formed as Birmingham Clerks by two Scots, J.Campbell Orr and John Carson, who was connected with the Queen's Park club of Glasgow, then the leading team in Scotland.

Clearly, Villa were not strong enough to meet the Clerks and so it was March 1874, some six weeks after they were founded, before Aston Villa Football Club could play their first match, and that was against a rugby team. The sides agreed to play 45 minutes under each code. So Aston Villa began their glorious history by fielding 15 players against Aston Brook St Mary's on a ground near Birchfield's present-day Wilson Road at Perry Barr.

The first half was played under rugby rules and Villa managed to reach half-time without any score being recorded for either side. In the second half, a round ball was produced and the teams continued the match under soccer rules — or Association (Sheffield) Rules as the code was named. Midway through the second period, Villa scored their first-ever goal when Jack Hughes neatly turned the ball past the rugby club's goalkeeper and when the final whistle sounded, Villa had won their inaugural match 1-0, despite the bizarre nature of its setting.

For the record, that first Aston Villa team was: W.Scattergood, W.H.Price, W.Weiss, D.J.Stevens, E.B.Lee, F.G.Matthews, H.Matthews, C.H. Midgley, J.Hughes, W.Such, H.Whateley, G.Page, A.H.Robbins, G.Greaves and T.Page. The attendance was said to be around 250.

Villa could not manage another game that season. Of the few other pure soccer teams around, none were considered weak enough to give Aston Villa a fair game. Besides Birmingham Clerks (later Calthorpe

FC after their ground at Calthorpe Park), other top teams, such as Wednesbury Old Athletic and Wolverhampton's Stafford Road Works FC, would have demolished that early Villa side.

In 1874-75, however, Villa managed games against such teams as St George's Excelsior and Aston Unity, and returned some creditable results, especially considering the youth of their club. Villa's early grounds included Aston Park, close to today's Villa Park, and Aston Lower Grounds Meadow, a venue which had also seen W.G.Grace play against the Australians and a team of American Indians introduce the game of lacrosse to Birmingham.

Just as we have seen that Victorian gaslamps seemed to play an important part in the early days of English soccer clubs, so too did the arrival of a few Scotsmen. Again, Aston Villa proved no exception to this rule and when a 21-year-old Scot called George Ramsey arrived in Birmingham in 1876, he was set to become one of the prime movers in taking the club on its first steps to greatness.

Ramsey was slightly built, but he made up for his lack of physical stature with a display of wizardry which soon had his teammates gasping with admiration. He dribbled around opposing defences wearing a tiny polo cap and soon captured the imagination of the faithful Villa supporters who were now turning up to see the new team play. Villa made him their skipper in 1876 and, as we shall see, Ramsey played an epic part in the club's rise to greatness, both on and off the field.

Yet another Scot was on his way to Birmingham to play a big part in the Villa story. In 1878, Archie Hunter arrived in the city from Ayr to play for the Calthorpe team of which he had heard so much. Fortunately for Villa, Hunter could not find the Calthorpe ground and instead ended up at the Villa ground. He became one of the club's most famous skippers — indeed, the first to lift the FA Cup — whilst Calthrope Football Club went out of existence as a major force in the game.

Meanwhile, the affairs of Aston Villa gathered momentum. Soccer was rapidly gaining a hold in the heavily industrialised Midlands and North, and Ramsey began to see that his club needed another ground if they were to take advantage of the ever-increasing attendances that were turning up on Villa match days.

It was on a fateful Sunday in 1876 that Ramsey and a fellow Scot called John Lindsay took a stroll to Perry Barr — then a village with a toll gate. Near Wellington Road, the visionary Ramsey spotted a piece of land used for grazing. He had found Villa's first real ground.

Quickly he discovered that the ground was rented from the Bridge Trust by a local butcher and soon drew up an agreement to sub-rent the field from the butcher for £5 per annum. Villa players used a nearby blacksmith's shed for dressing-rooms and made their headquarters at the Old Crown and Cushion pub, situated where Wellington Road met Aston Lane.

Villa's first game at Perry Barr was against Wednesbury Town, when just 21 people paid threepence each to watch the match. Villa's first 'gate' amounted, therefore, to 5s 3d (28p). But those figures would soon increase many times over as Ramsey and Hunter steered Villa onwards. The team at that time also included such players as Howard Vaughton and Eli Davis, who joined Villa from Wednesbury Strollers and played together as the club's left-wing attack. Sam Law played at centre-half, and two players wore headgear when they played: full-back Joe Simmonds sported a red cap and Charlie Johnstone appeared in a skull cap.

The Football League was still some years away from its formation (by Villa's William McGregor) but in 1879-80, the club entered the FA Cup for the first time and were drawn away to Stafford Road Works, the powerful Wolverhampton club who had lost only three games in five

Howard Vaughton, one of Villa's greatest forwards and the club's first full international when he scored five goals for England against Ireland in 1882. After his playing days were over, Vaughton continued to serve Villa as a director and club president.

years. Villa made the best possible start to their first Cup campaign. They drew 1-1 at Wolverhampton and won the replay 3-2 to earn a tie with Oxford University.

Oxford were then a power in the game and had already played in three FA Cup Finals, winning the trophy in 1874. Even so, Villa's attitude to the tie was astounding — they withdrew. To this day, no one knows why they took this drastic course of action. Whether the prospect of travelling to such a bastion of soccer supremacy daunted them we shall never know. But if it did, it was an act not in keeping with the Villa tradition. At any rate, Oxford went through and finally reached the Kennington Oval, where they lost the

FA Cup Final to Clapham Rovers.

Villa did win their first trophy in 1880, when they took the Birmingham Senior Cup, and in 1880-81 they again entered the FA Cup, despite their withdrawal of the previous season. In the second round they went to Nottingham and beat Forest 2-1.

The draw for the third round sent Villa back to Nottingham, this time to play the 'Notts Club', alias Notts County. They won 3-1, a victory which brought Villa face-to-face with Stafford Road Works again. The prospect of a home game against one of the Midlands most powerful sides filled the Perry Barr ground but, alas, Villa fell short of the occasion and the Wolverhampton team won 3-2 to reach the quarter-finals where they were knocked out by the Old Etonians, the eventual losing Finalists.

Villa's matches in the FA Cup and Birmingham Senior Cup were punctuated with top-class friendly games and on New Year's Day 1881, they had beaten Heart of Midlothian, the famous Edinburgh club, 4-1 with Richards, Hunter, Davis and Brown the Villa scorers.

In 1881-82, Villa received a bye into the third round of the FA Cup before beating Nottingham Forest 4-1 after two drawn games. In the next round, however, Wednesbury Old Athletic beat Villa 4-2 and their Cup involvement was over for another year.

But Aston Villa soon came bouncing back and the following season they reached the quarter-finals. Their Cup run started with a 4-1 win over Walsall Swifts at Perry Barr. Wednesbury Old Athletic were the next team to fall — by the same score and on the same ground — and then Villa faced Aston Unity in a local derby game. In their third successive home tie, Villa won 3-1 and when the draw for the fourth round was made, it pulled Villa out of the hat first yet again, this time against Walsall Town who were beaten 2-1.

In the last eight of the competition for the first time, Villa were forced to travel at last and they found themselves at Trent Bridge, Nottingham, where they faced Notts County. It was an epic Cup encounter in the best traditions. County went 3-0 ahead before Villa pulled right-

back into the game at 3-3. Then William Gunn, a famous name in both soccer and cricket, broke away from the Villa defence and scored the winner. Yet Villa might have forced a replay had the penalty-kick been invented at that time. A Notts defender used his hand to divert a shot from goal, but the resultant free-kick was not enough to rescue Villa.

The club had not much longer to wait, however, before it stamped its name on the coveted FA Cup for the first time. Although they travelled all the way to Glasgow for the 1883-84 fourth round and were soundly beaten 6-1 by Queen's Park, and despite being knocked out in the early stages of both the 1884-85 and 1885-86 competitions, there was glory just around the corner.

In 1886-87, Aston Villa became FA Cup holders at last, although it took them ten matches to lift the trophy, including four games with Wolverhampton Wanderers in a marathon tie.

Villa now had a magnificent side. George Ramsey had retired to concentrate his efforts on the post of Aston Villa secretary, but there were new faces in a Villa team which lined up in the more familiar positions of two full-backs, three half-backs and five forwards. Jimmy Warner had taken over in goal from Charlie Hobson and, in front of him, Villa had Frank Coulton and Joe Simmonds at full-back in place of Tom Riddell and Alf Jones. On the left wing, Dennis Hodgetts had joined Villa from the local side St George's FC and he lined up on the flank with Howard Vaughton who, along with Arthur Brown, had been capped by England against the other three Home Countries in the year that Villa had been knocked out of the FA Cup in that thrilling tie at Trent Bridge.

A record number of clubs — 132 — entered the FA Cup in 1886-87 and they represented England, Scotland, Ireland and Wales. There were Rangers, Hearts and Partick Thistle from North of the Border; Chirk, amongst several teams from the Principality; and Cliftonville from across the Irish Sea.

In the first round Villa started much closer to home, against their old rivals Wednesbury Old Athletic,

and won 13-0 with hat-tricks from Hodgetts, Hunter and Brown. Derby Midland were crushed 6-1 in the next stage and Villa moved on to the tie against Wolves. On 11 December 1886, Aston Villa and Wolves drew 2-2 at Perry Barr. Seven weeks later, and after seven and a half hours football, Villa finally won through 2-0, again at Perry Barr, after two matches at Wolverhampton had ended 1-1 and 3-3. The deciding match was played in the teeth of a gale but a record crowd of 11,500 braved the conditions to see the marathon finally ended.

Villa were rewarded with a bye in the fourth round — and how they must have needed the rest — before they beat the Lincolnshire side, Horncastle, 5-0 at Perry Barr. In the quarter-finals, Villa were given a much tougher time by the Lancashire club, Darwen, although they led 3-0 at half-time. Darwen almost pulled back into the game and at the end, Villa were more than happy with the 3-2 scoreline.

Glasgow Rangers at Crewe seems an incredible semi-final today, but that is the task which faced Aston Villa in March 1887 and they did well to beat a side comprised solely of Scottish internationals. Villa beat the Scots 3-1 with two goals from Hunter and one from Brown as Birmingham went wild — their team was in the FA Cup Final, where they met neighbours West Bromwich Albion at Kennington Oval.

Some 15,000 spectators saw the first-ever all-Midlands FA Cup Final, held on Saturday, 2 April 1887. Both sides fielded full-strength teams and in the Albion goal stood their huge goalkeeper Bob Roberts, complete in cricket flannels. Albion won the toss and attacked down the sloping Oval pitch with a strong wind gusting behind them. For the first quarter of an hour, Villa had their defence to thank for being level at 0-0.

It was essential to Villa's hopes that they hung on until half-time and this they did. In the second half, with the advantage of the slope and the fact that Albion had suffered the psychological blow of being unable to capitalise on their first-half advantages, Villa took charge of the game and won it convincingly, although

Aston Villa, FA Cup winners in 1887. Standing (left to right): Coulton, Warner, Dawson, Simmonds, Allen. Seated: Davies, Brown, Hunter, Vaughton, Hodgetts. On ground: Yates, Burton.

their first goal had something of a bizarre nature about it.

Roberts made no attempt to save Hodgett's shot, assuming that the winger was offside. Imagine his horror when referee Major Marindin, president of the FA, pointed to the centre-circle to signal a goal. Player protests are nothing new, but the Major stood his ground as Roberts and his Albion colleagues swarmed around the official. Villa were 1-0 ahead.

Two minutes from the end, they made it 2-0. Hunter snapped up a badly-judged back-pass from an Albion defender and although Roberts came out of his goal to collide with the Villa captain, Hunter was able to poke the ball over the line.

When they arrived home at three o'clock the following morning, the Villa party were met at the railway station by thousands of fans. Besides the FA Cup, Villa had also won the Birmingham Cup and the Birmingham Charity Cup that season, and on the Saturday after their FA Cup triumph, they entertained the

Action from the 1887 FA Cup Final between Aston Villa and West Bromwich Albion. This apparently started life as the oldest known action picture from a football match but has been heavily retouched over the years.

Scottish Cup winners, Hibernian, and beat them 3-0 to end a great season — the first of many.

It was to be 1892 before Villa reached the FA Cup Final again, but in those brief, ensuing years there happened events, not only significant

in the affairs of Aston Villa Football Club, but in the history of the game of football itself. By the time they made their second Cup Final appearance, Villa were members of the Football League.

Into the Football League

BY THE late 1880s, English football clubs and their spectators were tiring of the friendly matches which were played when there was no Cup football to whet the appetite. Friendlies lacked the spice of competitive football like Villa's fifth-round Cup tie against Preston North End in 1887-88 which packed in a record crowd of 26,849 to the Perry Barr ground amidst scenes of wild confusion.

That season, Villa's FA Cup campaign began with a 4-0 win at Oldbury Town, where 3,000 spectators saw the home side soundly beaten. In the second round, Villa were paired with Small Heath Alliance, the club who were later to become Birmingham City.

The clubs had first met in September 1879, when Small Heath won a friendly game at Muntz Street by 'one goal and a disputed goal to nil'. On 6 March 1886, they reached the semi-finals of the FA Cup before losing 4-0 to West Brom at the Aston Lower Grounds. And in July 1888, they dropped 'Alliance' and also became a limited company, thus becoming the first football club to introduce directors.

The previous November, Small Heath met Aston Villa in the FA Cup at Muntz Street. Tom Green (two), Brown and Allen scored the Villa goals in a 4-0 win before a 12,000 crowd. Over at the Aston Lower Grounds on the same day, Buffalo Bill Cody staged his travelling Wild West Show before a sparse attendance.

Now into the third round, Villa hammered the minnows of Shankhouse 9-0 before the idiosyncracy of the competition gave them a bye into the fifth round, where they met Preston at Perry Barr.

It was a tie which everyone wanted to see and well before kick-off on the afternoon of 7 January 1888, thousands were making their way to Wellington Road. The ground was a sight to behold, packed to the rafters with spectators. They stood on the roofs of vehicles, wedged themselves ten deep right up the touch-line and jostled and elbowed furiously for a glimpse of the action.

During the game, the crowd twice spilled on to the pitch and eventually the police had to summon assistance from their mounted branch and also call up a handful of Hussars stationed at nearby Brook Street Barracks.

Midway through the game, with Preston leading 3-1, conditions became so impossible that the teams conferred and agreed to regard the game as a friendly. There was no further score but the FA were having none of it and ruled that the match had, indeed, been a Cup tie and Villa were out of the competition. The decision was no doubt influenced by the fact that Villa had so obviously been unable to maintain order on their own ground. So, from Cup Final glory nine months earlier, the Villa were rather humiliatingly dumped out.

There were more significant things afoot, however, and the infamous Villa-Preston game was soon followed by the formation of the world's first football competition in which each club played every other club home and away — the Football League.

One of the League's prime instigators was Villa committeeman William McGregor, a draper with premises near Villa Park. He had often spoken of a 'Football League' and, after discussing the scheme with other members of Villa's committee, set off to visit the best clubs in the country. Eventually, the top sides in the Midlands and North showed enough interest for McGregor to call

William McGregor, the Villa member whose vision led to the formation of the Football League in 1888.

a meeting at the Anderton's Hotel in London's Fleet Street, in March 1888.

A subsequent meeting was held at the Royal Hotel, Manchester, the following month and the Football League was formed. It has never been called the 'English League' because McGregor always hoped that Scottish clubs would join.

When the 1888-89 season kicked-off, Aston Villa lined up with 11 other sides and at the end of that first season they had finished runners-up to Preston North End.

Villa's first Football League match was a 1-1 draw at Wolves before 2,500 spectators at Dudley Road on 8 September 1888. The following week

John Devey
— A Magnificent Skipper

JOHN Devey was a great captain of Aston Villa at a time when the team was sweeping everything before them in the 1890s. He was also a highly skilful forward — equally at home at inside-forward or leading the attack — who made over 300 League and Cup appearances for Villa, scoring 187 goals.

He was born at Newtown, Birmingham, on Boxing Day 1866 and played local football with Excelsior, Aston Unity, Mitchell St George's, and Aston Manor before signing for Villa in March 1891.

After making his League debut on the opening day of the following season, in a 5-1 home win over Blackburn Rovers, at the end of that campaign he appeared in an FA Cup Final against West Brom, which Villa lost 3-0. In the League, Villa finished fourth and Devey was their top scorer with 29 goals in 25 games.

He went on to win five League championship medals, two FA Cup winners' medals and a Cup runners-up medal. He also won two England caps, in 1892 and 1894, both against Ireland, and was also an excellent cricketer, scoring over 6,500 runs for Warwickshire between 1888 and 1907, including eight centuries. After retiring from football, Devey continued to run a sports shop at Lozells, and in 1902 he was appointed a Villa director, serving the club in that capacity until 1934.

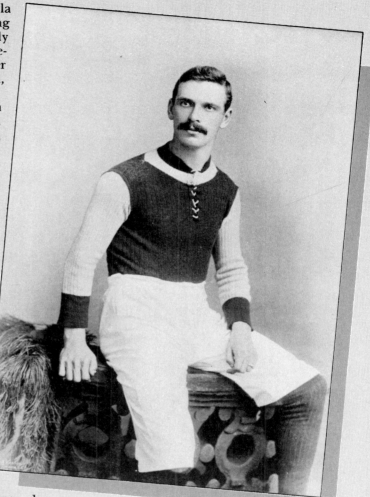

A contemporary writer said: 'John Devey was a splendid captain. He holds very strong ideas on the subject of captaincy, and is of opinion that club directorates do not attach sufficient importance to the appointment of skipper. A good man, he says, will get a maximum amount of work out of a team, an astute captain will artfully flatter one man and mildly bully another, cajole a third and bully a fourth.

'He acts as an invaluable go-between so far as directors and players are concerned, and can either keep an eleven in reasonable harmony, or set them by the ears.

'And in truth, Devey knows what he is talking about, for he knew how to lead men to victory. The Villa were a happy family when Devey was their skipper. He had an exceptional set of men to deal with, it may be, but the success of the club during the period of his leadership will ever remain the most convincing testimony to the genius he had for leadership.

'John Devey was a skilful, individual player. Fast and clever, he could work the ball through the defence at a greater rate than most men, and he usually made a bee-line for the goal. At his best he could dodge and dribble adroitly, and he had a good idea of finding where the posts stood.

'But it is as a partner, as a member of the homogeneous front rank, that John Devey will be best remembered. He did not aspire to do all the work himself; he was always content to sink his identity. I have seen Devey play as many matches as anyone living, and I never recall an instance in which a suspicion of selfishness manifested itself.

'As a matter of fact, he was unselfish to a fault; he liked to make openings for his partner or the centre man. Devey made Athersmith; no fleet wing ever had a more thoughtful partner. Devey used to skip along with the ball until the defenders were compelled to go with him, as his progress spelled danger. But the moment he had drawn the opposition away from Athersmith, the ball used to to fly from Devey's toe and roll gently towards the touch-line . . .Devey had a genius for getting the ball out to his partner . . .Devey and Athersmith were made for each other.'

John Devey died in Birmingham in October 1940.

Denny Hodgetts, bulky for a winger but a man who became a key figure in Villa's League championship and FA Cup successes of the 1890s. He won six England caps.

the first time when they beat a touring Canadian side 4-2. Earlier, they had trounced Ayr United 10-0 with Albert Brown scoring six.

That same season, Preston, the first League champions, won the FA Cup by beating Wolves 3-0 at Kennington Oval, thereby becoming the first team to do the double, a feat which Villa would emulate before long, although in 1888-89 they were drubbed 8-1 by Blackburn Rovers in what was, for Villa, a record defeat in the FA Cup competition.

Against Preston, who were now being hailed as the 'Invincibles', Villa lost at home — their only League defeat of the season at Perry Barr — but were the only side to take a point from Deepdale.

Considering what honours Villa would win in the next few seasons, the 1889-90 campaign was a poor one, as indeed was the following season. First, Villa finished in the bottom four and were saved from re-election only because of unique circumstances. The last four clubs had to apply for re-election but when Villa and Bolton finished eighth and ninth respectively, but equal on points, the League announced that the rules were to be suspended.

DIVISION 1	1889-90										
	P	W	D	L	F	A	W	D	L	F	A	Pts
Preston NE	22	8	1	2	41	12	7	2	2	30	18	33
Everton	22	8	2	1	40	15	6	1	4	25	25	31
Blackburn R	22	9	0	2	59	18	3	3	5	19	23	27
Wolves	22	6	3	2	28	14	4	2	5	23	24	25
WBA	22	8	1	2	37	20	3	2	6	10	30	25
Accrington	22	6	4	1	33	25	3	2	6	20	31	24
Derby Co	22	8	2	1	32	13	1	1	9	11	42	21
Aston Villa	22	6	2	3	30	15	1	3	7	13	36	19
Bolton W	22	6	1	4	37	24	3	0	8	17	41	19
Notts Co	22	4	3	4	20	19	2	2	7	23	32	17
Burnley	22	3	1	7	20	21	1	4	6	16	44	13
Stoke	22	2	3	6	18	20	1	1	9	9	49	10

Villa were also knocked out of the FA Cup in the second round, by Notts County, and then finished in the bottom four again the following season and this time were obliged to go cap in hand to the League. Their FA Cup run again ended in the second round, this time at the hands of Stoke.

Inspiration was at hand, however, in the shape of another Villa committee stalwart, Frederick Rinder, a Liverpudlian who had come to Birmingham to work for the local authority's surveying department. In 1892, Rinder called a special meeting of Villa members, attacked the record of the men in charge and gained

they gained their first League victory, beating Stoke 5-1 at Perry Barr in front of a 2,000 attendance. Then Everton were beaten 2-1 and Notts County hammered 9-1. Villa had two other big wins in that first League season, 6-1 over Blackburn Rovers

DIVISION 1	1888-89										
	P	W	D	L	F	A	W	D	L	F	A	Pts
Preston NE	22	10	1	0	39	7	8	3	0	35	8	40
Aston Villa	22	10	0	1	44	16	2	5	4	17	27	29
Wolves	22	8	2	1	30	14	4	2	5	20	23	28
Blackburn R	22	7	4	0	44	23	3	2	6	22	23	26
Bolton W	22	6	0	5	35	30	4	2	5	28	29	22
WBA	22	6	2	3	25	24	4	0	7	15	22	22
Accrington	22	5	3	3	26	17	1	5	5	22	31	20
Everton	22	8	0	3	24	17	1	2	8	11	29	20
Burnley	22	6	3	2	21	19	1	0	10	21	43	17
Derby Co	22	5	1	5	22	20	2	1	8	19	41	16
Notts Co	22	4	2	5	25	32	1	0	10	15	41	12
Stoke	22	3	4	4	15	18	1	0	10	11	33	12

and 6-2 over Bolton Wanderers. They signed off with a 5-2 defeat at Derby.

Villa's leading scorer in that first League campaign was 21-year-old Albert Allen, who had joined the club from local football. Allen played a big part in Villa's run to the 1887 Cup Final but missed the Final itself through injury. He laid on the club's first-ever League goal, scored by Tommy Green at Wolverhampton, and then hit Villa's first League hat-trick, against Notts County. Allen ended the 1888-89 campaign with 18 League goals, four more than Green.

In October that season, Villa entertained 'foreign' opposition for

Aston Villa in 1891. Standing (left to right): G.Campbell, unknown official, Dickson, Hinchley, Baird, Hare, Oxenbould (trainer), Evans, G.B.Ramsay (secretary). Seated: James Cowan, Athersmith, J.Brown, Devey, Hodgetts, L.Campbell.

control of the club as financial secretary with a new committee.

It was perhaps the most fundamental move in the entire history of a club which has known only too well the upheavals of committee and boardroom unrest. Within a decade, Villa had won the League championship five times, the FA Cup twice and reached another Cup Final in Rinder's very first season in charge, when they lost 3-0 to West Bromwich Albion.

As financial secretary, one of Rinder's first jobs was to tighten up security and he had turnstiles installed at Perry Barr. The first time they were used, the gate receipts trebled and there must have been at least one or two Villa gatemen whose standard of living dropped dramatically as a result.

The story of Aston Villa between 1893 and the start of World War One is one of extraordinary success in League and Cup as the Villa club became the giants of the game,

starting their epic run when Victoria was still on the throne and continuing it into the reign of George V.

Three men played as big a part as any in this rise to fame. They were John Devey, Charles Athersmith and James Cowan.

Devey was a fine inside-forward who joined the Villa club in March 1891, when he was 24, from Mitchell St George's. He was capped twice by England and only the tremendous form of the Derby County stars Steve Bloomer and John Goodall prevented Devey from adding to those caps.

Devey actually made his debut for the club as a baseball player. Villa, along with other professional teams, played the American game quite seriously in the 19th century. He went on to skipper Villa's soccer team to many honours. He also played cricket for Warwickshire and scored 7,000 runs for them between 1888 and 1907.

Devey's partner on the right wing was Charlie Athersmith, a signing

from Unity Gas FC in February 1891. Athersmith was born at Bloxwich in 1872 but he was soon immersed in the Villa legend and in all he won 12 England caps, playing against all three home countries in 1896-97, as well as gaining an FA Cup winners' medal and a League championship medal. It was, of course, impossible for a footballer to win more honours at that time.

James Cowan made his name as a great centre-half. He was a Scotsman, born near Dumbarton in 1868, and although he was a small man,

DIVISION 1	1890-91											
	P	W	D	L	F	A	W	D	L	F	A	Pts
Everton	22	9	0	2	39	12	5	1	5	24	17	29
Preston NE	22	7	3	1	30	5	5	0	6	14	18	27
Notts Co	22	9	1	1	33	11	2	3	6	19	24	26
Wolves	22	8	1	2	23	8	4	1	6	16	42	26
Bolton W	22	9	0	2	36	14	3	1	7	11	20	25
Blackburn R	22	7	1	3	29	19	4	1	6	23	24	24
Sunderland	22	7	2	2	31	13	3	3	5	20	18	*23
Burnley	22	7	1	3	33	24	2	2	7	19	39	21
Aston Villa	22	5	4	2	29	18	2	0	9	16	40	18
Accrington	22	5	1	5	19	19	1	3	7	9	31	16
Derby Co	22	6	1	4	38	28	1	0	10	9	53	15
WBA	22	3	1	7	17	26	2	1	8	17	31	12

*Sunderland deducted two points for unapproved registration

his tackling and speed off the mark were better than anything that football fans of that age had ever seen. Cowan even managed to win the famous Powderhall Sprint in 1896, obtaining time off for the race, and for training, by complaining to Villa of a back injury. Although he won £80 in prize money, Cowan was later suspended for a month by a Villa committee seething over the way they had been tricked.

Villa's epic run began in 1891-92 when they finished fourth in the League and reached the FA Cup Final. It was the last Final to be played at The Oval and Villa reached it with some outstanding performances. In the first round they beat the Derbyshire side Heanor Town 4-1 at Perry Barr; in the next they defeated Darwen 2-0 at home; and in the third round they made the short journey to Wolverhampton, where Wolves had recently opened their Molineux ground. Over 22,000 spectators saw Villa win 3-1. The semi-final brought them a game against Sunderland at Bramall Lane, Sheffield.

Charlie Athersmith, one of the game's fastest wingers in the 1890s. He spent ten years with Villa, winning League and FA Cup honours as well as playing for England.

DIVISION 1	1891-92												
	P	W	D	L	F	A	W	D	L	F	A	Pts
Sunderland	26	13	0	0	55	11	8	0	5	38	25	42
Preston NE	26	12	0	1	42	8	6	1	6	19	23	37
Bolton W	26	9	2	2	29	14	8	0	5	22	23	36
Aston Villa	26	10	0	3	63	23	5	0	8	26	33	30
Everton	26	8	2	3	32	22	4	2	7	17	27	28
Wolves	26	8	2	3	34	15	3	2	8	25	31	26
Burnley	26	9	1	3	34	14	2	3	8	15	31	26
Notts Co	26	9	3	1	41	12	2	1	10	14	39	26
Blackburn R	26	8	3	2	39	26	2	3	8	19	39	26
Derby Co	26	6	3	4	28	18	4	1	8	18	34	24
Accrington	26	7	3	3	24	20	1	1	11	16	58	20
WBA	26	6	3	4	37	24	0	3	10	14	34	18
Stoke	26	5	0	8	19	19	0	4	9	19	42	14
Darwen	26	4	1	8	31	43	0	2	11	7	69	11

Although Sunderland were powering to the League championship, Villa halted their thoughts of the double by winning 4-1 with Athersmith having a quite superb match. Seven days before the match at The Oval, where they faced West Brom, Villa primed themselves for the Cup Final with a record 12-2 League win over Accrington, when Devey and Louis Campbell, a winger from Hibernian, each scored four times.

But if Villa's attack was rampant, they still had problems. Just as Albion's defence had let them down when Villa took the FA Cup from them in 1887, now Villa's rearguard was largely to blame for their defeat in 1892. Geddes headed home Bassett's centre to put Albion a goal ahead, and then Bassett broke away

again, and this time it was Nicholl who met his cross to sink their near neighbours.

The Villa goalkeeper, Jimmy Warner, was hopelessly out of position when 'Baldy' Reynolds, who was to join Villa 11 months later, scored a third from some 40 yards out. Villa were thus beaten 3-0 by a much better side. There was more gloom for Warner when irate Villa fans smashed the windows of his public house at Spring Hill.

Aston Villa's team which reached the 1892 FA Cup Final was: J.Warner; W.Evans, G.Cox, H. Devey, J.Cowan, J.Baird, C.Athersmith, J.Devey, W.Dickson, D.Hodgetts, L.Campbell.

Season 1892-93 saw Villa in fourth place in the table and out of the FA

Cup in the first round when Darwen beat them 5-4 in a thrilling tie in Lancashire. But Villa had been edging up the Football League table and they did not have to wait any longer for the title.

In 1893-94, Villa sat on top of the 16-club division for the first time to win the Football League champion-

DIVISION 1	1892-93												
	P	W	D	L	F	A	W	D	L	F	A	Pts
Sunderland	30	13	2	0	58	17	9	2	4	42	19	48
Preston NE	30	11	2	2	34	10	6	1	8	23	29	37
Everton	30	9	3	3	44	17	7	1	7	30	34	36
Aston Villa	30	12	1	2	50	24	4	2	9	23	38	35
Bolton W	30	12	1	2	43	21	1	5	9	13	34	32
Burnley	30	10	2	3	37	15	3	2	10	14	29	30
Stoke	30	8	2	5	33	16	4	3	8	25	32	29
WBA	30	9	2	4	35	17	3	3	9	23	52	29
Blackburn R	30	5	8	2	29	24	3	5	7	18	32	29
Nottingham F	30	7	2	6	30	27	3	6	6	18	25	28
Wolves	30	11	2	2	32	17	1	2	12	15	51	28
Sheffield W	30	8	2	5	34	28	4	1	10	21	37	27
Derby Co	30	5	6	4	30	28	4	3	8	22	36	27
Notts Co	30	8	3	4	34	15	2	1	12	19	46	24
Accrington	30	5	5	5	29	34	1	6	8	28	47	23
Newton Heath	30	6	3	6	39	35	0	3	12	11	50	18

Aston Villa in 1894. Standing (left to right): Baird, Johnson (linesman), Dunkley (trainer), Dunning, Grierson (trainer), unknown official, W.McGregor (committee), Elliott. Seated: Athersmith, Chatt, Devey, Hodgetts, Woolley. On ground: Reynolds, Cowan, Russell.

ship. They took the title six points ahead of runners-up Sunderland and scored 84 goals in 30 matches. In the FA Cup, Villa might have reached the later stages but for appalling conditions at Sheffield Wednesday in the third round, where they lost 3-2 in a bog, only three days after winning a replay on an ice-rink of a pitch against Sunderland at Perry Barr.

DIVISION 1 1893-94											
	P	W	D	L	F	A	W	D	L	F	A	Pts
Aston Villa	30	12	2	1	49	13	7	4	4	35	29	44
Sunderland	30	11	3	1	46	14	6	1	8	26	30	38
Derby Co	30	9	2	4	47	32	7	2	6	26	30	36
Blackburn R	30	13	0	2	48	15	3	2	10	21	38	34
Burnley	30	13	0	2	43	17	2	4	9	18	34	34
Everton	30	11	1	3	63	23	4	2	9	27	34	33
Nottingham F	30	10	2	3	38	16	4	2	9	19	32	32
WBA	30	8	4	3	35	23	6	0	9	31	36	32
Wolves	30	11	1	3	34	24	3	2	10	18	39	31
Sheffield U	30	8	3	4	26	22	5	2	8	21	39	31
Stoke	30	13	1	1	45	17	0	2	13	20	62	29
Sheffield W	30	7	3	5	32	21	2	5	8	16	36	26
Bolton W	30	7	3	5	18	14	3	1	11	20	38	24
Preston NE	30	7	1	7	25	24	3	2	10	19	32	23
Darwen	30	6	4	5	25	28	1	1	13	12	55	19
Newton Heath	30	5	2	8	29	33	1	0	14	7	39	14

The following season the positions had been reversed. In 1894-95, Villa slipped off the top of the table and ended in third place, eight points behind the champions Sunderland

and three behind runners-up Everton. But they reached the FA Cup Final for the third time in their short history and won the trophy for the second time.

Incredibly, their opponents on each occasion had been West Brom. The Villa team had again undergone major surgery. Tom Wilkes played in goal and his full-backs were Howard Spencer and Jim Welford. Devey moved over to centre-forward to allow Bob Chatt to come into the inside berth and on the left wing, Steve Smith teamed up with Dennis Hodgetts. Smith came from Cannock Chase and along with Spencer would win full international honours in the England team.

Villa's first round match was against Derby County at Perry Barr and that was won 2-1; Newcastle United were thrashed 7-1 and Nottingham Forest 6-2, and Villa were through to the semi-finals where they met Sunderland at Blackburn.

Earlier, Villa had drawn 4-4 in a

DIVISION 1 1894-95											
	P	W	D	L	F	A	W	D	L	F	A	Pts
Sunderland	30	13	2	0	51	14	8	3	4	29	23	47
Everton	30	12	2	1	47	18	6	4	5	35	32	42
Aston Villa	30	12	2	1	51	12	5	3	7	31	31	39
Preston NE	30	9	3	3	32	14	6	2	7	30	32	35
Blackburn R	30	9	5	1	40	15	2	5	8	19	34	32
Sheffield U	30	10	2	3	33	17	4	2	9	24	38	32
Nottingham F	30	10	1	4	33	22	3	4	8	17	34	31
Sheffield W	30	10	2	3	36	19	2	2	11	14	36	28
Burnley	30	8	2	5	28	24	3	2	10	16	32	26
Bolton W	30	8	3	4	45	23	1	4	10	16	39	25
Wolves	30	7	4	4	24	25	2	3	10	19	38	25
Small Heath	30	6	6	3	35	28	3	1	11	15	46	25
WBA	30	9	2	4	38	21	1	2	12	13	45	24
Stoke	30	7	3	5	35	25	2	3	10	15	42	24
Derby Co	30	4	5	6	23	23	3	4	8	22	45	23
Liverpool	30	6	4	5	38	28	1	4	10	13	42	22

League game at Sunderland, although the Wearsiders later inflicted Villa's only home defeat of the season, and they took the field at Ewood Park full of confidence. In a tight semi-final, Villa squeezed home 2-1 and a third Cup Final appearance against the Throstles at the Crystal Palace.

The crowd which jammed into the South London ground was a record attendance of over 42,562 — and yet over half of them missed the winning goal. It was scored within 30 seconds of the kick-off when Athersmith's

Artist's impression of an incident from the 1895 FA Cup Final at the Crystal Palace when Villa's Devey and West Brom's Higgins collided. ''Both reeled back . . . .and after swaying about a moment, Higgins suddenly sat down.'' The Albion player had to leave the field for a while.

centre was hit goalwards by Chatt, Albion's Joe Reader only half-cleared and the ball cannoned off John Devey's knee for a sensational start. Albion battled away but it was to no avail and the FA Cup came to Perry Barr yet again.

In 1895-96, Villa once more exchanged trophies when they were knocked out of the FA Cup 4-2 at Derby in the first round, but went on to regain the League championship, this time finishing four points clear of runners-up Derby County. But before they had officially lost the

James Cowan
— Prince of Half-Backs

DURNG the latter years of the last century, there was apparently no better half-back in the country than Aston Villa centre-half, Jimmy Cowan, who with Jack Reynolds and Jimmy Crabtree either side of him, enjoyed great success in a side that swept all before it.

Yet Cowan, who was born near Dumbarton in October 1868, had not been a regular in the Vale of Leven first team before Villa snapped him up in August 1889. In fact, Cowan had come down to have a trial with Warwickshire CCC when George Ramsey offered him the same with Villa.

He soon settled into the Villa first team, however, and went on to win five League championship medals, two FA Cup winners' medals and a Cup runners-up medal. He was a member of the double-winning side and was capped three times for Scotland, who then had a policy of not selecting players with English clubs. He was also remarkably quick, so much so that he won the famous Powderhall Sprint in 1896, under an assumed name, for which Villa later fined him.

A contemporary writer said of Cowans: 'He will always be recalled as the prince of half-backs. . . . he had not been at Aston long before it was realised that the club had a treasure. He fitted the centre-half position to a niceity. There was a vigour and a skill about his tackling which assured the Villa that they had a recruit of the best type.

'Every club that met Villa talked about the remorseless tackling of James Cowan. Time after time did he play ducks and drakes with the reputations of the cleverest inside men in the country. And that is what I mean by saying that Cowan was the greatest player in the Villa eleven.

'I shall also regard him as the most expert tackler I have watched. The ball seemed to have a fascination for him. Wherever Cowan was, there was the ball. He had not to wander all over the field to get it; it literally seemed to follow him. And when he had wrested the ball from an opponent, how well he knew what to do with it!

'With an easy, quiet, long pass the ball would shoot out to an inside man or to a waiting wing player . . .and Cowan's tackle had meant not only the arrest of the other side's attacks, but an aggressive movement on the part of the Villa forwards.

'There was only one thing that Cowan could not do. He was a poor shot at goal. He often put good shots in, it is true, but oftener than not he would send the ball flying high over the bar. People would say, good-humourdley, "There goes another Cowan sky-scraper." '

James Cowan played for Aston Villa from 1889-90 to 1901-02, clocking up 354 League and Cup appearances in which he scored 26 goals. Towards the end of his playing career with Villa he began to put on weight and his powers began to wane.

After he decided to retire, he coached the young players at Villa Park and became licensee of the Grand Turk in High Street, Aston, before being appointed as Queen's Park Rangers' first-ever manager in 1906. He remained in that job until 1913, when he returned to Scotland. James Cowan died in his homeland in December 1918.

That writer can have the final word: 'Every player has his value in a team and the greatest team of all is that in which it is difficult to explain the precise manner in which superiority is manifested. But Cowan, while always willing to subdue his personality — no man played to the gallery less — had such a pronounced individuality that . . . .the spectator could not help his eye following the movements of the Vill's centre-half; he could not resist the animal magnetism which the man possesed.

Another scene from the 1895 Cup Final. The original caption said "Higgins skies the ball,".

General view of the 1897 Cup Final between Villa and Everton, also at the Crystal Palace. It seems that many of the crowd had a very poor view of the action.

DIVISION 1		1895-96									
	P	W	D	L	F	A	W	D	L	F	A	Pts
Aston Villa	30	14	1	0	47	17	6	4	5	31	28	45
Derby Co	30	12	2	1	42	13	5	5	5	26	22	41
Everton	30	10	4	1	40	17	6	3	6	26	26	39
Bolton W	30	12	2	1	34	14	4	3	8	15	23	37
Sunderland	30	10	5	0	36	14	5	2	8	16	27	37
Stoke	30	12	0	3	43	11	3	0	12	13	36	30
Sheffield W	30	10	2	3	31	18	2	3	10	13	35	29
Blackburn R	30	10	1	4	26	18	2	4	9	14	32	29
Preston NE	30	8	5	2	31	18	3	1	11	13	30	28
Burnley	30	8	5	2	33	11	2	2	11	15	33	27
Bury	30	7	1	7	32	24	5	2	8	18	30	27
Sheffield U	30	9	4	2	28	12	1	2	12	12	38	26
Nottingham F	30	11	1	3	34	16	0	2	13	8	41	25
Wolves	30	10	0	5	43	18	0	1	14	18	47	21
Small Heath	30	7	2	6	22	24	1	2	12	17	55	20
WBA	30	5	4	6	18	22	1	3	11	12	37	19

FA Cup on the field, Villa had already lost the actual silver trophy, which was in fact a comparatively small goblet weighing only 19 ounces.

Villa put the Cup on show in the window of William Shillcock, a football boot manufacturer of 73 Newtown Row. On the night of 11-12 September 1895 somebody stole it. There have been many theories — including the sensational 'confession' of an 83-year-old man in 1958 — but the Cup was never found and Villa were fined £25 by the FA (although they had wisely insured the trophy for £200). Perhaps it was as well that they were knocked out so quickly, once the competition proper got under way — there would have been few volunteers to look after a new FA Cup. Now, though, Villa stood on the brink of a glorious double.

Villa's in 1895 with the FA Cup. Standing (left to right): J.Grierson (trainer), J.Dunkley (hon secretary), Reynolds, C.S.Johnstone (director), Spencer, John Devey, Wilkes, J.T.Lees (director), Welford, F.W.Rinder (director), J.E.Margoschis (chairman). Seated: G.B.Ramsay (secretary), Athersmith, Chatt, James Cowan, Russell, Hodgetts, Smith.

Villa in 1896-97. Back row (players only, left to right): Spencer, Wilkes, Hodgetts, Welford. Middle row: Chatt, Crabtree, Reynolds, James Cowan, Devey, Burton, Athersmith, Campbell. On ground: Smith, John Cowan.

Double Winners

WHEN Aston Villa embarked on the 1896-97 season they surely could not have imagined just what a significant campaign it would be. This was the season in which Villa won both the FA Cup and the First Division championship, the last side to achieve this feat until the Spurs team of 1960-61. Towards the end of the season, Villa also moved to the ground which was to become known throughout the football world as Villa Park.

New players were also arriving at the club, not least of which was Jimmy Crabtree, a Scottish international full-back who joined Villa from Burnley. To further strengthen the defence, Villa also signed the Grimsby Town goalkeeper Jimmy Whitehouse for £200 — then a record transfer fee for a 'keeper.

One player going in the opposite direction was Dennis Hodgetts, who joined Villa's Birmingham rivals Small Heath and thus missed being part of an almost unique football team when his old club won the double. Villa also paid Small Heath £100 plus the proceeds of a testmimonial game when inside-forward Fred Wheldon came to Perry Barr. With these and other signings, Aston Villa began to rewrite soccer's record book. And they did it in style, taking the title 11 points clear of the runners-up and knocking three top First Division sides out of the FA Cup before beating the Second Division champions in the Final. Villa had already made sure of the title before they went to the Crystal Palace for the FA Cup Final.

They began the defence of the League championship with a 2-1 victory over Stoke at Perry Barr, where a 6,000 crowd saw John Cowan — James' brother — and John Devey score the Villa goals. There followed

Jimmy Crabtree, winner of 11 England caps, was one of the finest and most versatile defenders of his day. He won three League championship medals and an FA Cup winners' medal whilst with Villa.

something of a hiccup, however, and by the beginning of October, Villa had only six points from six matches. They lost 3-1 at West Brom's Stoney Lane ground, drew 2-2 at home to Sheffield United and then beat Everton 3-2 at Goodison.

The following week, however, it was Everton's turn to win at Perry Barr and then Sheffield United held Villa to a goalless draw at Bramall Lane.

So, there was little to suggest that such glory was around the corner.

Johnny Campbell, the man who scored the first-ever goal at Villa Park. A Scottish international, he spent two seasons with Villa before returning to Celtic.

Steve Smith, a speedy left winger with a terrific shot. He won five League championship medals with Villa as well as two FA Cup winners' medals and an England cap.

On 10 October 1896, however, Villa embarked on a run of four successive victories which saw them turn the corner. The run began with a 2-0 win over West Brom, then a double over Derby County — 3-1 at the Baseball Ground and 2-1 at Perry Barr — and finally a 2-0 victory at Stoke.

Thereafter, Villa burst through to head the table. A 1-1 draw at Bury was followed by four more consecutive victories — a double over Sheffield Wednesday (3-1 and 4-0), a 5-1 hammering of Blackburn Rovers at Ewood Park and a 3-2 win over Nottingham Forest just before Christmas.

On Christmas Day 1896, a 15,000 crowd saw Villa draw 3-3 at Anfield and on Boxing Day they travelled to Molineux and won 2-1.

Villa were to lose only two more League games all season and, strangely, they came in the next two matches — 3-0 at home to Burnley and 4-2 at Sunderland. After that, however, Villa just marched on and on, winning ten out of their last 11 League games. The only side to take a point off them was Liverpool, who earned a goalless draw at Perry Barr in mid-March.

After the Roker defeat, Villa beat Sunderland 2-1 in the return game,

then won 2-0 at Bury and 4-3 at Burnley, 3-1 at home to Preston and 4-2 at Nottingham Forest.

Their last five games brought victories over Bolton (6-2 and 2-1), Blackburn (3-0), Wolves (5-0) and Preston (1-0). The Villa had been two goals down at home to Bolton but their eventual emphatic victory over the Trotters left them high at the top of the First Division, the title theirs with four games still to play.

Villa used only 17 players to win the title and three of them — Athersmith, James Cowan and Wheldon — were ever-present. Wheldon was leading scorer with 18 goals, followed by Devey with 17 and Campbell with 13.

While Villa were storming to the championship, they were also making impressive progress in the FA Cup. In the first round they beat Newcastle United 5-0 at home (also appearing in that first-round draw were such long-forgotten names as Burton Town, Burton Swifts, Stockton and Glossop North End). Notts County came to Perry Barr for the second round and lost 2-1. And a third-round tie against Preston went to three games before Villa won the second replay.

The first two games ended 1-1 and 0-0 before Villa got through in a nail-biting game at Sheffield, where Athersmith (two) and John Campbell, signed from Celtic in May 1895, scored the goals.

Liverpool at Bramall Lane was their semi-final obstacle, one week after the sides had fought out a dour goalless draw at Perry Barr. Now some 10,000 Villa supporters swelled the crowd at Sheffield to over 30,000 and were rewarded for their journey with a one-sided game in which Villa powered to a 3-0 win to move into their fourth FA Cup Final.

At last, they had different opponents, for Everton had beaten Derby County in the other semi-final at Stoke, Liverpool thus missing out on what would have been an historic all-Merseyside final.

An official estimate put the attendance at the 1897 FA Cup Final at 65,891 and about 20,000 of those must have come from Birmingham, where a special works holiday had been declared.

The committee and team travelled in a special train provided by the North Western Railway Company and the players had been promised a special win bonus by the club as well as many gifts from local tradesman, who offered everything from cigars to clothing if Villa returned to Birmingham with the Cup.

Those fans lucky enough to have made the journey London witnessed one of the most entertaining of all FA Cup Finals with five goals being scored in a period of little more than half an hour.

After both sides had started brightly on a fine day, Villa took the lead after 18 minutes. Devey gave Johnny Campbell a perfectly measured through-ball and the centre-forward cracked a magnificent shot past Menham in the Everton goal.

But the Merseysiders were not to be outdone and within a short time it was the sky-blue shirted Everton players who were doing a victory jig. First Bell combined with Hartley before giving Whitehouse no chance, to make it 1-1; then Cowan conceded a free-kick and Boyle planted the ball past Whitehouse to give Everton the lead.

Ten minutes later, Villa were level again when Crabtree dropped a free-kick into the path of Wheldon, who made the score 2-2.

With the crowd still buzzing from this sensational spate of scoring, Villa won a corner and when the ball came over from the right-hand flag, Crabtree took full advantage of Everton's slack marking to run in and head the winner. In the second half both sides continued to thrill the crowd but there were no more goals and when the referee ended the game, Aston Villa were double champions.

Villa skipper John Devey — 'blushing,' according to a report in the *Birmingham Daily Post* — received the Cup from Lord Rosebery, who said: "I cannot judge the finer points of the game but I can judge the great qualities which both sides have displayed. These qualities we recognise as distinctly British. It was a true Olympian struggle."

After returning to Birmingham with the FA Cup, the Villa players attended a dinner at the Old Royal Restaurant, as guests of the Bir-

Jack 'Baldy' Reynolds, a wing-half who played international soccer for both England and Ireland. With Villa he won three League championship medals and two FA Cup winners' medals.

mingham Hotel and Restaurant Company.

Aston Villa were now installed in a new home. On Easter Saturday, 17 April 1897 — a cold, wet day — the club officially opened what was to become Villa Park, although then it was still known as Aston Lower Grounds. The first visitors were Blackburn Rovers in a First Division match and, as we have seen, Villa won 3-0, Johnny Campbell scoring the first goal on the new ground. A 15,000 crowd braved heavy rain to see

DIVISION 1 1896-97													
	P	W	D	L	F	A	W	D	L	F	A	Pts
Aston Villa	30	10	3	2	36	16	11	2	2	37	22	47
Sheffield U	30	6	4	5	22	16	7	6	2	20	13	36
Derby Co	30	10	2	3	45	22	6	2	7	25	28	36
Preston NE	30	8	4	3	35	21	3	8	4	20	19	34
Liverpool	30	7	6	2	25	10	5	3	7	21	28	33
Sheffield W	30	9	4	2	29	11	1	7	7	13	26	31
Everton	30	8	1	6	42	29	6	2	7	20	28	31
Bolton W	30	7	3	5	22	18	5	3	7	18	25	30
Bury	30	7	5	3	25	15	3	5	7	14	29	30
Wolves	30	6	4	5	26	14	5	2	8	19	27	28
Nottingham F	30	8	3	4	30	16	1	5	9	14	33	26
WBA	30	7	2	6	18	16	3	4	8	15	40	26
Stoke	30	8	3	4	30	18	3	0	12	18	41	25
Blackburn R	30	8	1	6	27	25	3	2	10	8	37	25
Sunderland	30	4	6	5	21	21	3	3	9	13	26	23
Burnley	30	4	5	6	25	25	2	2	11	18	36	19

this historic occasion, one week after Villa's Cup Final victory had earned them the double. Another seven days on and there were 35,000 to see Wolves beaten 5-0.

The Aston Lower Grounds had been a kind of pleasure park for working people and Villa's early matches had sometimes been played on the adjoining meadow before they moved to Perry Barr.

When the new ground was completed it had a stand which seated 5,500 fans with another 4,500 standing in front. A further 8,000 could find accommodation on the Trinity Road side of the stadium, and the rest had to be content with open terraces. A concrete cycle-track ran around the pitch.

Frederick Rinder and Charles Johnstone did the early work in negotiating a lease from the owners, Flowers Brewery, and it ran for 21 years at a starting rent of £250 per annum. By 1911, Villa were in a position to buy the freehold at about five shillings (25p) a square yard, together with further land from Ansells Brewery.

Villa were well on the way to owning a stadium which would compare with the best in the world and only World War One prevented them from developing the stadium into one which would have held a massive 130,000 people.

It was sad, however, that the famous old Perry Barr ground was to close. On Good Friday 1897, Aston Villa Reserves met Shrewsbury Town in a Birmingham League game. It was to be the last match ever played at this grand old venue.

So, Aston Villa said goodbye to an era and, at the same time, looked forward to even greater days ahead. The team which won the double was apparently delightful to watch. They

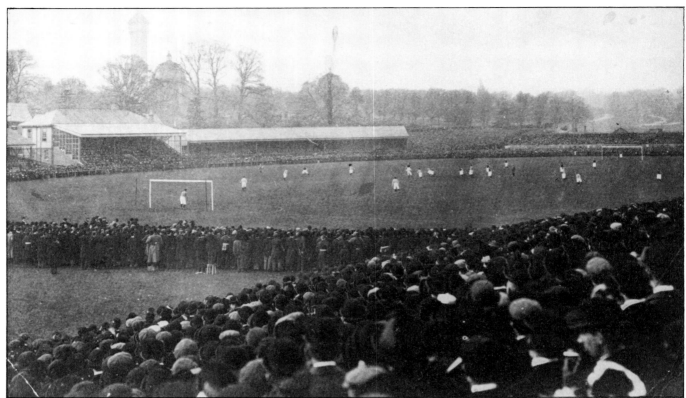

General view of the 1897 Cup Final between Villa and Everton.

Aston Villa, League and FA Cup double winners of 1896-97. Back row (left to right): G.B.Ramsey (secretary), J.Grierson (trainer), Spencer, Whitehouse, J.E.Margoschis (chairman), Evans, Crabtree, J.T.Lees (director), C.Johnstone (director). Front row: V.Jones (director), James Cowan, Athersmith, Campbell, Devey, Wheldon, John Cowan, Reynolds, F.W.Rinder (director).

played a passing game, keeping the ball on the ground and switching it quickly from man to man. But they also had some fine dribblers in Crabtree, Devey, Wheldon and Reynolds, and a real speed merchant in Athersmith.

The team was also immensely fit

and, indeed, they needed to be as the Cup campaign saw their resources stretched, particularly during March when they played four important League games and four in the Cup, including the marathon tie with Liverpool.

Much of the credit for this was

down to their trainer, Joe Grierson, who joined Villa from Middlesbrough Ironopolis and who took charge of every one of the club's League championship winning sides from 1894 to 1910.

The Golden Era

ASTON Villa were to add two more FA Cup wins and three League championships to their record before World War One intervened and closed down soccer for the duration. During that period of some 18 years between the move to Villa Park and the war, there were to be many more famous names associated with the legendary claret and blue shirt of the club which had become one of the greatest names in football.

However, in the months following their double success, Villa lost two stalwart players when Johnny Campbell returned to Glasgow Celtic and 'Baldy' Reynolds also joined the Parkhead club. At the end of the 1897-98 season, Celtic had lifted another Scottish League championship.

Jimmy Welford had also been transferred to Celtic, shortly after the start of the double-winning season. A Scot who had joined Villa from Mitchell St George's in 1893, Welford had proved a sturdy full-back who partnered Howard Spencer before the arrival of Albert Evans. His move to Celtic in November 1896 eventually proved ill-advised for Villa. Spencer was injured at the start of the following season and Villa had to sign a makeshift full-back when Welford would surely have done much better.

Villa also struggled to find a replacement for Campbell and the club began to ring the changes. John Cowan was switched to inside-right with Steve Smith returning on the left wing. Tommy Bowman, a Scottish-born defender who joined Villa from Blackpool in October 1897, took over from Bert Sharp at right-back. Sharp had been the

DIVISION 1				1897-98							
	P	W	D	L	F	A	W	D	L	F	A	Pts
Sheffield U	30	9	4	2	27	14	8	4	3	29	17	42
Sunderland	30	12	2	1	27	8	4	3	8	16	22	37
Wolves	30	10	4	1	36	14	4	3	8	21	27	35
Everton	30	11	3	1	33	12	2	6	7	15	27	35
Sheffield W	30	12	0	3	39	15	3	3	9	12	27	33
Aston Villa	30	12	1	2	47	21	2	4	9	14	30	33
WBA	30	8	5	2	25	16	3	5	7	19	29	32
Nottingham F	30	7	5	3	30	19	4	4	7	17	30	31
Liverpool	30	7	4	4	27	16	4	2	9	21	29	28
Derby Co	30	10	3	2	40	19	1	3	11	17	42	28
Bolton W	30	9	2	4	18	13	2	2	11	10	28	26
Preston NE	30	7	5	3	26	15	1	3	11	9	28	24
Notts Co	30	4	6	5	23	23	4	2	9	13	23	24
Bury	30	8	3	4	25	19	0	5	10	14	32	24
Blackburn R	30	4	7	4	20	22	3	3	9	19	32	24
Stoke	30	8	3	4	21	14	0	5	10	14	41	24

Billy George, the ex-Army goalkeeper who made nearly 400 senior appearances for Villa, winning two League championship medals and an FA Cup winners' medal. He played three times for England.

immediate replacement for the injured Spencer and he now moved to right-half to cover the gap left by Campbell. Jack Sharp, meanwhile, played a few games at centre-forward, although his greatest days were to be

with Everton, whom he joined in August 1899.

All these changes — Villa used 24 players in 1897-98 as opposed to 17 in the double-winning season — inevitably meant that their grip on both trophies was broken. In the First Division they finished sixth and in the FA Cup they were knocked out in the first round, going down 1-0 at Derby to a goal from former Liverpool player, Hugh McQueen. Derby eventually reached the Final where they lost to Nottingham Forest.

The great days, though, were about to return and Villa took the First Division titles in successive seasons in 1898-99 and 1899-1900, although some bizarre incidents surrounded the period.

First, Villa were fined £50 for alleged irregularities over the signing of goalkeeper Bill George, a regular soldier who was stationed in Wiltshire. They wanted a 'keeper to replace Jimmy Whitehouse, who had been transferred to Newton Heath (now Manchester United), and gave George a trial in a First Division game against West Brom at Stoney Lane in October 1897.

George, a well-built goalkeeper, gave a fine performance in the 1-1 draw and Villa signed him on. Somehow they infringed League registration rules and apart from the fine, Frederick Rinder, George Ramsey and Bill George himself were each suspended for a month.

It was worth it, though, for George eventually went on to become one of the greatest goalkeepers in the club's history, making 396 League and FA Cup appearances for Villa, gaining

Aston Villa, League champions 1898-99. Back row (players only, left to right): Bowman, Crabtree, Garraty, Spencer, George, Evans. Front row: Johnson, Athersmith, Devey, Wheldon, James Cowan, Smith.

League and Cup medals and winning three England caps.

In November 1898, Villa were also involved in a match which will go down as marking one of the silliest decisions ever made by the Football League.

With almost 80 minutes gone in the game against Wednesday at Sheffield, Villa were losing 3-1 when the referee ended the game due to bad light. The League ordered that the remaining ten minutes to be played *four months later* and Villa made the trek back to Yorkshire for the farce which saw Wednesday score another goal to win 4-1.

Villa made one change from their original team, Billy Garraty, a locally-born player, replacing Frank Bedingfield at centre-forward. In fact,

Billy Garraty, a key figure in Villa's attack for seven seasons.

	P	W	D	L	F	A	W	D	L	F	A	Pts
DIVISION 1 1898-99												
Aston Villa	34	15	2	0	58	13	4	5	8	18	27	45
Liverpool	34	12	3	2	29	10	7	2	8	20	23	43
Burnley	34	11	5	1	32	15	4	4	9	13	32	39
Everton	34	10	2	5	25	13	5	6	6	23	28	38
Notts Co	34	9	6	2	33	20	3	7	7	14	31	37
Blackburn R	34	9	5	3	41	23	5	3	9	19	29	36
Sunderland	34	11	3	3	26	10	4	3	10	15	31	36
Wolves	34	9	5	3	30	13	5	2	10	24	35	35
Derby Co	34	11	5	1	46	19	1	6	10	16	38	35
Bury	34	9	5	3	31	18	5	2	10	17	31	35
Nottingham F	34	6	6	5	22	18	5	5	7	20	24	33
Stoke	34	10	4	3	29	17	3	3	11	18	35	33
Newcastle U	34	9	3	5	33	18	2	5	10	16	30	30
WBA	34	11	1	5	28	9	1	5	11	14	48	30
Preston NE	34	10	4	3	29	14	0	5	12	15	33	29
Bolton W	34	6	5	6	24	21	3	2	12	13	30	25
Sheffield W	34	8	2	7	26	24	0	6	11	6	37	24

the 80 minutes of the first game marked Bedingfield's only appearance for Villa before he moved to QPR in May 1900.

That season Villa contested the title with Liverpool, finally finishing two points clear of the Merseysiders by beating them in the very last game of the season at Villa Park before over 41,000 fans, who saw John Devey (two), Fred Wheldon (two) and Jim Crabtree complete a resounding five-goal win.

Joe Bache
— The Schemer Who Scored Goals

THERE were few more skilful, cultured players in the Football League during the early years of this century than Joe Bache, who displayed such a wonderful awareness of the game as he schemed in Aston Villa's midfield, ruling as the general of the team.

More than that, though, Joe Bache could also score goals and in 473 League and Cup appearances for Villa between 1900-01 and 1914-15, he netted 185 times, including eight hat-tricks. And he achieved all this at the very highest level, whilst Villa were one of the leading clubs in the country.

Bache was a product of non-League West Midlands football. He was born in Stourbridge in February 1880 and began his career with the local club as a 17-year-old. In December 1900, when he was almost 21, he signed for Aston Villa and made his senior debut in a friendly match against the German club, FC Berlin.

He also made his League bow that season, at inside-left in a 2-0 defeat at Notts County. By the end of the season he had played seven times and opened his scoring account for the club with their goal in a 3-1 defeat at Nottingham Forest.

This was a moderate League season for Villa, the reigning champions, and they slumped to finish 15th in the table, although they did reach as FA Cup semi-final (a run in which the young Bache played no part).

The following season, Bache was a major player at Villa Park, playing in every game and scoring eight goals in the League as he helped the club to begin its climb back to the higher reaches of the First Division.

Twelve months later, they were runners-up and Bache, now so well established in the side, played in the first 25 games before injury again cost him his place. He was injured after winning his first international cap, scoring on his England debut against Wales at Portsmouth.

In 1905, when Villa won the FA Cup with Hampton's two goals against Newcastle United, Bache scored four times in six Cup games. And in 1909-10, as the League championship was lifted, he was second-highest scorer with 20 goals from 32 appearances. His contribution to Villa's 1913 Cup Final win was one goal in six games, although he made plenty more as Villa scored 18 just to reach the semi-final.

Between 1905 and 1912, Bache forged a marvellous partnership with Albert Hall and in 1910 they formed the England left wing against Ireland in Belfast. This was to become something of a Villa tradition, starting with Athersmith and Devey and continuing with Walker and Dorrell and then Walker and Houghton. Altogether, Bache won seven England caps.

He eventually succeeded Howard Spencer as the Villa captain and continued to give the club excellent service until the last season of peacetime football in 1914-15. When League football resumed in 1919-20, Joe Bache was 39 and he left top-flight soccer to become player-manager of Mid-Rhonnda FC.

After a spell with the Welsh club he moved to Grimsby Town as a coach and then worked in Germany, coaching Rot Weiss FC, the club based in Frankfurt. In 1927, Bache returned to Villa Park as coach to the reserve team and in later years he was the licensee of a public house in Aston. He died in November 1960, aged 80.

During the height of his career, one writer said this about him: 'In Bache, the Villa have a superb forward. He likes to dribble too closely and dallies with the ball too much, but he is a talented player.

'Until Hampton came along, Bache was one of the few real goal-getters the Villa had and although he wastes a good many chances, he is a great player.'

Aston Villa, League champions again in 1899-1900. Back row (players only, left to right): Noon, Bowman, Crabtree, George, Spencer, Evans. Front row: Wilkes, Cowan, Wheldon, Devey, Athersmith, Garraty, Smith, Templeton.

DIVISION 1 1899-1900											
	P	W	D	L	F	A	W	D	L	F	A	Pts
Aston Villa	34	12	4	1	45	18	10	2	5	32	17	50
Sheffield U	34	11	5	1	40	11	7	7	3	23	22	48
Sunderland	34	12	2	3	27	9	7	1	9	23	26	41
Wolves	34	8	4	5	28	16	7	5	5	20	21	39
Newcastle U	34	10	5	2	34	15	3	5	9	19	28	36
Derby Co	34	11	2	4	32	15	3	6	8	13	28	36
Manchester C	34	10	3	4	33	15	3	5	9	17	29	34
Nottingham F	34	12	3	2	42	16	1	5	11	14	39	34
Stoke	34	9	5	3	24	15	4	3	10	13	30	34
Liverpool	34	9	4	4	31	19	5	1	11	18	26	33
Everton	34	11	1	5	30	15	2	6	9	17	34	33
Bury	34	12	2	3	29	14	1	4	12	11	30	32
WBA	34	8	6	3	27	11	3	2	12	16	40	30
Blackburn R	34	12	2	3	38	22	1	2	14	11	39	30
Notts Co	34	5	7	5	29	22	4	4	9	17	38	29
Preston NE	34	9	3	5	28	20	3	1	13	10	28	28
Burnley	34	10	2	5	28	17	1	3	13	6	37	27
Glossop NE	34	4	6	7	19	22	0	4	13	12	52	18

Villa's overall leading scorers were Devey (21 goals) and Wheldon (16). Villa used 23 players, of whom only Tommy Bowman, a wing-half from Blackpool, was ever-present. Wheldon missed only one game, the opening match of the season which ended in a 3-1 home win over Stoke.

In the Cup, Villa's form was less impressive and defeat at Nottingham Forest meant that they had gone out in the first round for the third time in four seasons. The exception had been, of course, in 1897 when they beat Everton in the Final to complete the double.

Liverpool dropped right out of the race the following season but Villa kept right on until they completed their fifth League championship win in seven consecutive seasons, this time finishing two points ahead of runners-up Sheffield United.

Villa's rearguard was now well established. Bill George was ever-present in goal and at full-back, Howard Spencer had recovered and missed only six games, playing alongside Albert Evans.

Spencer was, indeed, the 'Prince of Full-backs'. Born at Edgbaston in August 1875, he had joined Villa from Birchfield Trinity in 1894, initially teaming up with Jim Welford to form one of the best full-back partnerships Villa have ever had. His partnership with Evans had been one of the key factors in Villa winning the double in 1896-97 and despite missing the entire 1900-01 season through injury, by the time he retired

in 1907 he had clocked up almost 300 League and FA Cup appearances.

Spencer, who also won six England caps, continued his association with the club as a director and when he retired from the board in May 1936, he had been with Villa in one role or another, for 42 years.

Up front, Bill Garraty, who would eventually win England honours, had taken over from John Devey as the main goalscorer. In 1899-1900, Garraty netted 27 League goals but Devey still weighed in with a useful 13.

In the Cup that year, Villa played six games to reach the quarter-finals. They drew 1-1 with Manchester City before winning the Villa Park replay 3-1 to move into the second round, then hammered Bristol City, also at home, 5-1 with Devey scoring four times.

That earned them a tie against Millwall of the Southern League. In those days the Southern League was a strong competition and Millwall were not going to be pushovers, far from it. After earning a 1-1 draw in a difficult away game at East Ferry Road, Villa would have felt fairly confident. But the the Londoners held Villa to another draw, this time 0-0, and still Southampton waited to see who their semi-final opponents would be.

The third game was staged at Elm Park, Reading, where Villa, perhaps now too cautious, went down 2-1. Millwall were beaten in the semi-finals and the following year, Villa scored an emphatic revenge over them.

In 1900-01, Aston Villa reached the semi-finals of the Cup and beat Millwall 5-0 in the first round. They then took two games each to beat

Nottingham Forest and Small Heath before losing another replay, this time to Sheffield United just one game from the Final.

The second-round tie against old rivals and near neighbours Small Heath at Muntz Street was a strange affair. The Heathens were on their way to promotion from the Second Division and when they drew Villa in the Cup, deciding to cash in on what was expected to be a record attendance. Small Heath doubled the basic admission charge from sixpence to one shilling (5p), but Villa fans then boycotted the game and only 18,000 saw the goalless draw.

Perhaps even more unusually, only some 15,000 attended the replay at Villa Park, although the fact that it

was staged on a Wednesday afternoon might explain this.

Small Heath duly won promotion and when they entertained Villa in a First Division game the following season, their directors left the admission price alone and were rewarded with a record attendance of 23,000.

Villa dropped down the table in 1900-01, finishing in 15th place and avoiding relegation by only five points after losing their last four games of the season. Indeed, after beating Sheffield Wednesday 2-1 at home on 9 March, they did not win any of their last seven matches.

In 1901-02, the Villains climbed back to finish eighth, but were knocked out of the Cup in the first round, going down 2-1 at home to Stoke after a 2-2 draw at the Victoria Ground. This season the leading

DIVISION 1 1900-01											
	P	W	D	L	F	A	W	D	L	F	A	Pts
Liverpool	34	12	2	3	36	13	7	5	5	23	22	45
Sunderland	34	12	3	2	43	11	3	10	4	14	15	43
Notts Co	34	13	2	2	39	18	5	2	10	15	28	40
Nottingham F	34	10	4	3	32	14	6	3	8	21	22	39
Bury	34	11	3	3	31	10	5	4	8	22	27	39
Newcastle U	34	10	5	2	27	13	4	5	8	15	24	38
Everton	34	10	4	3	37	17	6	1	10	18	25	37
Sheffield W	34	13	2	2	38	16	0	8	9	14	26	36
Blackburn R	34	9	4	4	24	18	3	5	9	15	29	33
Bolton W	34	10	5	2	21	12	3	2	12	18	43	33
Manchester C	34	12	3	2	32	16	1	3	13	16	42	32
Derby Co	34	10	4	3	43	18	2	3	12	12	24	31
Wolves	34	6	10	1	21	15	3	3	11	18	40	31
Sheffield U	34	8	4	5	22	23	4	3	10	13	29	31
Aston Villa	34	8	5	4	32	18	2	5	10	13	33	30
Stoke	34	8	3	6	23	15	3	2	12	23	42	27
Preston NE	34	6	4	7	29	30	3	3	11	20	45	25
WBA	34	4	4	9	21	27	3	4	10	14	35	22

Left: Villa on the attack against Bury in January 1902, in a First Division game at Villa Park. *Below:* Villa pack their defence as Stoke prepare to take a close-range free-kick in a first-round FA Cup replay at Villa Park in January 1902.

scorer was Jimmy McLuckie, who had joined Villa from Bury at the start of the season. McLuckie scored 16 League goals in 1901-02, including a hat-trick against Grimsby Town just before Christmas.

But the most significant signing was that of Joe Bache, a young inside-forward who had joined Villa from Stourbridge in December 1900 at the age of 20. In his first season, Bache made only seven appearances and in 1901-02, despite playing in every game, he managed only eight goals.

But this was the start of a quite magnificent career which saw Bache score 184 goals in 473 League and Cup games, win two FA Cup medals, in 1905 and 1913, and a League championship medal in 1910. At Villa he formed a brilliant left-wing partnership with Albert Evans, a

Joe Bache, a great goalscoring career after a slow start.

DIVISION 1 1901-02											
	P	W	D	L	F	A	W	D	L	F	A	Pts
Sunderland	34	12	3	2	32	14	7	3	7	18	21	44
Newcastle U	34	11	3	3	41	14	3	6	8	7	20	37
Blackburn R	34	12	2	3	36	16	3	4	10	16	32	36
Nottingham F	34	11	4	2	32	13	2	5	10	11	30	35
Derby Co	34	11	5	1	26	10	2	4	11	13	31	35
Bury	34	11	5	1	31	9	2	3	12	13	29	34
Aston Villa	34	9	5	3	27	13	4	3	10	15	27	34
Sheffield W	34	9	5	3	30	14	4	3	10	18	38	34
Sheffield U	34	10	5	2	38	13	3	2	12	15	35	33
Liverpool	34	8	3	6	28	16	2	9	6	14	22	32
Bolton W	34	10	6	1	38	17	2	2	13	13	39	32
Notts Co	34	12	2	3	44	19	2	2	13	7	38	32
Wolves	34	12	3	2	32	13	1	3	13	14	44	32
Grimsby T	34	11	3	3	33	16	2	3	12	11	44	32
Stoke	34	10	4	3	31	12	1	5	11	14	43	31
Small Heath	34	8	5	4	31	14	3	3	11	16	31	30
Manchester C	34	10	3	4	28	17	1	3	13	14	41	28

partnership which they carried into the England team with great success.

Indeed, such partnerships were becoming part of Aston Villa tradition. There had been John Devey and Charlie Athersmith on the right flank, and later Billy Walker and Arthur Dorrell, then Walker and Eric Houghton.

Below: **Spurs' goalkeeper George Clawley in various trouble during Villa's FA Cup win at White Hart Lane in March 1903.**

DIVISION 1 1902-03											
	P	W	D	L	F	A	W	D	L	F	A	Pts
Sheffield W	34	12	3	2	31	7	7	1	9	23	29	42
Aston Villa	34	11	3	3	43	18	8	0	9	18	22	41
Sunderland	34	10	5	2	27	11	6	4	7	24	25	41
Sheffield U	34	11	0	6	36	22	6	5	6	22	22	39
Liverpool	34	11	3	3	48	21	6	1	10	20	28	38
Stoke	34	11	2	4	29	11	4	5	8	17	27	37
WBA	34	10	2	5	37	27	6	2	9	17	26	36
Bury	34	14	1	2	41	14	2	2	13	13	29	35
Derby Co	34	13	2	2	34	11	3	1	13	16	36	35
Nottingham F	34	10	3	4	33	22	4	4	9	16	25	35
Wolves	34	12	2	3	34	17	2	3	12	14	40	33
Everton	34	10	2	5	28	18	3	4	10	17	29	32
Middlesbrough	34	10	3	4	27	16	4	1	12	14	34	32
Newcastle U	34	12	1	4	31	11	2	3	12	10	40	32
Notts Co	34	8	5	4	25	16	4	2	11	16	33	31
Blackburn R	34	9	2	6	27	24	3	3	11	17	39	29
Grimsby T	34	6	5	6	28	22	2	4	11	15	40	25
Bolton W	34	6	2	9	18	20	2	1	14	19	53	19

Season 1902-03 saw Villa back near the top of the First Division when they finished runners-up behind Sheffield Wednesday, who scraped to the title by just one point. Villa also reached the semi-finals of the FA Cup before losing 3-0 to the eventual winners, Bury. Now it was felt at Villa Park that the lapses of the previous two years were only temporary affairs.

Yet Villa had made a poor start to the 1902-03 season, when they did not win until their fourth game, a 2-0 success at Ewood Park. By the middle of November they had won only twice and a relegation battle looked a greater certainty than a championship challenge.

Then three successive wins, the last of them a 7-0 defeat of Newcastle

Alex Leake, a 'character' who joined Villa from Small Heath in 1902.

United in late November, heralded something of a revival and five consecutive victories at the season's end brought Villa so close to another title.

Garraty and McLuckie shared top spot with 15 League goals each.

The big games of the season included those against West Brom. In November, a crowd of over 35,000 saw the Throstles win 3-0 at Villa Park. At The Hawthorns in February, some 28,000 fans saw Villa gain revenge with a 2-1 win. The biggest Villa Park League attendance of the season was the 40,000 who saw Billy Garraty's penalty beat Sheffield Wednesday on Boxing Day.

In the FA Cup, though, a crowd of 47,000 at Villa Park saw Sunderland beaten 4-0 in the first round. Villa then removed Barnsley and Spurs before losing 3-0 to Bury in the semi-final at Goodison Park.

Into Villa's side now stepped Alex Leake, who had joined the club from Small Heath in June 1902. Leake was an exceptional defender and a real 'character' as well, often to be seen chatting to an opponent who was about to take a corner. By the time he left for Burnley in December 1907, he had gained England honours and an FA Cup winners' medal. At Turf Moor, Leake continued to prosper and in 1912, at the age of 40, he was chosen as an England reserve. With Small Heath, Villa and Burnley, Leake clocked up a total of 464 League and Cup appearances.

In 1903-04, Villa finished fifth in

Villa have the Sheffield Wednesday defence in trouble during the Boxing Day game in 1903.

DIVISION 1 1903-04											
	P	W	D	L	F	A	W	D	L	F	A	Pts
Sheffield W	34	14	3	0	34	10	6	4	7	14	18	47
Manchester C	34	10	4	3	35	19	9	2	6	36	26	44
Everton	34	13	0	4	36	12	6	5	6	23	20	43
Newcastle U	34	12	3	2	31	13	6	3	8	27	32	42
Aston Villa	34	13	1	3	41	16	4	6	7	29	32	41
Sunderland	34	12	3	2	41	15	5	2	10	22	34	39
Sheffield U	34	9	6	2	40	21	6	2	9	22	36	38
Wolves	34	10	6	1	29	23	4	2	11	15	43	36
Nottingham F	34	7	3	7	29	26	4	6	7	28	31	31
Middlesbrough	34	9	3	5	30	17	0	9	8	16	30	30
Small Heath	34	8	5	4	25	19	3	3	11	14	33	30
Bury	34	6	8	3	25	20	1	7	9	15	33	29
Notts Co	34	9	3	5	27	26	3	2	12	10	35	29
Derby Co	34	7	3	7	41	33	2	7	8	17	27	28
Blackburn R	34	7	5	5	29	23	4	1	12	19	37	28
Stoke	34	9	2	6	45	26	1	5	11	9	31	27
Liverpool	34	7	5	5	24	20	2	3	12	25	42	26
WBA	34	4	8	5	19	19	3	2	12	17	41	24

Division One — six points behind Sheffield Wednesday, who won the title for the second successive season — and lost 1-0 at home to Tottenham Hotspur in the second round of the FA Cup, albeit in remarkable fashion.

There were some remarkable score-lines this season: in only their second game, Villa lost 6-1 at Sunderland; in December they won 7-3 at Nottingham Forest; and in late February beat Sheffield United 6-1 at home.

Bache was now the outright leading scorer with 15 League goals, helped by a hat-trick against Newcastle United in November. Again there were some big attendances, the highest being 38,920 against West Brom in mid-September.

The Cup tie against Tottenham was a dramatic affair. Villa took a big following to White Hart Lane and at half-time, with Villa leading

1-0, part of the big crowd spilled on to the pitch. Efforts to clear the playing area were doomed to failure and the game was abandoned.

Spurs were fined £350 and the tie was ordered to be replayed at Villa Park the following Thursday afternoon, where Spurs had the last laugh, going through with a goal from Jack Jones.

In 1904-05, however, Aston Villa were back in the Cup Final and also found a hero in that season in Harry Hampton, who joined the club from Wellington Town. A fiery centre-forward, as Villa marched towards another Final, Hampton came to full prominence.

The Cup trail started with a 5-1

win over Leicester Fosse at Villa Park. There followed a 3-2 win over Bury, also at home, and then in the quarter-finals Villa demolished Fulham 5-0 in Birmingham.

Safely into the semi-finals, Villa

DIVISION 1 1904-05											
	P	W	D	L	F	A	W	D	L	F	A	Pts
Newcastle U	34	14	1	2	41	12	9	1	7	31	21	48
Everton	34	14	2	1	36	11	7	3	7	27	25	47
Manchester C	34	14	3	0	46	17	6	3	8	20	20	46
Aston Villa	34	11	2	4	32	15	8	2	7	31	28	42
Sunderland	34	11	3	3	37	19	5	5	7	23	25	40
Sheffield U	34	13	0	4	39	20	6	2	9	25	36	40
Small Heath	34	11	1	5	32	17	6	4	7	22	21	39
Preston NE	34	9	5	3	28	13	4	5	8	14	24	36
Sheffield W	34	10	3	4	39	22	4	2	11	22	35	33
W Arsenal	34	9	5	3	19	12	3	4	10	17	28	33
Derby Co	34	9	4	4	29	19	3	4	10	8	29	32
Stoke	34	10	3	4	26	18	3	1	13	14	40	30
Blackburn R	34	9	3	5	28	18	2	2	13	12	33	27
Wolves	34	10	2	5	30	23	1	2	14	17	50	26
Middlesbrough	34	7	3	7	21	24	2	5	10	15	32	26
Nottingham F	34	5	3	9	24	28	4	4	9	16	33	25
Bury	34	8	2	7	34	26	2	2	13	13	41	24
Notts Co	34	1	7	9	16	33	4	1	12	20	36	18

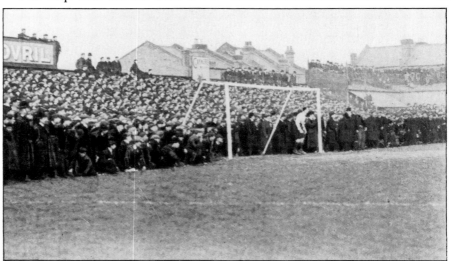

The crowd are already wedged up to the goal-line at White Hart Lane in February 1904. The Cup tie was eventually abandoned with Villa leading 1-0.

After the game had been called off, thousands more fans streamed on to the Tottenham ground.

Villa's Albert Hall leaves a Fulham defender stranded in the 5-0 Cup win over the Cottagers in March 1905.

The players gather round as Fulham's Harry Ross receives attention.

found the going much tougher against Everton, the eventual First Division runners-up, and after drawing 1-1 at Stoke, finally edged their way through 2-1 at Nottingham to face an even more daunting task in the Final — Newcastle United, the League champions who had done the League double over a Villa side which eventually finished fourth.

But the fans need not have worried. In the third minute, Hampton gave Villa the lead with a superb goal. The Midlanders got straight on to the attack and Hampton exchanged passes with Bache before hitting the ball home past Jimmy Lawrence in the Magpies' goal.

After Billy Brawn squandered a good chance to put Villa 2-0 ahead, Hampton might have scored and then Brawn again fluffed a chance. Billy Garraty was playing a deeper role, feeding Hall on the left wing and Villa reached the half-time whistle wondering just how their lead was still only a slender one goal. Indeed, Newcastle might have equalised when Howie shot at George with only the goalkeeper to beat.

With 15 minutes remaining, Hall got past his full-back and sent in a cracking shot which Lawrence could only block. The ball ran to Hampton, who rammed home his second goal, and Villa had won the Cup for the fourth time in their history.

Up stepped Villa captain Howard Spencer to receive the trophy from Lord Kinnaird and also collect his third winners' medal. The Villa party delayed their return to Birmingham until the following Monday evening, until after the funeral of the city's Lord Mayor that afternoon, and when they arrived at New Street Station they found the place decked out in claret and blue bunting. A huge crowd cheered them off the train and then they were taken by charabancs to the Holte Hotel in Trinity Road.

But if those Villa supporters hoped for more stirring deeds in the immediate future, then they were to be disappointed for in 1905-06 and 1906-07, Villa had only modest seasons.

In the first of those campaigns they finished eighth in the First Division and were knocked out of the Cup by Manchester United, going down

Harry Hampton scores Villa's first goal against Newcastle in the 1905 FA Cup Final.

A long-range view of Villa's first goal, scored after only three minutes.

Aston Villa before the start of the 1904-05 season with the Mayor of Birmingham's Charity Cup, Birmingham League Shield and Birmingham Senior Cup. Standing (left to right): Noon, Evans, Johnson, George, Miles, Wood, Niblo. Seated: Wilkes, McLuckie, Pearson, Spencer, Hall, Garraty, Bache, Lockett. On ground: Brown, Leake.

5-1 at Clayton in the third round after establishing what is still their record FA Cup win with an 11-0 hammering of King's Lynn in the first round.

In the next season, they ended it in fifth place and Bolton beat them 2-0 at Burnden Park in the second round of the Cup.

The 1907-08 season saw the final appearance in a Villa shirt of the

Harry Hampton
— The Wellington Whirlwind

NO man in the history of the club scored more League goals for Aston Villa than Harry Hampton, the man they called the 'Wellington Whirlwind'. Between 1904-05 and 1919-20, Hampton hit the back of the net 215 times, once more than the great Billy Walker. And overall, in League and Cup, he was only two goals behind Walker on 242 in the list of Villa's all-time great goalscorers.

And it was not just the amount of goals he scored, but the manner in which he scored them which made him such a huge favourite with the Villa fans, for he terrorised opposing defences, particularly the goalkeepers who were often bundled into the back of the net — all perfectly fair in those days.

Hampton, though, was no mere bulldozing forward. He had plenty of skill and one of the most delightful aspects of his game were the long, sweeping passes out to the wings. By the time the ball came back into the middle, Hampton was usually there to connect. A contemporary writer said: 'Hampton has that indescribable dash that no man can acquire unless nature has placed it upon him.'

He was born in the Shropshire town of Wellington in April 1885 and played for Shifnal Juniors before graduating to more senior football with Wellington Town. Fifty-four goals in two seasons with Wellington were enough to persuade Villa to take him on and he joined the staff in April 1904. He made his League debut at Hyde Road the following November, in a 2-1 defeat at the hands of Manchester City, and scored his first goal for Villa in a 4-2 home win over Notts County the following week.

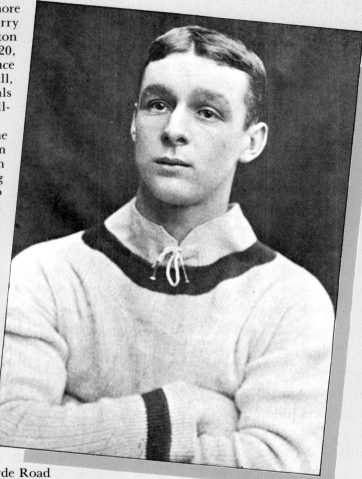

He missed only one League game for the remainder of that season, scoring 15 goals altogether, and had certainly arrived as a major force. Moreover, he was about to solve a centre-forward problem that had dogged Villa since Johnny Campbell had returned to Scotland.

But it was in the FA Cup that Hampton truly exploded on the national scene. As Villa marched to the Final, Hampton played in every game, scoring seven goals in six appearances. Two of those goals came in the Final itself, against Newcastle United at the Crystal Palace, and they helped Villa to lift the trophy yet again.

When Villa won the League championship in 1909-10, Hampton was their leading scorer with 26 goals, despite missing the first six games of the season through injury. He scored four League hat-tricks that season and another in the FA Cup. Surprisingly, though, Hampton had to wait until the 1912-13 season for his first England cap and he won only four altogether. In 1913 he also collected another Cup

winners' medal, when Villa beat Sunderland 1-0 in the Final.

That same season, when Villa finished runners-up in the First Division, he scored five goals when they hammered Sheffield Wednesday 10-0 (two weeks later Harold Halse emulated his feat with all five against Derby County). He was an utterly fearless player who possessed an almost reckless approach — and the crowd just loved him.

During World War One, he suffered in a German gas attack on his platoon's position. Yet when peacetime football resumed in 1919-20, Hampton was ready to take his place for the opening game and played seven times before being transferred to Birmingham in February 1920.

The Blues were battling to get out of the Second Division and Hampton scored 11 goals in only ten games before he was injured. His absence from the last six games almost certainly cost Birmingham promotion but the following season they went up as champions and Hampton was their top scorer with 16 goals. His job done, he moved to Newport County in September 1922. Harry Hampton died at Wrexham in March 1963.

Aston Villa, 1905-06. Back (left to right): Spencer, George, Miles. Middle: Pearson, Leake, Windmill. Front: Brawn, Garraty, Hampton, Bache, Hall.

Aston Villa, 1907-08. Back row (left to right): H.Toney (director), J.Devey (director), Garraty, Spencer, Logan, Miles, F.W.Rinder (director), George, J.Ansell (director), J.E.Margoschis (chairman), Riley, Logan, Dr H.Jessop (director), P.W.M.Bate (director), E.W.Strange (director). Middle row: J.Whitehouse (director), F.Cooper (director), Greenhalgh, Walters, Millington, Hampton, J.Jones (director), Evans, E.Cox (director), W.McGregor (director). Front row: Hall, Buckley, Cantrell, Codling, Leake, Bache, Boden.

DIVISION 1 1905-06											
	P	W	D	L	F	A	W	D	L	F	A	Pts
Liverpool	38	14	3	2	49	15	9	2	8	30	31	51
Preston NE	38	12	5	2	36	15	5	8	6	18	24	47
Sheffield W	38	12	5	2	40	20	6	3	10	23	32	44
Newcastle U	38	12	4	3	49	23	6	3	10	25	25	43
Manchester C	38	11	2	6	46	23	8	3	8	27	31	43
Bolton W	38	13	1	5	51	22	4	6	9	30	45	41
Birmingham	38	14	2	3	49	20	3	5	11	16	39	41
Aston Villa	38	13	2	4	51	19	4	4	11	21	37	40
Blackburn R	38	10	5	4	34	18	6	3	10	20	34	40
Stoke	38	12	5	2	41	15	4	2	13	13	40	39
Everton	38	12	1	6	44	30	3	6	10	26	36	37
W Arsenal	38	12	4	3	43	21	3	3	13	19	43	37
Sheffield U	38	10	4	5	33	23	5	2	12	24	39	36
Sunderland	38	13	2	4	40	21	2	3	14	21	49	35
Derby Co	38	10	5	4	27	16	4	2	13	12	42	35
Notts Co	38	8	9	2	34	21	3	3	13	21	50	34
Bury	38	8	5	6	30	26	3	5	11	27	48	32
Middlesbrough	38	10	4	5	41	23	0	7	12	15	48	31
Nottingham F	38	11	2	6	40	27	2	3	14	18	52	31
Wolves	38	7	5	7	38	28	1	2	16	20	71	23

DIVISION 1 1906-07											
	P	W	D	L	F	A	W	D	L	F	A	Pts
Newcastle U	38	18	1	0	51	12	4	6	9	23	34	51
Bristol C	38	12	3	4	37	18	8	5	6	29	29	48
Everton	38	16	2	1	50	10	4	3	12	20	36	45
Sheffield U	38	13	4	2	36	17	4	7	8	21	38	45
Aston Villa	38	13	4	2	51	19	6	2	11	27	33	44
Bolton W	38	10	4	5	35	18	8	4	7	24	29	44
W Arsenal	38	15	1	3	38	15	5	3	11	28	44	44
Manchester U	38	10	6	3	33	15	7	2	10	20	41	42
Birmingham	38	13	5	1	41	17	2	3	14	11	35	38
Sunderland	38	10	4	5	42	31	4	5	10	23	35	37
Middlesbrough	38	11	2	6	33	21	4	4	11	23	42	36
Blackburn R	38	10	3	6	40	25	4	4	11	16	34	35
Sheffield W	38	8	5	6	33	26	4	6	9	16	34	35
Preston NE	38	13	4	2	35	19	1	3	15	9	38	35
Liverpool	38	9	2	8	45	32	4	5	10	19	33	33
Bury	38	9	4	6	30	23	4	2	13	28	45	32
Manchester C	38	7	7	5	29	25	3	5	11	24	52	32
Notts Co	38	6	9	4	31	18	2	6	11	15	32	31
Derby Co	38	8	6	5	29	19	1	3	15	12	40	27
Stoke	38	7	6	6	27	22	1	4	14	14	42	26

Villa Park in 1907, during the game between Aston Villa and Liverpool.

Aston Villa, League champions 1909-10. Back row (players only, left to right): Lyons, Layton, Hogan, George, Cartlidge, Miles, Kearns. Middle row: Gerrish, Hunter, Eyre, Bache, Tranter, Buckley, Hall. Front row: Walters, Moss, Hampton, Wallace.

great Howard Spencer, who bowed out after the 3-3 draw with Newcastle United at Villa Park on 30 November, when there were 24,000 spectators to see the end of a remarkable career.

That season also saw Villa finish runners-up in Division One and, although they were well behind the champions Manchester United, this paved the way for Villa's sixth title in 1909-10.

Inevitably, new faces were arriving at Villa Park including Chris Buckley, a classy centre-half, Manchester-born but signed from Brighton & Hove Albion in August 1906. The brother of Frank Buckley, later to win fame as manager of Wolves, amongst other clubs, Chris Buckley recovered from a broken ankle, suffered in the opening game of 1907-08, to help Villa win the title two years later.

In 1908-09, Villa dropped a little to seventh place and lost to Nottingham Forest in the first round of the Cup. Twelve months earlier they had again gone out to Manchester United, this time in the third round.

The following season they took the title for the sixth time — and the last occasion until Ron Saunders' team over 70 years later.

Villa lost only eight League matches in 1909-10 and were unbeaten at home, scoring 84 goals in 38 matches, a fine striking rate even in those days. They finished five

DIVISION 1 1907-08											
	P	W	D	L	F	A	W	D	L	F	A	Pts
Manchester U	38	15	1	3	43	19	8	5	6	38	29	52
Aston Villa	38	9	6	4	47	24	8	3	8	30	35	43
Manchester C	38	12	5	2	36	19	4	6	9	26	35	43
Newcastle U	38	11	4	4	41	24	4	8	7	24	30	42
Sheffield W	38	14	0	5	50	25	5	4	10	23	39	42
Middlesbrough	38	12	2	5	32	16	5	6	9	22	29	41
Bury	38	8	7	4	29	22	6	4	9	29	39	39
Liverpool	38	14	2	6	43	24	5	4	10	25	37	38
Nottingham F	38	11	6	2	42	21	2	5	12	17	41	37
Bristol C	38	8	7	4	29	21	4	5	10	29	40	36
Everton	38	11	4	4	34	24	4	2	13	24	37	36
Preston NE	38	9	7	3	33	18	3	5	11	14	35	36
Chelsea	38	8	3	8	30	35	6	5	8	23	27	36
W Arsenal	38	9	8	2	32	18	3	4	12	19	45	*36
Blackburn R	38	10	7	2	35	23	2	5	12	16	40	*36
Sunderland	38	11	2	6	53	31	5	1	13	25	44	35
Sheffield U	38	8	6	5	27	22	4	5	10	25	36	35
Notts Co	38	9	3	7	24	19	4	5	10	15	32	34
Bolton W	38	10	3	6	30	16	4	2	13	22	40	33
Birmingham	38	6	6	7	22	28	3	6	10	18	32	30
*Woolwich Arsenal & Blackburn Rovers finished in equal 14th place												

DIVISION 1 1908-09											
	P	W	D	L	F	A	W	D	L	F	A	Pts
Newcastle U	38	14	1	4	32	20	10	4	5	33	21	53
Everton	38	11	3	5	51	28	7	7	5	31	29	46
Sunderland	38	14	0	5	41	23	7	2	10	37	40	44
Blackburn R	38	6	6	7	29	26	8	7	4	32	24	41
Sheffield W	38	15	0	4	48	24	2	6	11	19	37	40
W Arsenal	38	9	3	7	24	18	5	7	7	28	31	38
Aston Villa	38	8	7	4	31	22	6	3	10	27	34	38
Bristol C	38	7	7	5	24	25	6	5	8	21	33	38
Middlesbrough	38	11	2	6	38	21	3	7	9	21	32	37
Preston NE	38	8	7	4	34	24	4	6	9	13	24	37
Chelsea	38	8	7	4	33	22	6	2	11	23	39	37
Sheffield U	38	9	5	5	31	25	5	4	10	20	34	37
Manchester U	38	10	3	6	37	33	5	4	10	21	35	37
Nottingham F	38	9	2	8	39	24	5	6	8	27	33	36
Notts Co	38	9	4	6	31	23	5	4	10	20	25	36
Liverpool	38	9	5	5	36	25	6	1	12	21	40	36
Bury	38	9	6	4	35	27	5	2	12	28	50	36
Bradford C	38	8	7	6	27	20	4	4	10	20	27	34
Manchester C	38	12	3	4	50	23	3	1	15	17	46	34
Leicester F	38	6	6	7	32	41	2	3	14	22	61	25

points ahead of runners-up Liverpool.

Manchester United were hammered 7-1, Woolwich Arsenal 5-1 and Sheffield Wednesday also suffered a five-goal defeat. Villa also smashed six goals past Derby in a second-round FA Cup tie before losing 2-1 to Manchester City at Villa Park.

So, Villa had won the League

DIVISION 1 1909-10												
	P	W	D	L	F	A	W	D	L	F	A	Pts
Aston Villa	38	17	2	0	62	19	6	5	8	22	23	53
Liverpool	38	13	3	3	47	23	8	3	8	31	34	48
Blackburn R	38	13	6	0	47	17	5	3	11	26	38	45
Newcastle U	38	11	3	5	33	22	8	4	7	37	34	45
Manchester U	38	14	2	3	41	20	5	5	9	28	41	45
Sheffield U	38	10	5	4	42	19	6	5	8	20	22	42
Bradford C	38	12	3	4	38	17	5	5	9	26	30	42
Sunderland	38	12	3	4	40	18	6	2	11	26	33	41
Notts Co	38	10	5	4	41	26	5	5	9	26	33	40
Everton	38	8	6	5	30	28	8	2	9	21	28	40
Sheffield W	38	11	4	4	38	28	4	5	10	22	35	39
Preston NE	38	14	2	3	36	13	1	3	15	16	45	35
Bury	38	8	3	8	35	30	4	6	9	27	36	33
Nottingham F	38	4	7	8	19	34	7	4	8	35	38	33
Tottenham H	38	10	6	3	35	23	1	4	14	18	46	32
Bristol C	38	9	5	5	28	18	3	3	13	17	42	32
Middlesbrough	38	8	4	7	34	36	3	5	11	22	37	31
W Arsenal	38	6	5	8	17	19	5	4	10	20	48	31
Chelsea	38	10	4	5	32	24	1	3	15	15	46	29
Bolton W	38	7	2	10	31	34	2	4	13	13	37	24

championship six times in the first 35 years of the club's existence and they were to finish runners-up three more times before 1914.

Harry Hampton was leading scorer with 26 goals, followed by Joe Bache with 20. Villa used only 18 players, of whom only Charlie Wallace was ever-present.

Wallace, a tricky outside-right, was born in Sunderland but joined Villa in 1907 from Crystal Palace, to embark on a career which saw him make 349 League and Cup appearances despite losing four seasons to the war, and gain a League championship medal and two FA Cup winners' medals as well as playing three times for England.

And Wallace's Villa days did not end when he retired from playing. After a short spell with Oldham Athletic, he returned to Villa Park and worked as a steward until 1960.

In 1910-11, Villa finished runners-up — pipped by a point by Manchester United — and yet again went out of the Cup at the hands of United, this time 2-1 in the second round.

In October 1910, a young clerk applied for the post of office junior at Villa Park. Eighteen-year-old William Smith got the job and began a 45-year association with the club. He died in August 1957, after watching Villa win the FA Cup for the

Harry Hampton, leading scorer as Villa won the title again.

seventh time, and after helping to sign some of the greatest players in the club's history.

In the two years following Smith's introduction to the world of football administration, there were several comings and goings at Villa Park. Clem Stephenson, a scheming forward from County Durham, was already on the books and farmed out to the Villa nursery side, Stourbridge.

Another player to lose out to the war, Stephenson still managed 216 League and Cup appearances before being rather surprisingly transferred to Huddersfield Town in 1921. With the Terriers he won an England cap

DIVISION 1 1910-11												
	P	W	D	L	F	A	W	D	L	F	A	Pts
Manchester U	38	14	4	1	47	18	8	4	7	25	22	52
Aston Villa	38	15	3	1	50	18	7	4	8	19	23	51
Sunderland	38	10	6	3	44	22	5	9	5	23	26	45
Everton	38	12	3	4	34	17	7	4	8	16	19	45
Bradford C	38	13	1	5	33	16	7	4	8	18	26	45
Sheffield W	38	10	5	4	24	15	7	3	9	23	33	42
Oldham A	38	13	4	2	30	12	3	5	11	14	29	41
Newcastle U	38	8	7	4	37	18	7	3	9	24	25	40
Sheffield U	38	8	3	8	27	21	7	5	7	22	22	38
W Arsenal	38	9	6	4	24	14	4	6	9	17	35	38
Notts Co	38	9	6	4	21	16	5	4	10	16	29	38
Blackburn R	38	12	2	5	40	14	1	9	9	22	40	37
Liverpool	38	11	3	5	38	19	4	4	11	15	34	37
Preston NE	38	8	5	6	25	19	4	6	9	15	30	35
Tottenham H	38	10	5	4	40	23	3	1	15	12	40	32
Middlesbrough	38	9	5	5	31	21	2	5	12	18	42	32
Manchester C	38	7	5	7	26	26	2	8	9	17	32	31
Bury	38	8	9	2	27	18	1	2	16	16	53	29
Bristol C	38	8	4	7	23	21	3	1	15	20	45	27
Nottingham F	38	5	4	10	28	31	4	3	12	27	44	25

Clem Stephenson, a scheming forward who made over 200 senior appearances despite losing several years to the war.

and helped them to a hat-trick of League championships and a Cup Final win, adding these to two FA Cup winners' medals gained with Villa.

Jimmy Leach, a strong wing-half from North-East non-League soccer, arrived in 1912. Tommy Weston, from Birmingham junior football, began to partner Tommy Lyons at full-back. George Tranter, another local product, became a regular at right-half.

And in 1912, Villa signed Harold Halse, Manchester United's high-

A Villa defender heads clear at White Hart Lane in November 1911.

scoring forward who had netted 50 goals in 124 appearances for the Manchester club. Halse played for Villa for only one season but made his mark with 28 goals in 37 games including five against Derby County in only his ninth match, a feat which equalled Harry Hampton's club record for most goals in a game.

DIVISION 1 1911-12											
	P	W	D	L	F	A	W	D	L	F	A	Pts
Blackburn R	38	13	6	0	35	10	7	3	9	25	33	49
Everton	38	13	5	1	29	12	7	1	11	17	30	46
Newcastle U	38	10	4	5	37	25	8	4	7	27	25	44
Bolton W	38	14	2	3	35	15	6	1	12	19	28	43
Sheffield W	38	11	3	5	44	17	5	6	8	25	32	41
Aston Villa	38	12	2	5	48	22	5	5	9	28	41	41
Middlesbrough	38	11	6	2	35	17	5	2	12	21	28	40
Sunderland	38	10	6	3	37	14	4	5	10	21	37	39
WBA	38	10	6	3	23	15	5	3	11	20	32	39
W Arsenal	38	12	3	4	38	19	3	5	11	17	40	38
Bradford C	38	12	3	4	31	15	3	5	11	15	35	38
Tottenham H	38	10	4	5	35	20	4	5	10	18	33	37
Manchester U	38	9	5	5	29	19	4	6	9	16	41	37
Sheffield U	38	10	4	5	47	29	3	6	10	16	27	36
Manchester C	38	10	5	4	39	20	3	4	12	17	38	35
Notts Co	38	9	4	6	26	20	5	3	11	20	43	35
Liverpool	38	8	4	7	27	23	4	6	9	22	32	34
Oldham A	38	10	3	6	32	19	2	7	10	14	35	34
Preston NE	38	8	4	7	26	25	5	3	11	14	32	33
Bury	38	6	5	8	23	25	0	4	15	9	34	21

Albert Hall, formed a wonderful under-standing with Joe Bache on Villa's left wing.

At the end of the 1911-12 season, Villa made a double swoop into the transfer market to bring Jimmy Harrop and Sam Hardy from Liverpool to Villa Park. Centre-half Harrop went on to skipper Villa, whilst Hardy was already one of the best goalkeepers the game had ever seen. The pair cost less than £1,250, a real bargain considering their future contributions.

A few weeks after they signed, Harrop and Hardy were joined by Andrew Ducat, who was transferred from Woolwich Arsenal for £1,000. Ducat, a fine wing-half who had played both soccer and cricket for England, also went on to skipper Villa, taking over for the 1920 Cup Final when Harrop missed the game through injury.

In 1911-12, Villa slipped back to sixth in the First Division and after

Aston Villa in 1911-12. Back row (left to right): J.Carland (assistant trainer), Greaves, Anstey, Edwards, Henshall, R.Moseley (commisionaire), Renville, Kearns, Lyons, Tranter, R.Leeson (groundsman), Littlewood, Hall, Miles, Logan, Kimberley, Keyworth, Smith. Middle row: E.W.Strange (assistant secretary), Edgley, George, J.Whitehouse (vice-president), H.Spencer (director), F.Cooper (vice-president), J.Ansell (president), F.W.Rinder (chairman), Dr H.Jessop (director), J.E.Margoschis (director), Doe, J.Grierson (trainer), G.B.Ramsay (secretary). Seated: P.W.M.Bate (director), Wallace, Gerrish, Buckley, Bache, Walters, Hampton, J.E.Jones (vice-chairman). On ground: Moss, Whittaker, Eyre, Hunter, Mann, Stephenson, Goods.

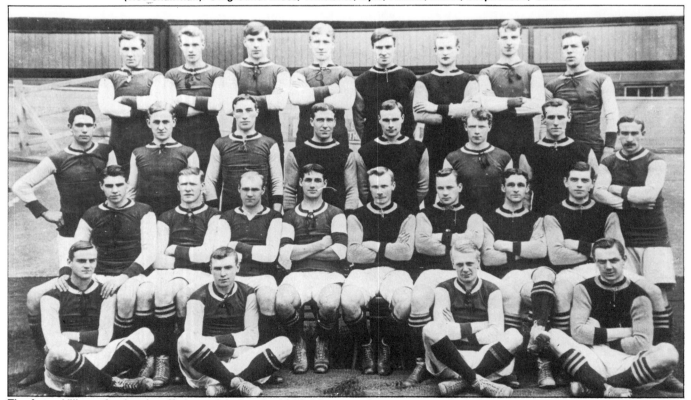

The Aston Villa professional staff pictured during the 1912-13 season. It was not a particularly successful season by Villa's standards, for they finished sixth in Division One and were knocked out of the FA Cup in the second round.

thumping Walsall 6-0 in the first round of the Cup, were embarrassingly knocked out by Reading, who won a second-round replay 1-0 at Elm Park.

Villa, though, were to make one more FA Cup Final appearance before World War One, when they won the trophy for the fifth time, beating Sunderland 1-0 at the Crystal Palace in 1913.

By the time they reached the semi-finals, Villa had scored 18 goals in four ties, against Derby County (3-1 after the first game at Derby had been abandoned because of a blizzard), West Ham United (5-0), Crystal Palace (5-0) and Bradford (5-0).

In the semi-final they met Oldham Athletic at Ewood Park and beat them 1-0 with a goal from Clem Stephen-

son, whilst Sunderland scraped through 3-2 against Burnley after the first game had ended goalless.

There were two survivors from Villa's previous FA Cup Final appearance in 1905 — Harry Hampton and Joe Bache. For Hampton in particular it was a memorable year, for he had scored the only goal of England's win over Scotland in April

Joe Bache meets the Oldham captain David Wilson before the FA Cup semi-final at Ewood Park in March 1913.

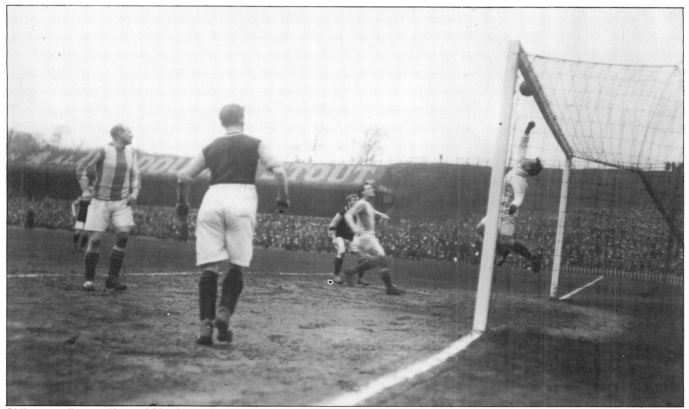

Oldham goalkeeper Howard Matthews tips the ball over the bar during the 1913 semi-final. Matthews was still playing, for Halifax, in his 45th year.

Villa's winning goal, scored by Tommy Barber, in the 1913 FA Cup Final against Sunderland at the Crystal Palace.

that year, when he bundled the Scottish goalkeeper Jimmy Brownlie over the line at Stamford Bridge.

In Villa's goal against Sunderland — the Wearsiders' first appearance in a Cup Final — was the legendary Sam Hardy, who had taken over from Billy George and who had already won ten England caps before he joined Villa from Liverpool.

It was an FA Cup Final with a difference, for the participants were also first and second in the First Division — Sunderland the eventual champions and Villa runners-up, four points behind.

The occasion was reflected by the size of the crowd which, at 121,919, was a record attendance and although the match was not an epic, there was plenty of good football to please the paying spectators.

Aston Villa, FA Cup winners 1913. Back row (players only, left to right): Lyons, Weston, Hardy. Middle row: Bache, Halse, Hampton, Stephenson. Front row: Wallace, Barber, Harrop, Leach.

DIVISION 1 1912-13	P	W	D	L	F	A	W	D	L	F	A	Pts
Sunderland	38	14	2	3	47	17	11	2	6	39	26	54
Aston Villa	38	13	4	2	57	21	6	8	5	29	31	50
Sheffield W	38	12	4	3	44	23	9	3	7	31	32	49
Manchester U	38	13	3	3	41	14	6	5	8	28	29	46
Blackburn R	38	10	5	4	54	21	6	8	5	25	22	45
Manchester C	38	12	3	4	34	15	6	5	8	19	22	44
Derby Co	38	10	2	7	40	29	7	6	6	29	37	42
Bolton W	38	10	6	3	36	20	6	4	9	26	43	42
Oldham A	38	11	7	1	33	12	3	7	9	17	43	42
WBA	38	8	7	4	30	20	5	5	9	27	30	38
Everton	38	8	2	9	28	31	7	5	7	20	23	37
Liverpool	38	12	5	2	40	24	4	3	12	21	47	37
Bradford C	38	10	5	4	33	22	2	6	11	17	38	35
Newcastle U	38	8	5	6	30	23	5	3	11	17	24	34
Sheffield U	38	10	5	4	36	24	4	1	14	20	46	34
Middlesbrough	38	6	9	4	29	22	5	1	13	26	47	32
Tottenham H	38	9	3	7	28	25	3	3	13	17	47	30
Chelsea	38	7	2	10	29	40	4	4	11	22	33	28
Notts Co	38	6	4	9	19	20	1	5	13	9	36	23
W Arsenal	38	1	8	10	11	31	2	4	13	15	43	18

Villa should have taken the lead in the 15th minute when they were awarded a penalty but Wallace, overcome by the tension, shot wide. Then Hardy was carried off with a knee injury and his former Liverpool teammate, Jimmy Harrop, took his place in goal with Hampton moving back to centre-half.

Sunderland's Harry Martin twice saw his shots hit a Villa post wth Harrop well beaten, but eventually Hardy returned and Villa regained their composure. Late in the game

they scored the only goal. Wallace took a low corner and Barber headed it home.

Sunderland had fielded such stars as Charlie Buchan, who combined with Cuggy and Mordue to form one of the best right-wing triangles of the day, but they had been only second best in the 1913 FA Cup Final.

During the game, Villa's Harry Hampton and Sunderland's tough defender Charlie Thomson were involved in a series of unsavoury incidents. Nottingham referee

Villa goalkeeper Sam Hardy punches away from a Chelsea forward at Stamford Bridge in February 1914.

DIVISION 1 1913-14											
	P	W	D	L	F	A	W	D	L	F	A	Pts
Blackburn R	38	14	4	1	51	15	6	7	6	27	27	51
Aston Villa	38	11	3	5	36	21	8	3	8	29	29	44
Middlesbrough	38	14	2	3	55	20	5	3	11	22	40	43
Oldham A	38	11	5	3	34	16	6	4	9	21	29	43
WBA	38	11	7	1	30	16	4	6	9	16	26	43
Bolton W	38	13	4	2	41	14	3	6	10	24	38	42
Sunderland	38	11	3	5	32	17	6	3	10	31	35	40
Chelsea	38	12	3	4	28	18	4	4	11	18	37	39
Bradford C	38	8	6	5	23	17	4	8	7	17	23	38
Sheffield U	38	11	4	4	36	19	5	1	13	27	41	37
Newcastle U	38	9	6	4	27	18	4	5	10	12	30	37
Burnley	38	10	4	5	43	20	2	8	9	18	33	36
Manchester C	38	9	3	7	28	23	5	5	9	23	30	36
Manchester U	38	8	4	7	27	23	7	2	10	25	39	36
Everton	38	8	7	4	32	18	4	4	11	14	37	35
Liverpool	38	8	4	7	27	25	6	3	10	19	37	35
Tottenham H	38	9	6	4	30	19	3	4	12	20	43	34
Sheffield W	38	8	4	7	34	34	5	4	10	19	36	34
Preston NE	38	9	4	6	39	31	3	2	14	13	38	30
Derby Co	38	6	5	8	34	32	2	6	11	21	39	27

DIVISION 1 1914-15											
	P	W	D	L	F	A	W	D	L	F	A	Pts
Everton	38	8	5	6	44	29	11	3	5	32	18	46
Oldham A	38	11	5	3	46	25	6	6	7	24	31	45
Blackburn R	38	11	4	4	51	27	7	3	9	32	34	43
Burnley	38	12	1	6	38	18	6	6	7	23	29	43
Manchester C	38	9	7	3	29	15	6	6	7	20	24	43
Sheffield U	38	11	5	3	28	13	4	8	7	21	28	43
Sheffield W	38	10	7	2	43	23	5	6	8	18	31	43
Sunderland	38	11	3	5	46	30	7	2	10	35	42	41
Bradford	38	11	4	4	40	20	6	3	10	29	45	41
WBA	38	11	5	3	31	9	4	5	10	18	34	40
Bradford C	38	11	7	1	40	18	2	7	10	15	31	40
Middlesbrough	38	10	6	3	42	24	3	6	10	20	50	38
Liverpool	38	11	5	3	45	34	3	4	12	20	41	37
Aston Villa	38	10	5	4	39	32	3	6	10	23	40	37
Newcastle U	38	8	4	7	29	23	6	3	10	17	25	32
Notts Co	38	8	7	4	28	18	1	6	12	13	39	31
Bolton W	38	8	5	6	35	27	3	3	13	33	57	30
Manchester U	38	8	6	5	27	19	1	6	12	19	43	30
Chelsea	38	8	6	5	32	25	0	7	12	19	40	29
Tottenham H	38	7	7	5	30	29	1	5	13	27	61	28

The great Sam Hardy, an England international who joined Villa from Liverpool. Hardy went on to make 183 League and Cup appearances for Villa.

A.Adams decided, perhaps as this was a Cup Final, to largely ignore the trouble but after the game the FA suspended both players and the referee for a month each for 'failing to maintain order'.

Villa finished runners-up in the First Division in 1913-14 — seven points behind Blackburn Rovers — and reached the semi-finals of the Cup again before losing 2-0 to Liverpool at White Hart Lane. Halse had now been transferred to Chelsea and one new face was Harold Edgley, who joined Villa from Crewe and who, six years later, was to be one of the unluckiest of footballers.

The following season was foot-ball's last until peace was restored and Villa slipped to 13th place in the table and were beaten 1-0 by Manchester City in the second round of the Cup. Then the lights went out over Europe and many Aston Villa footballers went to do battle of a different kind.

Since their formation in 1874, Villa had won the FA Cup five times in six Finals and taken the Football League championship six times, finishing runners-up a further six. It was an incredible performance and ensured that the name of Aston Villa would stand amongst the giants of the game, no matter what happened after the war.

Between Two Wars

WHEN war was declared in August 1914, there were many who felt that football should be suspended. In November that year, the historian A.F.Pollard, writing in *The Times*, said, "Every club that employs a professional football player is bribing a much-needed recruit from enlistment and every spectator who pays his gate money is contributing so much towards a German victory."

Others, however, saw the game as a necessary morale-booster for troops at home on leave and weary workers in munitions factories. So, the 1914-15 season was played to a conclusion and after Lord Derby presented the FA Cup to Sheffield United in April 1915, he said, "The clubs and their supporters had seen the Cup played for and now it was the duty of everyone to join with each other and play a sterner game for England."

The Football League and the FA Cup competitions were then suspended but most clubs played throughout the war in regionalised leagues and cups. For Villa, however, there was little football and the

Andy Ducat, captain of Aston Villa, and Fred Bullock, the Huddersfield Town skipper, inspect the coin at the toss-up for the 1920 Cup Final.

biggest disappointment was that Frederick Rinder had to abandon plans to turn Villa Park into a 120,000 capacity stadium,

There were a few matches against West Brom, in aid of the War Fund, but it was not until 1918-19 that Aston Villa played serious competitive football again when they took part in the Midland Victiory League. It comprised only four clubs — Villa, West Brom, Wolves and Derby — and Villa finished bottom with three points from their six games. West Brom won the mini league.

For Villa, though, there was real glory just around the corner, although the club now had an overdraft of £2,726, whereas before the war they had been one of the wealthiest clubs in the Football League.

When football proper resumed for the 1919-20 season, the Football League arranged the programme so that the clubs played each other on succeeding weeks — for instance, Villa would be at home to West Brom one week and then away at The Hawthorns the next. It was an arrangement which suited West Brom far better than it did Villa. Whilst the Throstles went on to become League champions, Villa had to wait until the first Saturday in October for their first League win — a 1-0 victory over Bradford — and by the middle of the month they were bedded firmly at the foot of the table with only three points from ten games.

But a transformation was on the way and it coincided with the signing of a player who was to become a major part of the Aston Villa story in those early post-war years.

Frank Barson, the Barnsley centre-half, joined Villa in October 1919 and made his debut at Middlesbrough when Villa scored a sensational 4-1 win to begin their fight back. Barson was joined at Villa by an inside-forward called Billy Kirton, who came to the club from Leeds City, the club expelled from the Football League for financial irregularities.

DIVISION 1 1919-20											
	P	W	D	L	F	A	W	D	L	F	A	Pts
WBA	42	17	1	3	65	21	11	3	7	39	26	60
Burnley	42	13	5	3	43	27	8	4	9	22	32	51
Chelsea	42	15	3	3	33	10	7	2	12	23	41	49
Liverpool	42	12	5	4	35	18	7	5	9	24	26	48
Sunderland	42	17	2	2	45	16	5	2	14	27	43	48
Bolton W	42	11	3	7	35	29	8	6	7	37	36	47
Manchester C	42	14	5	2	52	27	4	4	13	19	35	45
Newcastle U	42	11	5	5	31	13	6	4	11	13	26	43
Aston Villa	42	11	3	7	49	36	7	3	11	26	37	42
Arsenal	42	11	5	5	32	21	4	7	10	24	37	42
Bradford	42	8	6	7	31	26	7	6	8	29	37	42
Manchester U	42	6	8	7	20	17	7	6	8	34	33	40
Middlesbrough	42	10	5	6	35	23	5	5	11	26	42	40
Sheffield U	42	14	5	2	43	20	2	3	16	16	49	40
Bradford C	42	10	6	5	36	25	4	5	12	18	38	39
Everton	42	8	6	7	42	29	4	8	9	27	39	38
Oldham A	42	12	4	5	33	19	3	4	14	16	33	38
Derby Co	42	12	5	4	36	18	1	7	13	11	39	38
Preston NE	42	9	6	6	35	27	5	4	12	22	46	38
Blackburn R	42	11	4	6	48	30	2	7	12	16	47	37
Notts Co	42	9	8	4	39	25	3	4	14	17	49	36
Sheffield W	42	6	4	11	14	23	1	5	15	14	41	23

Both men were to play a big part in Villa's drive that season when they went on to win the FA Cup.

Like most sides, Villa had lost several players to the war. Tommy Barber and Arthur Dobson, a young centre-half, had been killed in the fighting, whilst Bache, Halse and Lyons had left the club and that made a big hole in the 1913 FA Cup-winning side. But with Barson, Kirton and another young player — Billy Walker — Villa were rebuilding

Ducat steps up to receive the FA Cup from Prince Henry, third son of King George V, at Stamford Bridge.

Billy Walker
— The Goal Machine

THERE can be few players who have enjoyed such a dramatic entry into football as Aston Villa's Billy Walker, who signed on with two goals on his debut in an FA Cup third-round tie against Queen's Park Rangers at Villa Park in January 1920. In the semi-final, Walker again scored twice and one month later he was climbing up to receive a winners' medal when Villa lifted the Cup by beating Huddersfield Town at Stamford Bridge.

Born at Wednesbury, Staffordshire, in October 1897, the son of a former Wolves player, Walker scored 80 goals in the Walsall Boys' League in 1910-11 and then continued that devastating form with Hednesford Town, Darlaston and Wednesbury Old Athletic, once scoring nine goals inside 40 minutes for the Wednesbury club in 1915.

It was that sort of form that saw a number of leading clubs show interest but it was Villa who snapped him up in March 1915, on amateur forms, and hang on to him until he could be signed as a full-time professional after the war ended.

Walker began as a centre-forward but Villa converted him to inside-left and in a career which lasted until he retired in November 1933, Walker scored 244 goals in 531 League and Cup games for the club, skippered Villa for six seasons and won 18 caps for England, captaining his country twice, as well as that FA Cup winners' medal in 1920 and a runners-up medal in 1924, when Villa were beaten by Newcastle United in the Final.

For England he partnered both Arthur Dorrell and the young Eric Houghton, both Villa teammates. He made his international debut against Ireland in 1920-21, his first full season, and played his last game against Austria in 1932-33, in a game that saw Eric Houghton make his England debut.

Walker really did burst on the scene in sensational fashion and on the opening day of the 1920-21 season, still only a novice in terms of games played, he netted four goals in a 5-0 win over Arsenal at Villa Park.

That was only one of many memorable days in his football career. He was one of the few players to score a hat-trick of penalties in a Football League game — against Bradford City at Villa Park in November 1921 — and he was also a good deputy goalkeeper, not only taking over for Villa in emergencies but once keeping goal for England, against France in Paris in 1925 when Gillingham's Fred Fox was injured during the second half. Five years later, when Fred Biddleston was hurt against Derby County, Walker agains stepped between the posts.

Only Harry Hampton scored more League goals for Aston Villa than Billy Walker, but Walker is the club's overall top scorer with two more than Hampton's tally of 242 in all matches.

He was renowned for long, sweeping passes to either wing and a body-swerve that had defenders falling over, and not since Hampton was in his prime had the Villa Park fans idolised a player in the way that they did Walker. Throughout the 1920s and well into the '30s, he practically *was* Aston Villa.

A month after retiring from playing, he took over as manager of Sheffield Wednesday and helped them win the FA Cup in 1935, then had a short spell in charge of Southern League club Chelmsford City before being appointed manager of Nottingham Forest in March 1939. He became the longest-serving manager in Forest's history and took them from the Third Division South to the First Division and to victory in the 1959 FA Cup Final before retiring through ill health in July 1960. Even then he served on the Forest committee until his death in Sheffield in November 1964.

Aston Villa, FA Cup winners in 1920. Back row (players only, left to right): Smart, Hardy, Moss. Middle row: Kirton, Ducat, Walker, Stephenson. Front row: Wallace, Barson, Weston, Dorrell.

that side around men like Hardy, Weston, Harrop and Stephenson, who were now veterans.

In January, with Villa now climbing slowly up the table, the FA Cup came around and Queen's Park Rangers arrived at Villa Park and were beaten 2-1 in the first round. It was in that game that Walker made his debut.

The son of George Walker, a former Wolverhampton Wanderers defender, Billy Walker was set to become a great player, both at club and international level, and a great manager. When Villa fans first saw his dazzling performance in the Cup game, they sensed that the club had signed a 'good 'un'.

Villa beat Manchester United at Old Trafford and Sunderland at Villa Park to reach the quarter-finals and a game at White Hart Lane where Spurs full-back, Tommy Clay, put through his own goal to send Villa into the semi-final against Chelsea at Bramall Lane.

Chelsea had the added incentive of knowing that if they won through to the FA Cup Final, then the game would be on their own ground of Stamford Bridge. They did not have the opportunity of that advantage, however, and two goals from Billy Walker put Aston Villa into their seventh Final, against Huddersfield Town, the team which would finish Second Division runners-up that season.

Harold Edgley missed the 1920 Final. Three weeks before the game he suffered a broken leg against Chelsea in a League match, at Stamford Bridge of all places. Thus, Villa would have been forgiven for thinking that a Cup hoodoo had overtaken them as they ran out to take on Huddersfield on the same pitch on which their winger had suffered his tragic accident.

Town were confident of a unique double of FA Cup and Second Division championship. From eight League matches up to the Final, the Yorkshire club had taken 14 points. However, the double eluded them as Tottenham eventually took the title and Aston Villa lifted the FA Cup.

Villa went into the game with a side naturally much changed from the one which contested the 1913 Final. Besides the changes already mentioned, Jimmy Harrop was injured before the Final and the Villa skipper had to hand over the captaincy to Andy Ducat, the wing-half who had joined Villa from Woolwich Arsenal in 1912.

Another addition to the Villa side was left-half Frank Moss, the only Aston-born player in the team. Moss had signed for Villa in 1914 but had to wait until the 1920 semi-final for a Cup debut more in keeping with a boy's comic-book hero.

Only 50,018 fans watched the first post-war Final, many others believing that the crowd would be so great that they would not stand a chance

of gaining admittance to what was not an all-ticket match. With record receipts of almost £10,000, one wonders what the takings would have been from a full house. Six months later, Stamford Bridge housed a crowd of 76,000 for a League game between Chelsea and Spurs.

For 90 minutes the sides in the 1920 FA Cup Final battled without a goal being scored and, for the first time, a Final went into extra-time. In the seventh minute of that extra period, Villa scored the only goal of the game — and what a lucky goal it was too.

Arthur Dorrell took a corner and Billy Kirton went up for it with the Huddersfield goalkeeper Alex Mutch and their centre-half, Tommy Wilson. Kirton got his head to the ball and nodded it goalwards, where it flew off Wilson and past Mutch to take the FA Cup to Villa Park for the sixth time in seven Finals.

It was a fluke of a goal and one not worthy of an FA Cup Final, but Villa had the edge on the day and at least it served to ensure that justice was done, although there were many Yorkshiremen who felt otherwise. It was also a particularly significant moment for Villa secretary Billy Smith. It was Smith who had signed Tommy Barber, the man who headed the Villa winner in the 1913 Final. Now his latest signing, Billy Kirton, had done likewise.

Kirton was one of the players 'auctioned off' when Leeds City were expelled and his Villa career covered 261 senior games and 59 goals before he had a brief spell with Coventry City.

Arthur Dorrell, the man who took the corner for Villa's Cup-winning goal, had joined the club from Army football, although he was locally

DIVISION 1 1920-21												
	P	W	D	L	F	A	W	D	L	F	A	Pts
Burnley	42	17	3	1	56	16	6	10	5	23	20	59
Manchester C	42	19	2	0	50	13	5	4	12	20	37	54
Bolton W	42	15	6	0	53	17	4	8	9	24	36	52
Liverpool	42	11	7	3	41	17	7	8	6	22	18	51
Newcastle U	42	14	3	4	43	18	6	7	8	23	27	50
Tottenham H	42	15	2	4	46	16	4	7	10	24	32	47
Everton	42	9	8	4	40	26	8	5	8	26	29	47
Middlesbrough	42	10	6	5	29	21	7	6	8	24	32	46
Arsenal	42	9	8	4	31	25	6	6	9	28	38	44
Aston Villa	42	11	4	6	39	21	7	3	11	24	49	43
Blackburn R	42	7	9	5	36	27	6	6	9	21	32	41
Sunderland	42	11	4	6	34	19	3	9	9	23	41	41
Manchester U	42	9	4	8	34	26	6	6	9	30	42	40
WBA	42	8	7	6	31	23	5	7	9	23	35	40
Bradford C	42	7	9	5	38	28	6	10	23	35	39	
Preston NE	42	10	4	7	38	25	5	5	11	23	40	39
Huddersfield T	42	11	4	6	26	16	4	5	12	16	33	39
Chelsea	42	7	9	5	38	28	6	6	10	23	35	39
Oldham A	42	6	9	6	23	26	3	6	12	26	60	33
Sheffield U	42	5	11	5	22	19	1	7	13	20	49	30
Derby Co	42	3	12	6	21	23	2	4	15	11	35	26
Bradford	42	6	5	10	29	35	2	3	16	14	41	24

Billy Kirton (left) and Dickie York, two Villa stalwarts of the 1920s. Together they made over 650 appearances for the club.

born. His career spanned the decade and when he moved to Port Vale in June 1931 he had played 390 times in Villa's first team, scoring 65 goals. He won his place in the 1920 Cup Final because of the injury to Harold Edgley.

Frank Moss, who had made his League debut in 1914-15, had recovered from a knee injury sustained in the fighting in World War One and his Villa days saw him make 283 League and Cup appearances and win five England caps before being transferred to Cardiff City in January 1929.

In contrast to their Cup campaign of 1919-20, Villa's League season had been something of a disappointment.

After their poor start, a run of seven consecutive wins from 22 November to 27 December, helped them back up the table. But thereafter their form deteriorated again and they won only five of their last 15 games to finish ninth.

Back in January 1920, when Billy Walker was making his debut for Aston Villa at the start of a wonderful career, Harry Hampton, the legendary Villa centre-forward, was being transferred to Birmingham. The following season, Hampton, having recovered from being gassed during the war, helped the Blues to the Second Division title.

In 1920-21, Walker established

himself with 27 League goals in 37 games as Villa finished tenth in the First Division. In the Cup they got as far as the quarter-finals before Tottenham Hotspur loosened their grip on the trophy by winning 1-0 at White Hart Lane.

Spurs' goal that day, scored by the quick-thinking Jimmy Banks, was only the fourth Villa had conceded in 11 Cup ties since the end of World War One. The game also marked the last Cup appearance for Villa of the great Sam Hardy, who was to leave for Nottingham Forest before the start of the following season.

Attendances were now booming at Villa Park. The first post-war season

Villa goalkeeper Cyril Spiers is well supported by his defenders at Stamford Bridge in September 1923.

had seen an average home crowd of over 32,000. Now Villa pushed that up to over 35,000, helped by a 66,000 gate for the home game against West Brom in early November. Their final position owed much to the fact that they won their last five games of the season.

In February 1921, Villa had transferred Clem Stephenson to Huddersfield Town, who beat off Sunderland for his signature. Many people thought that Stephenson's best days were behind him but he proved them wrong with League and Cup honours for Huddersfield as well as an England cap.

Although Aston Villa were to reach another FA Cup Final before another world war was declared, and despite the fact that they would finish First Division runners-up twice in that period, the writing was on the wall for the club which had dominated the early history of English soccer. Even the arrival of such famous names as 'Pongo' Waring, Eric Houghton and Jimmy Gibson would not alter the

fact that the Villa machine was running out of steam and that there would soon be new names like Bolton Wanderers, Huddersfield Town and Arsenal coming up to take over Villa's place as League and Cup experts.

In 1921-22 Villa climbed up to fifth place in the League and again reached the FA Cup quarter-finals, this time losing 4-3 to Notts County at Villa Park after a 2-2 draw at Meadow Lane. Their Cup campaign had started with a bang when Billy Walker's hat-trick helped beat Derby County 6-1.

That season, Tommy Jackson took over in goal from Sam Hardy. Jackson, a schoolteacher by profession after graduating from Durham University, had joined Villa as an amateur in 1919 and signed professional forms the following year. He missed only three League games in his first season in the first team and altogether had made 186 League and Cup appearances by the time he joined Kidderminster Harriers in 1930.

Another new name establishing himself in the Villa side was Dickie

DIVISION 1 1921-22											
	P	W	D	L	F	A	W	D	L	F	A	Pts
Liverpool	42	15	4	2	43	15	7	9	5	20	21	57
Tottenham H	42	15	3	3	43	17	6	6	9	22	22	51
Burnley	42	16	3	2	49	18	6	2	13	23	36	49
Cardiff C	42	13	2	6	40	26	6	8	7	21	27	48
Aston Villa	42	16	3	2	50	19	6	0	15	24	36	47
Bolton W	42	12	4	5	40	24	8	3	10	28	35	47
Newcastle U	42	11	5	5	36	19	7	5	9	23	26	46
Middlesbrough	42	12	6	3	46	19	4	8	9	33	50	46
Chelsea	42	9	6	6	17	16	8	6	7	23	27	46
Manchester C	42	13	7	1	44	21	5	2	14	21	49	45
Sheffield U	42	11	3	7	32	17	4	7	10	27	37	40
Sunderland	42	13	4	4	46	23	3	4	14	14	39	40
WBA	42	8	6	7	26	23	7	4	10	25	40	40
Huddersfield T	42	12	3	6	33	14	3	6	12	20	40	39
Blackburn R	42	7	6	8	35	31	6	6	9	19	26	38
Preston NE	42	12	7	2	33	20	1	5	15	9	45	38
Arsenal	42	10	6	5	27	19	5	1	15	20	37	37
Birmingham	42	9	2	10	25	29	6	5	10	23	31	37
Oldham A	42	8	7	6	21	15	5	4	12	17	35	37
Everton	42	10	7	4	42	22	2	5	14	15	33	36
Bradford C	42	8	5	8	28	30	3	5	13	20	42	32
Manchester U	42	7	7	7	25	26	1	5	15	16	47	28

York, who took over from Charlie Wallace on the right wing. York was a truly local boy, who was born almost opposite where the Villa club was founded. As a boy he ran for the famous Birchfield Harriers club and during World War One, in which he served in the Royal Flying Corps, he guested at right-half for Chelsea.

Villa signed York in May 1919 and he played a few games at wing-half behind Wallace before replacing him

Full-back Tommy Mort, who formed a remarkable defensive partnership with Tommy Smart through the 1920s.

League and Cup appearances for Aston Villa. Smart also won England caps and when he left for Brierley Hill Alliance in 1932, he had clocked up even more games for Villa, making 452 appearances in League and Cup.

In 1922-23, Aston Villa finished sixth — Liverpool won the title for the second year running — and went out of the Cup as early as the first round when Blackburn Rovers won 1-0 at Villa Park, although Villa were by now without Frank Barson who had signed for Manchester United.

DIVISION 1 1922-23												
	P	W	D	L	F	A	W	D	L	F	A	Pts
Liverpool	42	17	3	1	50	13	9	5	7	20	18	60
Sunderland	42	15	5	1	50	25	7	5	9	22	29	54
Huddersfield T	42	14	2	5	35	15	7	9	5	25	17	53
Newcastle U	42	13	6	2	31	11	5	6	10	14	26	48
Everton	42	14	4	3	41	20	6	3	12	22	39	47
Aston Villa	**42**	**15**	**3**	**3**	**42**	**11**	**3**	**7**	**11**	**22**	**40**	**46**
WBA	42	12	7	2	38	10	5	4	12	20	39	45
Manchester C	42	14	6	1	38	16	3	5	13	12	33	45
Cardiff C	42	15	2	4	51	18	3	5	13	22	41	43
Sheffield U	42	11	7	3	41	20	5	3	13	27	44	42
Arsenal	42	13	4	4	38	16	3	6	12	23	46	42
Tottenham H	42	11	3	7	34	22	6	4	11	16	28	41
Bolton W	42	11	8	2	36	17	3	4	14	14	41	40
Blackburn R	42	12	7	2	32	19	2	5	14	15	43	40
Burnley	42	12	3	6	39	24	4	3	14	19	35	38
Preston NE	42	12	3	6	41	26	1	8	12	19	38	37
Birmingham	42	10	4	7	25	19	3	7	11	16	38	37
Middlesbrough	42	11	4	6	41	25	2	6	13	16	38	36
Chelsea	42	5	13	3	29	20	4	5	12	16	33	36
Nottingham F	42	12	2	7	25	23	1	6	14	16	47	34
Stoke	42	7	9	5	28	19	3	1	17	19	48	30
Oldham A	42	9	6	6	21	20	1	4	16	14	45	30

Barson's replacement in the Villa team for that Cup defeat by Blackburn was Tom Ball, who was to meet a violent death when he was shot by his policeman neighbour, George Stagg, at Brick Kiln Lane, Perry Barr, after an argument. Ball was only 24.

Teddy Bowen was another new face. Signed from local football in August 1923, he was a steady performer at full-back until leaving for Norwich City in November 1934, after 199 senior appearances. His transfer was hastened by Danny Blair and Joe Nibloe establishing themselves at full-back.

Villa were sixth again in 1923-24, but this time they reached their eighth FA Cup Final. The first round sent them to Ashington, then of the Third Division North, where Villa won 5-1. In the second round they beat Swansea Town 2-0 at Vetch Field, and in the third, Leeds United visited Villa Park and lost 3-0.

In the quarter-finals, West Brom had home advantage but Villa won the game at The Hawthorns 2-0 and advanced once more into the semi-finals, where they trounced Burnley 3-0 at Bramall Lane and so looked

on the wing. Thereafter, he was a regular in that position for nine seasons and was capped by England.

Yet another new man was full-back Tommy Mort. Signed from Rochdale in April 1922, Mort became a regular the following season. His full-back partnership with Tommy Smart, signed from Halesowen in January 1920 became legendary and they were known as 'Death and Glory'.

When Mort — who was capped by England — retired at the end of the 1934-35 season, he had made 368

A West Brom defender clears his lines during the FA Cup tie between Albion and Villa at The Hawthorns in March 1924 as Billy Kirton challenges.

forward to Newcastle United at Wembley — only the second time that the Final had been played at the stadium.

Five days before the Final, Newcastle came to Villa Park for an Easter holiday First Division match but the

DIVISION 1   1923-24

	P	W	D	L	F	A	W	D	L	F	A	Pts
Huddersfield T	42	15	5	1	35	9	8	6	7	25	24	57
Cardiff C	42	14	5	2	35	13	8	8	5	26	21	57
Sunderland	42	12	7	2	38	20	10	2	9	33	34	53
Bolton W	42	13	6	2	45	13	5	8	8	23	21	50
Sheffield U	42	12	5	4	39	16	7	7	7	30	33	50
Aston Villa	42	10	10	1	33	11	8	3	10	19	26	49
Everton	42	13	7	1	43	18	5	6	10	19	35	49
Blackburn R	42	14	5	2	40	13	3	6	12	14	37	45
Newcastle U	42	13	5	3	40	21	4	5	12	20	33	44
Notts Co	42	9	7	5	21	15	5	7	9	23	34	42
Manchester C	42	11	7	3	34	24	4	5	12	20	47	42
Liverpool	42	11	5	5	35	20	4	6	11	14	28	41
West Ham U	42	10	6	5	26	17	3	9	9	14	26	41
Birmingham	42	10	4	7	25	19	3	9	9	16	30	39
Tottenham H	42	9	6	6	30	22	3	8	10	20	34	38
WBA	42	10	6	5	43	30	2	8	11	8	32	38
Burnley	42	10	5	6	39	27	2	7	12	16	33	36
Preston NE	42	8	4	9	34	27	4	6	11	18	40	34
Arsenal	42	8	5	8	25	24	4	4	13	15	39	33
Nottingham F	42	7	9	5	19	15	3	3	15	23	49	32
Chelsea	42	7	9	5	23	21	2	5	14	8	32	32
Middlesbrough	42	6	4	11	23	23	1	4	16	14	37	22

Aston Villa's Len Capewell heads the first goal of his hat-trick against Spurs at White Hart Lane in March 1924.

Villa on the attack at the City Ground in April 1924, when they drew 0-0 with Nottingham Forest.

Villa fans parade through the streets of London before the start of the 1924 FA Cup Final.

Villa take the field before the 1924 Final against Newcastle United in only the second Cup Final to be staged at Wembley.

40,000 crowd were bitterly disappointed. United fielded only one player who was to play at Wembley and Villa won 6-1, whilst the Football League fined Newcastle the considerable sum of £750 for that and other offences concerning fielding weakened sides before the Final.

Frank Moss — who with Walker and York was now an England international — skippered Villa as the teams walked out in pouring rain to be presented to the Duke of York.

The Villa team showed many changes from that which had begun the post-war period. Of course, there was Jackson in goal for Hardy; Stephenson had joined Huddersfield;

Villa take the ball away but it was the Magpies who eventually emerged triumphant.

Goalmouth action as Aston Villa's Tommy Jackson flails at the ball. Villa went down 2-0 to goals from Harris and Seymour.

and York played on the right wing. Now George Blackburn replaced Jimmy Harrop at left-half and Dr Vic Milne, a sturdy Scottish centre-half, became the first Scot to play in an FA Cup Final for Aston Villa since 1897.

Milne had graduated from Aberdeen University and it was from Aberdeen FC that he joined Villa in 1923, thus appearing in an FA Cup Final in his first season in English

Aston Villa in 1924. Back row (left to right): Blackburn, F.Miles (trainer), Smart, Moss, Jackson, Milne, Johnstone, G.B.Ramsay (secretary), Stephens. Front row: York, Kirton, Capewell, Walker, Dorrell, Mort.

football. He was to become Villa's regular centre-half for six seasons and after he retired he was appointed club doctor.

Although Villa began the 1924 Cup Final by attacking furiously — they hit the Newcastle woodwork twice — they could not find the back of the net and with only five minutes still to play, extra-time seemed inevitable.

But then Newcastle struck — and struck again. First Neil Harris took a clearance from Jackson — a clearance which either Villa back could have snapped up — and fired the ball back past the unfortunate Villa goalkeeper; then Stan Seymour ran through the Villa defence without having to evade one tackle and made it 2-0 via the underside of the Villa crossbar. The Cup went to Newcastle and it would be 33 years before Aston Villa played in another Final.

The next 12 years were a curious mixture of hope and despair for Villa fans. In the season immediately

DIVISION 1 1924-25											
	P	W	D	L	F	A	W	D	L	F	A	Pts
Huddersfield T	42	10	8	3	31	10	11	8	2	38	18	58
WBA	42	13	6	2	40	17	10	4	7	18	17	56
Bolton W	42	18	2	1	61	13	4	9	8	15	21	55
Liverpool	42	13	5	3	43	20	7	5	9	20	35	50
Bury	42	13	4	4	35	20	4	11	6	19	31	49
Newcastle U	42	11	6	4	43	18	5	10	6	18	24	48
Sunderland	42	13	6	2	39	14	6	4	11	25	37	48
Birmingham	42	10	8	3	27	17	7	4	10	22	36	46
Notts Co	42	11	6	4	29	12	5	7	9	13	19	45
Manchester C	42	11	7	3	44	29	6	2	13	32	39	43
Cardiff C	42	11	5	5	35	19	5	6	10	21	32	43
Tottenham H	42	9	8	4	32	16	6	4	11	20	27	42
West Ham U	42	12	7	2	37	12	3	5	13	25	48	42
Sheffield U	42	10	5	6	34	25	3	8	10	21	38	39
Aston Villa	42	10	7	4	34	25	3	6	12	24	46	39
Blackburn R	42	7	6	8	31	26	4	7	10	22	40	35
Everton	42	11	4	6	25	20	1	7	13	15	40	35
Leeds U	42	9	8	4	29	17	2	4	15	17	42	34
Burnley	42	7	8	6	28	31	4	4	13	18	44	34
Arsenal	42	12	3	6	33	17	2	2	17	13	41	33
Preston NE	42	8	2	11	29	35	2	4	15	8	39	26
Nottingham F	42	5	6	10	17	23	1	6	14	12	42	24

following that Wembley defeat, they were to see their team knocked out of the Cup in the third round and finish 15th in the First Division, a record which was similarly matched for the next few seasons until 1928-29, when Villa climbed to third place in the table and fought through to the FA Cup semi-finals.

There were highlights in between

those years — like Villa's 10-0 win over Burnley at Villa Park on the opening day of the 1925-26 season, although that result was tempered by the news that Villa owed £55,000 to the bank and various creditors.

That Villa managed double-figures against Burnley was partly explained by the fact that the offside law had just been changed and now only two instead of three players were needed to play a man onside. While defences became used to the new law, goals fairly rained in all over the country.

In the romp against Burnley, Len Capewell scored five and Billy Walker three. Capewell was, indeed, one of the great sharpshooters of the inter-war years. He had joined Villa from Wellington Town for £700 in August 1920 and by the time he joined Walsall in 1929 he had scored exactly 100 goals in 156 League and Cup games for the club.

Apart from his five against Burnley, Capewell's feats also included four

Billy Walker scores Villa's eighth goal in their remarkable 10-0 win over Burnley at Villa Park in September 1925. The change in the offside law led to many more goals being scored in the Football League that season.

goals in a Cup game against Port Vale in 1925 and a hat-trick against Everton in December 1926 when, despite dislocating a shoulder early in the game, he helped Villa bounce back from 3-2 down to win 5-3.

Villa also introduced two new players to their side — 'Pongo' Waring and Eric Houghton — and both were to become synonymous with the name of Aston Villa FC in the 1930s.

Houghton signed in August 1927, from a Lincolnshire village side, and

Len Capewell, who scored five goals in the romp against Burnley. By the time his Villa career was over he had netted exactly 100 goals for the club.

DIVISION 1 1925-26													
	P	W	D	L	F	A	W	D	L	F	A	Pts	
Huddersfield T	42	14	6	1	50	17	9	5	7	42	43	57	
Arsenal	42	16	2	3	57	19	6	6	9	30	44	52	
Sunderland	42	17	2	2	67	30	4	4	13	29	50	48	
Bury	42	12	4	5	55	34	8	3	10	30	43	47	
Sheffield U	42	15	3	3	72	29	4	5	12	30	53	46	
Aston Villa	42	12	7	2	56	25	4	5	12	30	51	44	
Liverpool	42	9	8	4	43	27	5	8	8	27	36	44	
Bolton W	42	11	6	4	46	31	6	4	11	29	45	44	
Manchester U	42	12	4	5	40	26	7	2	12	26	47	44	
Newcastle U	42	13	3	5	59	33	3	7	11	25	42	42	
Everton	42	9	9	3	42	26	3	9	9	30	44	42	
Blackburn R	42	11	6	4	59	33	4	5	12	32	47	41	
WBA	42	13	5	3	59	29	3	3	15	20	49	40	
Birmingham	42	14	2	5	35	25	2	6	13	31	56	40	
Tottenham H	42	11	4	6	45	36	4	5	12	21	43	39	
Cardiff C	42	8	5	8	30	25	8	2	11	31	51	39	
Leicester C	42	11	3	7	42	32	3	7	11	28	48	38	
West Ham U	42	14	2	5	45	27	1	5	15	18	49	37	
Leeds U	42	11	5	5	38	28	3	3	15	26	48	36	
Burnley	42	7	7	7	43	35	6	3	12	42	73	36	
Manchester C	42	8	7	6	48	42	4	4	13	41	58	35	
Notts Co	42	11	4	6	37	26	2	3	16	17	48	33	

became a great Villa star; Waring came in February 1928 as a free-scoring forward from Tranmere Rovers. Villa were tempted to pay £4,700 for his signature after he scored six of the 11 goals which Tranmere hammered past Durham City in a Third Division North game.

When Waring made his debut in a Villa shirt, against Birmingham Reserves in a Central League game, a crowd of 23,000 turned up and saw him mark his first game with a hat-trick.

He went straight into the first team after that and repaid his big fee with 167 goals in 226 League and Cup games before being controversially transferred to Barnsley in 1935.

Houghton took a little longer to establish himself. His League debut came against Leeds United in January 1930 when he was entrusted with a penalty-kick and missed it. That was ironic, since Houghton went on to become one of the deadliest penalty-takers in the game.

DIVISION 1	1926-27											
	P	W	D	L	F	A	W	D	L	F	A	Pts
Newcastle U	42	19	1	1	64	20	6	5	10	32	38	56
Huddersfield T	42	13	6	2	41	19	4	11	6	35	41	51
Sunderland	42	15	3	3	70	28	6	4	11	28	42	49
Bolton W	42	15	5	1	54	19	4	5	12	30	43	48
Burnley	42	15	4	2	55	30	4	5	12	36	50	47
West Ham U	42	9	6	6	50	36	10	2	9	36	34	46
Leicester C	42	13	4	4	58	33	4	8	9	27	37	46
Sheffield U	42	12	6	3	46	33	5	4	12	28	53	44
Liverpool	42	13	4	4	47	27	5	3	13	22	34	43
Aston Villa	42	11	4	6	51	34	7	3	11	30	49	43
Arsenal	42	12	5	4	47	30	5	4	12	30	56	43
Derby Co	42	14	4	3	60	28	3	3	15	26	45	41
Tottenham H	42	11	4	6	48	33	5	5	11	28	45	41
Cardiff C	42	12	3	6	31	17	4	6	11	24	48	41
Manchester U	42	9	8	4	29	19	4	6	11	23	45	40
Sheffield W	42	15	3	3	49	29	0	6	15	26	63	39
Birmingham	42	13	3	5	36	17	4	1	16	28	56	38
Blackburn R	42	9	5	7	40	40	6	3	12	37	56	38
Bury	42	8	5	8	43	38	4	7	10	25	39	36
Everton	42	10	6	5	35	30	2	4	15	29	60	34
Leeds U	42	9	7	5	43	31	2	1	18	26	57	30
WBA	42	10	4	7	47	33	1	4	16	18	53	30

He went on to score 170 goals in 392 League and Cup games for Villa and later managed the club and served it in a number of other capacities including director.

Yet another name to become a great part of Villa's history in this period was that of Jimmy Gibson, a cultured half-back who was signed from Partick Thistle in April 1927 for what was then a record fee of £7,500. Gibson

became part of a famous Villa half-back line of Gibson, Alex Talbot and Joe Tate.

He served Villa for the next nine seasons, making a total of 225 League and Cup appearances and adding four Scottish caps to the four he had gained as a Partick player.

His half-back partners served Villa equally well. Talbot had joined the club from local football but after taking some time to break into the first team he made 263 appearances before a move to Bradford in June 1935.

Tate ran up 193 senior appearances between 1927-28 and 1933-34 and was capped three times for England. He, too, came from local football and had to wait until Frank Moss left Villa Park before gaining a regular place. A series of injuries eventually forced him out of League football and he became player-manager of Brierley Hill Alliance in May 1935.

Billy Kingdon, who had joined Villa from Kidderminster Harriers in

Dickie York scores Villa's second goal at White Hart Lane in December 1925. The ball is just passing through Kaine's feet.

Eric Houghton
— Villa's Cannonball

IN the mid-1920s, Eric Houghton was already a legend in football circles in his native Lincolnshire. The young man from Billingborough, where he was born in June 1910, was setting the game alight with his performances for his village side and for Boston Town, and local goalkeepers dreaded coming up against Houghton and his devastating shooting from centre-forward.

Inevitably, news of Houghton's prowess spread and in August 1927, Aston Villa were the lucky club who signed him on amateur forms after one of their scouts, Cecil Harris, sent him down for a trial. The following year, Houghton became a full-time professional at Villa Park and launched a career that would bring him 170 goals in almost 400 League and Cup games.

He made his League debut in a 4-3 home defeat by Leeds United on 4 January 1930. Even though his deadly shooting from dead-ball situations was already apparent, it was still remarkable that, as a debutant, Houghton should be asked to take a penalty against Leeds that day. Perhaps nerves overcame him, for he missed the spot-kick. He soon put the experience behind him, however, and became one of the most consistent penalty-takers in the history of the Football League.

The following season was Houghton's best in terms of goals, for in 1930-31 he scored 30, missing only one League game as Villa finished runners-up in the First Division. Even that did not make him Villa's leading scorer, however, as this was the season that Pongo Waring scored 49 League goals.

Houghton scored many spectacular goals for Villa, but none more sensational than one of the two he netted against Derby County at Villa Park on 5 December 1931. Taking a free-kick from fully 40 yards out, Houghton hammered the ball past Harry Wilkes, the astonished Derby goalkeeper.

Although he had been a centre-forward his his amateur days, Houghton was switched to outside-left by Villa, playing with the great Billy Walker as his partner. Walker had played alongside Villa's Arthur Dorrell as his wing partner in the England team and in December 1932, Eric Houghton was on the left wing with Walker at inside-left when England beat Austria 4-3 at Stamford Bridge. Houghton celebrated his first cap with a goal. It was the first of seven international appearances for Houghton, who also played for the Football League.

Besides his Second Division championship medal, Houghton's only other honour as a Villa player came in 1944, when he helped them win a wartime Cup Final. His last game in a Villa shirt was for the Reserves in a Central League match against Huddersfield Town on Boxing Day 1946 and, perhaps inevitably, he signed off with a penalty, struck as fiercely as any he had netted in his remarkable career. Apparently he missed only seven out of 79 penalties for Villa and also scored direct from some 40 free-kicks. Add 87 goals in 157 wartime games and the statistics are even more remarkable.

He moved to Notts County in December 1946 and took over as manager at Meadow Lane in April 1949, helping the Magpies into the Second Division in his first season in charge, with former Villa teammate Frank Broome and England centre-forward Tommy Lawton in the side.

In September 1953, Eric Houghton returned to Villa Park as manager and within four years he had taken Villa to an FA Cup Final and a Wembley victory over Manchester United.

Houghton remained with Villa until November 1958 and then scouted for Nottingham Forest and Walsall, managed Rugby Town and was a director at both Fellows Park and Villa Park. A good cricketer, he also played for Warwickshire 2nd XI and for Lincolnshire in the Minor Counties.

Jimmy Seed scores for Spurs against Villa in November 1926. Tottenham won 3-2 and Seed netted twice.

Aston Villa's Joe Beresford challenges the Arsenal defence at Highbury in November 1928 during a 5-2 Villa win.

Top left: **Tommy Smart leads Villa out for their FA Cup tie against Clapton Orient at Homerton in January 1929.** *Bottom left:* **Pongo Waring is beaten to the ball by Wood and Morley of Orient.** *Right:* **Wood is beaten for Villa's second goal. They eventually won 8-0 with Waring getting a hat-trick.**

March 1926, had enjoyed some early successes. A small but lion-hearted wing-half, Kingdon soon won a regular place and although he dropped into the Reserves in 1930-31 and 1931-32, he bounced back to regain his place and when he was transferred to Southampton in 1935, he had made 241 senior appearances for Villa.

After their defeat in the 1924 Final, one of Villa's most impressive Cup campaigns before the war came in 1928-29. In the third round they hammered Cardiff City 6-1 in front of a 51,000 crowd at Villa Park. And although Clapton Orient's giant goalkeeper Arthur Wood managed to help his team to a goalless draw in the fourth round at Villa Park, even his considerable frame could not prevent Villa winning 8-0 in the replay, when Waring scored a hat-trick at Millfields Road.

Reading were beaten 3-1 at Elm Park in the fifth round and in the quarter-finals Villa defeated Arsenal 1-0 at Villa Park. 'Pongo' Waring added the only goal of this match to the hat-trick he had scored at Clapton and the two he had netted at Reading.

DIVISION 1   1927-28

	P	W	D	L	F	A	W	D	L	F	A	Pts
Everton	42	11	8	2	60	28	9	5	7	42	38	53
Huddersfield T	42	15	1	5	57	31	7	6	8	34	37	51
Leicester C	42	14	5	2	66	25	4	7	10	30	47	48
Derby Co	42	12	4	5	59	30	5	6	10	37	53	44
Bury	42	13	1	7	53	35	7	3	11	27	45	44
Cardiff C	42	12	7	2	44	27	5	3	13	26	53	44
Bolton W	42	12	5	4	47	26	4	6	11	34	40	43
Aston Villa	**42**	**13**	**3**	**5**	**52**	**30**	**4**	**6**	**11**	**26**	**43**	**43**
Newcastle U	42	9	7	5	49	41	6	6	9	30	40	43
Arsenal	42	10	6	5	49	33	3	9	9	33	53	41
Birmingham	42	10	7	4	36	25	3	8	10	34	50	41
Blackburn R	42	13	5	3	41	22	3	4	14	25	56	41
Sheffield U	42	12	4	5	56	43	3	6	12	23	44	40
Sheffield W	42	9	6	6	45	29	4	7	10	36	49	39
Sunderland	42	9	5	7	37	29	6	4	11	37	47	39
Liverpool	42	10	6	5	54	36	3	7	11	30	51	39
West Ham U	42	9	7	5	48	34	5	4	12	33	54	39
Manchester U	42	12	6	3	51	27	4	1	16	21	53	39
Burnley	42	12	5	4	55	31	4	2	15	27	67	39
Portsmouth	42	13	4	4	40	23	3	3	15	26	67	39
Tottenham H	42	12	3	6	47	34	3	5	13	27	52	38
Middlesbrough	42	7	9	5	46	35	4	6	11	35	53	37

DIVISION 1   1928-29

	P	W	D	L	F	A	W	D	L	F	A	Pts
Sheffield W	42	18	3	0	55	16	3	7	11	31	46	52
Leicester C	42	16	5	0	67	22	5	4	12	29	45	51
Aston Villa	**42**	**16**	**2**	**3**	**62**	**30**	**7**	**2**	**12**	**36**	**51**	**50**
Sunderland	42	16	2	3	67	30	4	5	12	26	45	47
Liverpool	42	11	4	6	53	28	6	8	7	37	36	46
Derby Co	42	12	5	4	56	24	6	5	10	30	47	46
Blackburn R	42	11	6	4	42	26	6	5	10	30	37	45
Manchester C	42	12	3	6	63	40	6	6	9	32	46	45
Arsenal	42	11	6	4	43	25	5	7	9	34	47	45
Newcastle U	42	15	2	4	48	29	4	4	13	22	43	44
Sheffield U	42	12	5	4	57	30	3	6	12	29	55	41
Manchester U	42	8	8	5	32	23	6	5	10	34	53	41
Leeds U	42	11	5	5	42	28	5	4	12	29	56	41
Bolton W	42	10	6	5	44	25	4	6	11	29	55	40
Birmingham	42	8	7	6	37	32	7	3	11	31	45	40
Huddersfield T	42	9	6	6	45	23	5	5	11	25	38	39
West Ham U	42	11	6	4	55	31	4	3	14	31	65	39
Everton	42	11	2	8	38	31	6	2	13	25	44	38
Burnley	42	12	5	4	55	32	3	3	15	26	71	38
Portsmouth	42	13	2	6	43	26	2	4	15	13	54	36
Bury	42	9	5	7	38	35	3	2	16	24	64	31
Cardiff C	42	7	7	7	34	26	1	6	14	9	33	29

Villa's Ben Olney stretches for the ball in the 1929 semi-final against Portsmouth at Highbury.

Arsenal, though, enjoyed some kind of revenge when Villa went to Highbury for the semi-final against Portsmouth and lost 1-0 to a Jack Smith penalty.

The following season of 1929-30 saw Aston Villa into the quarter-finals. Along the way they beat near-neighbours Walsall 3-1, when a record attendance of 74,626 packed into Villa Park.

The game is also memorable for the fact that after its conclusion, Villa signed the Walsall goalkeeper Fred

Action from the sixth-round FA Cup tie against Huddersfield Town at Villa Park in March 1930. Tommy Mort tries to block Huddersfield's Kelly.

DIVISION 1 1929-30													
	P	W	D	L	F	A	W	D	L	F	A	Pts
Sheffield W	42	15	4	2	56	20	11	4	6	49	37	60
Derby Co	42	16	4	1	61	32	5	4	12	29	50	50
Manchester C	42	12	5	4	51	33	7	4	10	40	48	47
Aston Villa	**42**	**13**	**1**	**7**	**54**	**33**	**8**	**4**	**9**	**38**	**50**	**47**
Leeds U	42	15	2	4	52	22	5	4	12	27	41	46
Blackburn R	42	15	2	4	65	36	4	5	12	34	57	45
West Ham U	42	14	2	5	51	26	5	3	13	35	53	43
Leicester C	42	12	5	4	57	42	5	4	12	29	48	43
Sunderland	42	13	3	5	50	35	5	4	12	26	45	43
Huddersfield T	42	9	7	5	32	21	8	2	11	31	48	43
Birmingham	42	13	5	3	40	21	3	6	12	27	41	41
Liverpool	42	11	5	5	33	29	5	4	12	30	50	41
Portsmouth	42	10	6	5	43	25	5	4	12	23	37	40
Arsenal	42	10	2	9	49	26	4	9	8	29	40	39
Bolton W	42	11	5	5	46	24	4	4	13	28	50	39
Middlesbrough	42	11	3	7	48	31	5	3	13	34	53	38
Manchester U	42	11	4	6	39	34	4	4	13	28	54	38
Grimsby T	42	8	6	7	39	39	7	1	13	34	50	37
Newcastle U	42	13	4	4	52	32	2	3	16	19	60	37
Sheffield U	42	12	2	7	59	39	3	4	14	32	57	36
Burnley	42	11	5	5	53	34	3	3	15	26	63	36
Everton	42	6	7	8	48	46	6	4	11	32	46	35

Aston Villa in 1930-31. Back row (left to right): Bowen, H.Cooch (trainer), Talbot, Biddlestone, Smart, Gibson, Walker, Tate, York. Front row: Mandley, Mort, Dorrell, Waring, Chester, Brown, Houghton. On ground: Kingdon, Beresford.

Biddlestone, who went on to serve them well, although he was often left out of the side in favour of other goalkeepers, only to come fighting back each time. In 1937-38 he made 39 appearances to help Villa win the Second Division championship.

Huddersfield Town beat them 2-1 at Villa Park in the quarter-final on their way to Wembley. Huddersfield's manager that day was Clem Stephenson, whose name had continued to grab the headlines ever since the day Villa let him go.

The 1930s started with anything but a depression for Aston Villa, who finished second, fifth and second in the First Division in successive seasons.

In 1930-31 there were some remarkable scorelines. Waring netted all Villa's goals when they opened the season with a 4-3 win at Old Trafford. At Villa Park, Middlesbrough were

beaten 8-1, Manchester United 7-0, Huddersfield Town and West Ham United 6-1 each, and champions Arsenal 5-1. Away from home, Villa beat Huddersfield 6-1 (thus scoring a 12-goal double), won 4-0 at St Andrew's and were involved in a breathtaking 5-5 draw at Upton Park. Back at Villa Park, Derby County won 6-4 in November.

Waring, in particular, had a magnificent season. His 49 League goals are still a club record for one season and with one in the FA Cup he neatly reached the half-century mark.

Altogether, Villa scored a club-record 128 League goals and Joe Beresford weighed in with 14 from 28 games. Beresford had joined Villa from Mansfield Town in May 1927 and soon became a great favourite with the Holte End crowd. A bustling forward with a powerful shot, Beresford scored 73 goals in 251 League

DIVISION 1 1930-31											
	P	W	D	L	F	A	W	D	L	F	A	Pts
Arsenal	42	14	5	2	67	27	14	5	2	60	32	66
Aston Villa	42	17	3	1	86	34	8	6	7	42	44	59
Sheffield W	42	14	3	4	65	32	8	5	8	37	43	52
Portsmouth	42	11	7	3	46	26	7	6	8	38	41	49
Huddersfield T	42	10	8	3	45	27	8	4	9	36	38	48
Derby Co	42	12	6	3	56	31	6	4	11	38	48	46
Middlesbrough	42	13	5	3	57	28	6	3	12	41	62	46
Manchester C	42	13	2	6	41	29	5	8	8	34	41	46
Liverpool	42	11	6	4	48	28	4	6	11	38	57	42
Blackburn R	42	14	3	4	54	28	3	5	13	29	56	42
Sunderland	42	12	4	5	61	38	4	5	12	28	47	41
Chelsea	42	13	4	4	42	19	2	6	13	22	48	40
Grimsby T	42	13	2	6	55	31	4	3	14	27	56	39
Bolton W	42	12	6	3	45	26	3	3	15	23	55	39
Sheffield U	42	10	7	4	49	31	4	3	14	29	53	38
Leicester C	42	12	4	5	50	38	4	2	15	30	57	38
Newcastle U	42	9	2	10	41	45	6	4	11	37	42	36
West Ham U	42	11	3	7	56	44	3	5	13	23	50	36
Birmingham	42	11	3	7	37	28	2	7	12	18	42	36
Blackpool	42	8	7	6	41	44	3	3	15	30	81	32
Leeds U	42	10	3	8	49	31	2	4	15	19	50	31
Manchester U	42	6	6	9	30	37	1	2	18	23	78	22

and Cup appearances for Villa and won an England cap in 1934.

In 1931-32, when Villa finished fifth, Waring scored 30 goals and, again, there were some big scores. Leicester City were beaten 8-3 at Filbert Street, although the hero that day was George Brown, the England

Villa goalkeeper Percy Maggs is beaten by West Ham's Vivian Gibbins at Upton Park in January 1931 in a 5-5 draw.

Billy Walker waits to pounce as Arsenal goalkeeper Charlie Preedy collects the ball at Highbury in October 1931. Tom Park is the other Arsenal defender.

Tom 'Pongo' Waring, who scored a club record 50 goals in 1930-31.

DIVISION 1 1931-32											
	P	W	D	L	F	A	W	D	L	F	A	Pts
Everton	42	18	0	3	84	30	8	4	9	32	34	56
Arsenal	42	14	5	2	52	16	8	5	8	38	32	54
Sheffield W	42	14	4	3	60	28	8	2	11	36	54	50
Huddersfield T	42	11	8	2	47	21	8	2	11	33	42	48
Aston Villa	42	15	1	5	64	28	4	7	10	40	44	46
WBA	42	12	4	5	46	21	8	2	11	31	34	46
Sheffield U	42	13	3	5	47	32	7	3	11	33	43	46
Portsmouth	42	14	2	5	37	21	5	5	11	25	41	45
Birmingham	42	13	5	3	48	22	5	3	13	30	45	44
Liverpool	42	12	4	4	56	38	6	2	13	25	55	44
Newcastle U	42	13	5	3	52	31	5	1	15	28	56	42
Chelsea	42	12	4	5	43	27	4	4	13	26	46	40
Sunderland	42	11	4	6	42	29	4	6	11	25	44	40
Manchester C	42	10	5	6	49	30	3	7	11	34	43	38
Derby Co	42	13	5	3	51	25	1	5	15	20	50	38
Blackburn R	42	12	3	6	57	41	4	3	14	32	54	38
Bolton W	42	15	1	5	51	25	2	3	16	21	55	38
Middlesbrough	42	12	3	6	41	29	3	5	13	23	60	38
Leicester C	42	11	3	7	46	39	4	4	13	28	55	37
Blackpool	42	9	4	8	42	40	3	5	13	23	62	33
Grimsby T	42	11	4	6	39	28	2	2	17	28	70	32
West Ham U	42	9	5	7	35	37	3	2	16	27	70	31

Liverpool's great goalkeeper Elisha Scott at Villa Park.

In late November that season, a goalkeeper called Harry Morton made his League debut for Villa in dramatic circumstances. He was in the stand when Fred Biddlestone was injured in the pre-match kick-in against Manchester City. Morton was called up to play, helped Villa draw 3-3 and launched a career in which he made 207 League and Cup appearances before being transferred to Everton in Match 1937.

In 1932-33, when Villa were again runners-up, Brown scored four goals in a 6-1 home win over Bolton Wanderers. Waring was injured for most of the season and Brown finished leading scorer with 33 League goals.

DIVISION 1 1932-33											
	P	W	D	L	F	A	W	D	L	F	A	Pts
Arsenal	42	14	3	4	70	27	11	5	5	48	34	58
Aston Villa	42	16	2	3	60	29	7	6	8	32	38	54
Sheffield W	42	15	5	1	46	20	6	4	11	34	48	51
WBA	42	16	1	4	50	23	4	8	9	33	47	49
Newcastle U	42	15	2	4	44	24	7	3	11	27	39	49
Huddersfield T	42	11	6	4	32	17	7	5	9	34	36	47
Derby Co	42	11	8	2	49	25	4	6	11	27	44	44
Leeds U	42	10	6	5	39	24	5	8	8	20	38	44
Portsmouth	42	14	3	4	39	22	4	4	13	35	54	43
Sheffield U	42	14	3	4	50	30	3	6	12	24	50	43
Everton	42	13	6	2	54	24	3	3	15	27	50	41
Sunderland	42	8	7	6	33	31	7	3	11	30	49	40
Birmingham	42	13	3	5	40	23	1	8	12	17	34	39
Liverpool	42	10	6	5	53	33	4	5	12	26	51	39
Blackburn R	42	11	6	4	48	41	3	4	14	28	61	38
Manchester C	42	12	3	6	47	30	4	2	15	21	41	37
Middlesbrough	42	8	5	8	35	33	6	4	11	28	40	37
Chelsea	42	9	4	8	38	29	5	3	13	25	44	35
Leicester C	42	9	9	3	43	25	2	4	15	32	64	35
Wolves	42	10	4	7	56	48	3	5	13	24	48	35
Bolton W	42	10	7	4	49	33	2	2	17	29	59	33
Blackpool	42	11	2	8	44	35	3	3	15	25	50	33

The same season, 'Mush' Callaghan made his debut for Villa, at centre-half against Bradford City in the FA Cup in January. The following month, Callaghan made his League bow, at home to Portsmouth at Villa Park. Although he took some

Above: Villa winger Arthur Cunliffe challenges Tottenham goalkeeper Nicholls at White Hart Lane in September 1933. **Below:** Harry Morton gets his hand to a penalty from Spurs' Evans but cannot prevent the goal.

and former Huddersfield forward. Brown scored five against Leicester.

Villa scored seven goals past both Grimsby and Middlesbrough, six at Stamford Bridge and six against

Back at White Hart Lane in February 1934, Nicholls punches clear from a Villa attack. Villa won with a goal from Dai Astley.

Danny Blair leads Villa out for their 1934 quarter-final tie at Highbury, where Astley and Houghton put Villa into the last four of the Cup.

Harry Morton cannot prevent Manchester City's Fred Tilson scoring his side's second goal in the 1934 semi-final at Leeds Road. City went on to win 6-1.

Dai Astley, the Welsh international who scored 100 goals for Villa before being transferred to Derby County.

	P	W	D	L	F	A	W	D	L	F	A	Pts
DIVISION 1 1933-34												
Arsenal	42	15	4	2	45	19	10	5	6	30	28	59
Huddersfield T	42	16	3	2	53	19	7	7	7	37	42	56
Tottenham H	42	14	3	4	51	24	7	4	10	28	32	49
Derby Co	42	11	8	2	45	22	6	3	12	23	32	45
Manchester C	42	14	4	3	50	29	3	7	11	15	43	45
Sunderland	42	14	6	1	57	17	2	6	13	24	39	44
WBA	42	12	4	5	49	28	5	6	10	29	42	44
Blackburn R	42	16	5	0	57	21	2	2	17	17	60	43
Leeds U	42	13	5	3	52	21	4	3	14	23	45	42
Portsmouth	42	11	5	5	31	21	4	7	10	21	34	42
Sheffield W	42	9	5	7	33	24	7	4	10	29	43	41
Stoke C	42	11	5	5	33	19	4	6	11	25	52	41
Aston Villa	**42**	**10**	**5**	**6**	**45**	**34**	**4**	**7**	**10**	**33**	**41**	**40**
Everton	42	9	7	5	38	27	3	9	9	24	36	40
Wolves	42	13	4	4	50	28	1	8	12	24	58	40
Middlesbrough	42	13	3	5	51	27	3	4	14	17	53	39
Leicester C	42	10	6	5	36	26	4	5	12	23	48	39
Liverpool	42	10	6	5	52	37	4	4	13	27	50	38
Chelsea	42	12	3	6	44	24	2	5	14	23	45	36
Birmingham	42	8	6	7	29	20	4	6	11	25	36	36
Newcastle U	42	6	11	4	42	29	4	3	14	26	48	34
Sheffield U	42	11	5	5	40	25	1	2	18	18	76	31

time to establish himself, Callaghan later starred at full-back and was one of the mainstays of the Second Division championship side of 1937-38.

After starting the decade in such splendid fashion in the League, Villa again reached the FA Cup semi-finals in 1933-34. It was their 13th appearance in the semis, but this time they went down 6-1 to Manchester City at Leeds Road, Huddersfield, where City's Freddie Tilson scored four goals.

By now Villa's League position was giving cause for concern. Whilst gaining some Cup glory, the club had been sliding down the First Division and at the end of that season they were in 13th place, losing 16 matches and conceding 75 goals.

It was a long way from the previous season's triumphs of runners-up position when Villa had finished only four points behind the champions, Arsenal.

But in 1933-34 it was obvious that Villa's troubles lay in their defence

DIVISION 1 1934-35												
	P	W	D	L	F	A	W	D	L	F	A	Pts
Arsenal	42	15	4	2	74	17	8	8	5	41	29	58
Sunderland	42	13	4	4	57	24	6	12	3	33	27	54
Sheffield W	42	14	7	0	42	17	4	6	11	28	47	49
Manchester C	42	13	5	3	53	25	7	3	11	29	42	48
Grimsby T	42	13	6	2	49	25	4	5	12	29	35	45
Derby Co	42	10	4	7	44	28	8	5	8	37	38	45
Liverpool	42	13	4	4	53	29	6	3	12	32	59	45
Everton	42	14	5	2	64	32	2	7	12	25	56	44
WBA	42	10	8	3	55	33	7	2	12	28	50	44
Stoke C	42	12	5	4	46	20	6	1	14	25	50	42
Preston NE	42	11	5	5	33	22	4	7	10	29	45	42
Chelsea	42	11	5	5	49	32	5	4	12	24	50	41
Aston Villa	**42**	**11**	**6**	**4**	**50**	**36**	**3**	**7**	**11**	**24**	**52**	**41**
Portsmouth	42	10	5	6	41	24	5	5	11	30	48	40
Blackburn R	42	12	5	4	42	23	2	6	13	24	55	39
Huddersfield T	42	11	5	5	52	27	3	5	13	24	44	38
Wolves	42	13	3	5	65	38	2	5	14	23	56	38
Leeds U	42	10	6	5	48	35	3	6	12	27	57	38
Birmingham	42	10	3	8	36	36	3	7	11	27	45	36
Middlesbrough	42	8	9	4	38	29	2	5	14	32	61	34
Leicester C	42	9	4	8	39	30	3	5	13	22	56	33
Tottenham H	42	8	8	5	34	31	2	2	17	20	62	30

and when Manchester City whipped six goals past them in the semi-final, the truth had to be faced. Late in that season, Villa appointed their first team manager, Jimmy McMullan, then manager of Oldham Athletic and a former Manchester City and Scotland wing-half.

McMullan began to add players to the Villa staff. One of them was a young forward called Frank Broome, who came from Berkhamstead Town in November 1934 and who soon made his mark, scoring six goals against Moor Green in a Birmingham Combination game.

Broome was another Villa player to win international honours and before the war he became the first man to have played for England in four different forward positions.

McMullan also bought Jimmy McLuckie, a Scottish international wing-half, from his old club, and also signed England player Jimmy Allen from Portsmouth for a record fee of £10,755.

Allen, a classic 'stopper' type of centre-half, came in for some criticism from Villa Park fans who were used to a more attacking kind of centre-half.

Despite these signings, and despite the brilliance of players like Houghton, George Cummings (a hard-tackling Scottish international full-back signed from Partick Thistle for £9,500 in December 1935), Dai Astley (a Welsh international forward signed from Charlton in June 1931), Ronnie Dix (another forward who would win international honours, from Bristol Rovers in May 1933) and the great Alex Massie (a Scottish international wing-half who cost

Harry Morton grabs the ball from a Brentford forward at Griffin Park in September 1935.

Villa's Billy Kingdon and Norman Young in action against Brentford. At the end of the season Villa lost their First Division place.

£6,000 when he was signed from Hearts in December 1935), Villa were on the downward path.

In 1935-36, the club reached its nadir. After 48 years of First Division soccer, Aston Villa were relegated to the Second Division. They finished next-to-bottom of the table, two points ahead of Blackburn Rovers, and conceded 110 goals, 56 of them at Villa Park where even Blackburn won 4-2 on the very last day of a dreadful season.

Goals galore were piled past the

George Cummings of Villa and Chelsea's George Mills in a high-kicking tussle at Stamford Bridge in March 1936.

George Cummings joined Villa from Partick Thistle in December 1935.

Charlie Philips, scored the first against runners-up Derby at the Baseball Ground.

DIVISION 1 1935-36											
	P	W	D	L	F	A	W	D	L	F	A	Pts
Sunderland	42	17	2	2	71	33	8	4	9	38	41	56
Derby Co	42	13	5	3	43	23	5	7	9	18	29	48
Huddersfield T	42	12	7	2	32	15	6	5	10	27	41	48
Stoke C	42	13	3	5	35	24	7	4	10	22	33	47
Brentford	42	11	5	5	48	25	6	7	8	33	35	46
Arsenal	42	9	9	3	44	22	6	6	9	34	26	45
Preston NE	42	15	3	3	44	18	3	5	13	23	46	44
Chelsea	42	11	7	3	39	27	4	6	11	26	45	43
Manchester C	42	13	2	6	44	17	4	6	11	24	43	42
Portsmouth	42	14	4	3	39	22	3	4	14	15	45	42
Leeds U	42	11	5	5	41	23	4	6	11	25	41	41
Birmingham	42	10	6	5	38	31	5	5	11	23	32	41
Bolton W	42	11	4	6	41	27	3	9	9	26	49	41
Middlesbrough	42	12	6	3	56	23	3	4	14	28	47	40
Wolves	42	13	7	1	59	28	2	3	16	18	48	40
Everton	42	12	5	4	61	31	1	8	12	28	58	39
Grimsby T	42	13	4	4	44	20	4	1	16	21	53	39
WBA	42	12	3	6	54	31	4	3	14	35	57	38
Liverpool	42	11	4	6	43	23	2	8	11	17	41	38
Sheffield W	42	9	8	4	35	23	4	4	13	28	54	38
Aston Villa	42	7	6	8	47	56	6	3	12	34	54	35
Blackburn R	42	10	6	5	32	24	2	3	16	23	72	33

Villa defence and on 14 December 1935, Arsenal's Ted Drake had eight shots at the Villa goal and scored with seven of them as Arsenal won 7-1. Never before, or since, has a player scored so many goals on an opponent's ground in the Football League.

West Brom and Middlesbrough scored seven times and Grimsby Town six at Villa Park and manager McMullan resigned during October.

Amazingly, Villa managed to beat both the eventual champions, Sunderland, and the runners-up, Derby County, at Roker Park and the Baseball Ground respectively. But when the season ended, Villa fans had to face the fact that they would be watching Second Division soccer in 1936-37.

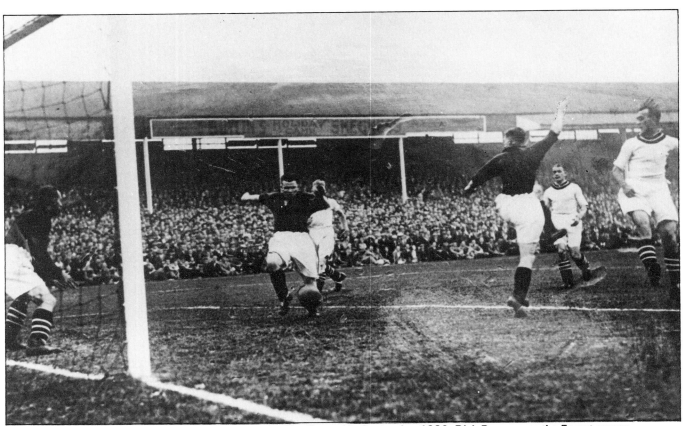

Villa go behind to Nottingham Forest at the City Ground in September 1936. Dick Brown was the Forest scorer.

Freddie Haycock scores for Villa at Tottenham in March 1937.

DIVISION 2 1936-37	P	W	D	L	F	A	W	D	L	F	A	Pts
Leicester C	42	14	4	3	56	26	10	4	7	33	31	56
Blackpool	42	13	4	4	49	19	11	3	7	39	34	55
Bury	42	13	4	4	46	26	9	4	8	28	29	52
Newcastle U	42	11	3	7	45	23	11	2	8	35	33	49
Plymouth A	42	11	6	4	42	22	7	7	7	29	31	49
West Ham U	42	14	5	2	47	18	5	6	10	26	37	49
Sheffield U	42	16	4	1	48	14	2	6	13	18	40	46
Coventry C	42	11	5	5	35	19	6	6	9	31	35	45
Aston Villa	**42**	**10**	**6**	**5**	**47**	**30**	**6**	**6**	**9**	**35**	**40**	**44**
Tottenham'H	42	13	3	5	57	26	4	6	11	31	40	43
Fulham	42	11	5	5	43	24	4	8	9	28	37	43
Blackburn R	42	11	3	7	49	32	5	7	9	21	30	42
Burnley	42	11	5	5	37	20	5	5	11	20	41	42
Barnsley	42	11	6	4	30	23	5	3	13	20	41	41
Chesterfield	42	12	3	6	54	34	4	5	12	30	55	40
Swansea T	42	14	2	5	40	16	1	5	15	10	49	37
Norwich C	42	8	6	7	38	29	6	2	13	25	42	36
Nottingham F	42	10	6	5	42	30	2	4	15	26	60	34
Southampton	42	10	8	3	38	25	1	4	16	15	52	34
Bradford	42	10	4	7	33	33	2	5	14	19	55	33
Bradford C	42	8	8	5	36	31	1	4	16	18	63	30
Doncaster R	42	6	6	9	18	29	1	4	16	12	55	24

Money had been spent on new players but the plain truth was that Villa had no divine right to success, despite their great pedigree.

Another boardroom upheaval preceded the season and the new regime secured the signature of Jimmy Hogan as team manager. A Lancashire lad who had played for Fulham, Swindon Town and Bolton, Hogan had made his name as a coach in Austria and Hungary and he set about the task of returning Aston Villa to the First Division.

In their first season in the Second Division, Villa finished in ninth position as Hogan began to sort out the team. Several players either retired or were transferred, although the legendary 'Pongo' Waring had left in November 1935.

The season started in fine style with ten points from the first six games including a 5-1 win over Bradford City at Villa Park. Former Liverpool player Gordon Hodgson scored a hat-trick and Villa Park fans looked forward to an early return to the First Division.

But slowly it dawned on them that it would not be that easy to return to the top flight straight away. Fulham won at Villa Park and Doncaster Rovers took both points at Belle Vue. When Sheffield United beat Villa 5-1 at Bramall Lane and Leicester City won 3-1 at Villa Park in early December, it was even more obvious.

At the end of the campaign, Villa had dropped 16 points at home, their illusions of a place in the top two finally shattered when Newcastle won 2-0 at Villa Park on Easter Tuesday.

Villa fans had not got to wait long

Frank Broome, Aston Villa's versatile forward who won seven full England caps plus two in unofficial wartime internationals. He scored 90 goals in 151 games for Villa.

for First Division soccer to return to their beloved Villa Park, however.

In 1937-38 Villa romped away with the Second Division title, finishing four points ahead of Manchester United. They also finished the season with a flourish when they won through to the semi-finals of the FA Cup.

In the League, it was Villa's defence that took the honours. The forwards managed only 73 goals but the defence conceded only 35.

Villa took up the challenge for the title on New Year's Day 1938, when a 1-1 draw at West Ham put them on top of the table for the first time. They stayed there until February and then fought it out with Manchester United, Sheffield United and Coventry before clinching the championship with a draw at Bramall Lane.

Left: Charlton's Tadman is tackled by Jimmy Allen while George Cummings looks on at The Valley in the fifth-round FA Cup tie in February 1938. *Right:* Action from the same game showing (from left to right) Iverson (Villa), Robinson (Charlton), Haycock (Villa), Owen (Charlton) and Allen (Villa). The crowd of 75,031 is still the record attendance for The Valley.

From left to right are Alec Massie, Jimmy Allen and Bob Iverson.

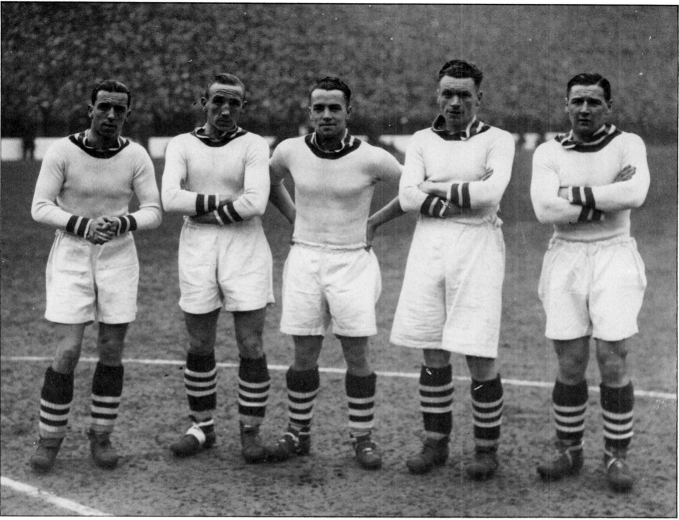

Villa's forward line in 1938. From left to right: Frank Broome, Freddie Haycock, Frank Shell, Ronnie Starling and Eric Houghton.

Their two games with Coventry produced record League attendances for both clubs — 68,029 at Villa Park in October, and 44,930 at Highfield Road in March.

In the FA Cup too, attendance records fell. When Villa beat Manchester City 3-2 in the sixth round on 5 March 1938, 75,540 fans paid over £5,500 into the Villa Park turnstiles.

Villa also found a new star in centreforward Frank Shell. Shell joined Villa from Ford Sports of Dagenham in May 1937 and on his second appearance for the club, against Stockport County on 11 December 1937, he scored a hat-trick in a 7-1 win.

Shell linked up with Frank Broome to provide a fearsome striking force for the rest of that season. Although Villa lost the FA Cup semifinal, 2-1 to Preston at Bramall Lane — the Preston winner was a controversial affair with the Villa defence standing still, believing George Mutch to be offside — they finished the season in magnificent style. After that goalless draw at Sheffield United which virtually gave them the title, they rounded off the season with wins over Swansea Town at Villa Park (4-0), Stockport, Bradford and Nor-wich. Villa were back in the First Division.

Broome was the club's leading League scorer with 20 goals, followed by Haycock (14) and Houghton (12). Shell netted eight in his 20 games.

The average League attendance at Villa Park for this championshipwinning season was 41,956.

DIVISION 2 1937-38

	P	W	D	L	F	A	W	D	L	F	A	Pts
Aston Villa	42	17	2	2	50	12	8	5	8	23	23	57
Manchester U	42	15	3	3	50	18	7	6	8	32	32	53
Sheffield U	42	15	4	2	46	19	7	5	9	27	37	53
Coventry C	42	12	5	4	31	15	8	7	6	35	30	52
Tottenham H	42	14	3	4	46	16	5	3	13	30	38	44
Burnley	42	15	4	2	35	11	2	6	13	19	43	44
Bradford	42	13	4	4	51	22	4	5	12	18	34	43
Fulham	42	10	7	4	44	23	6	4	11	17	34	43
West Ham U	42	13	5	3	34	16	1	9	11	19	36	42
Bury	42	12	3	6	43	26	6	2	13	20	34	41
Chesterfield	42	12	2	7	39	24	4	7	10	24	39	41
Luton T	42	10	6	5	53	36	5	4	12	36	50	40
Plymouth A	42	10	7	4	40	30	4	5	12	17	35	40
Norwich C	42	11	5	5	35	28	3	6	12	21	47	39
Southampton	42	12	6	3	42	26	3	3	15	13	51	39
Blackburn R	42	13	6	2	51	30	1	4	16	20	50	38
Sheffield W	42	10	5	6	27	21	4	5	12	22	35	38
Swansea T	42	12	6	3	31	21	1	6	14	14	52	38
Newcastle U	42	12	4	5	38	18	2	4	15	13	40	36
Nottingham F	42	12	3	6	29	21	2	5	14	18	39	36
Barnsley	42	7	11	3	30	20	4	3	14	20	44	36
Stockport Co	42	8	6	7	24	24	3	3	15	19	46	31

DIVISION 1 1938-39

	P	W	D	L	F	A	W	D	L	F	A	Pts
Everton	42	17	3	1	60	18	10	2	9	28	34	59
Wolves	42	14	6	1	55	12	8	5	8	33	27	55
Charlton A	42	16	3	2	49	24	6	3	12	26	35	50
Middlesbrough	42	13	6	2	64	27	7	3	11	29	47	49
Arsenal	42	14	3	4	34	14	5	6	10	21	27	47
Derby Co	42	12	3	6	39	22	7	5	9	27	33	46
Stoke C	42	13	6	2	50	25	4	6	11	21	43	46
Bolton W	42	10	6	5	39	25	5	9	7	28	33	45
Preston NE	42	13	7	1	44	19	3	5	13	19	40	44
Grimsby T	42	11	6	4	38	26	5	5	11	23	43	43
Liverpool	42	12	6	3	40	24	2	8	11	22	39	42
Aston Villa	42	11	3	7	44	25	5	6	10	27	35	41
Leeds U	42	11	5	5	40	27	5	4	12	19	40	41
Manchester U	42	7	9	5	30	20	4	7	10	27	45	38
Blackpool	42	9	8	4	37	26	3	6	12	19	42	38
Sunderland	42	7	7	7	30	29	6	5	10	24	38	38
Portsmouth	42	10	7	4	25	15	2	6	13	22	55	37
Brentford	42	11	2	8	30	27	3	6	12	23	47	36
Huddersfield T	42	11	4	6	38	18	1	7	13	20	46	35
Chelsea	42	10	5	6	43	29	2	4	15	21	51	33
Birmingham	42	10	5	6	40	27	2	3	16	22	57	32
Leicester C	42	7	6	8	35	35	2	5	14	13	47	29

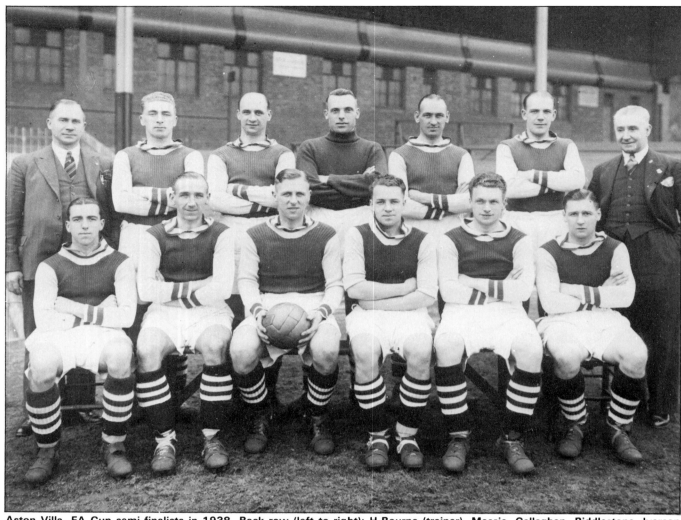

Aston Villa, FA Cup semi-finalists in 1938. Back row (left to right): H.Bourne (trainer), Massie, Callaghan, Biddlestone, Iverson, Cummings, Jimmy Hogan (manager). Front row: Broome, Haycock, Allen, Shell, Starling, Houghton.

Villa line up before the start of their game in the Olympic Stadium, Berlin, in 1938.

Jimmy Hogan (right) of Aston Villa meets Ipswich Town's Scott Duncan before the FA Cup replay at Portman Road in January 1939.

Aston Villa's Frank O'Donnell heads over the Ipswich bar following a corner but Villa won 2-1 with goals from Freddie Haycock.

There was to be only one season of First Division soccer, however, before World War Two intervened — Villa players had refused to emulate the England team and give the Nazi salute when they made a close-season tour to Germany in the summer of 1938 — and in that one season, Villa finished 12th in the table and reached the fourth round of the FA Cup before losing 2-0 to Preston North End.

On Christmas Day 1938, Frederick Rinder died. In his 80s, Rinder had devoted his life to football and to Villa and was senior vice-president of the Football Association at his death.

The same month, Bob Iverson scored the fastest goal ever netted by a Villa player — less than ten seconds after the start of the game against Charlton Athletic at Villa Park.

Iverson had been transferred from Wolves in December 1936 and proved a versatile player, appearing at half-back and in the forward line. He was one of the few Villa players whose career spanned World War Two and when he retired in 1947 he had made 153 League and Cup appearances, despite missing six seasons due to the war.

Villa had played only three matches of the 1939-40 season when war was declared. On the last Saturday of peace, Jack Nicholas' penalty beat them at Derby's Baseball Ground before the League programme was curtailed.

Brentford's Cheetham is brought down in the penalty area and from the spot-kick Reid scored, but Villa still won 4-2 in February 1939.

'Mush' Callaghan and George Cummings, two great Villa servants pictured here in 1939.

Villa goalkeeper Fred Biddlestone is out of position but this header from Chelsea's Joe Payne went just wide at Stamford Bridge in March 1939.

Joe Rutherford, the Aston Villa goalkeeper grabs the ball from Charlton's Blott at The Valley in April 1939, near the end of the last pre-war season.

Big Games and Big Crowds

LIKE almost all other clubs, Aston Villa played in wartime competitions, often with 'guest' players from whichever servicemen happened to be stationed near Villa Park at the time. In Villa's case this was so different from World War One, when the club had practically closed for the duration.

Nevertheless, they did not have the use of Villa Park in the early seasons of wartime football. After war was declared, the ground was closed for football and given over to the military with the Trinity Road stand converted into an air-raid shelter and stores and the home dressing-room being used by a rifle company of the 9th Royal Warwickshire Regiment.

Just before the war it had been planned to extend the terracing at the Holte End and although there were now severe restrictions on the building industry, the work was allowed to be completed by February 1940, after which the terracing, along with the rest of Villa Park, stood empty for three seasons as Villa played at Solihull Town's ground in 1940-41 and 1941-42, in the Birmingham & District League.

In 1942-43, Villa returned to Villa Park and could now take their place in the Football League North. The football, though, was sometimes bordering on the bizarre.

Teams were made up of guest players and those pre-war Villa men still in the city, employed in the police force or in munitions factories. Some clubs even had to call spectators out of the crowd when the selected men failed to show up, probably due to the difficulty of travelling in wartime Britain.

This sometimes led to some big scores and in 1942-43, Villa beat West Brom 8-2 at home with Eric

Houghton helping himself to a hat-trick.

The other confusing part of football in World War Two was that one match sometimes counted for two and even three competitions. There were two championships, one played until Christmas and the other to the end of the year. After Christmas, many league games also counted as cup ties and in this way, Villa reached the semi-finals of the Football League War Cup (North).

A qualifying competition began on Boxing Day 1942 and so Villa were competing in the league and the cup every Saturday. Eventually they won through to the knock-out stage of the cup — the games in this phase still counting towards the second championship — and reached the semi-finals before going out 4-3 on aggregate to Blackpool. They then had to finish off the season with two 'league only' matches and eventually finished fourth in the second championship. In the first they had ended in 14th place.

During the season, Birmingham City also played some of their home games at Villa Park after St Andrew's was damaged by German bombs.

In 1943-44, Villa gained revenge over Blackpool by beating them in the League War Cup North Final, 5-4 on aggregate. That pitted them against Charlton Athletic, winners of the War Cup South, at Stamford Bridge, where Eric Houghton scored Villa's goal in a 1-1 draw before a crowd of 38,540.

The following season, a third competition — the Midland Cup — was organised and Villa reached the Final of this, but after losing 3-0 at home to Derby County in the first leg, they went down 6-0 at the Baseball Ground where Peter

Harry Parkes, made a big impact when League football resumed in 1946.

Doherty, then still a guest player with Derby, scored five.

Like the previous conflict, World War Two had changed the lives of thousands of sportsmen and many, including some Villa players, were too old to continue when peace came. Others had six years taken out of the middle of their careers and when football resumed in something like its old form, for the 1945-46 FA Cup — played for the first and only time on a two-legged basis — teams in the Football League were a curious mixture of ageing skill and raw experience.

In that 1945-46 season, the Football League was divided into two premier sections of Leagues North and South, comprised of the pre-war First and Second Divisions, going back to the familiar 42-match programme. Black Country soccer fans enjoyed the fact that Birmingham City won League South with Aston Villa coming second.

Harry Parkes had joined the club from Boldmere St Michael's in 1939 and he made an immediate impact when peacetime football resumed. Parkes became a permanent fixture in Villa's defence for the first eight post-war seasons. He was a versatile player who excelled practically anywhere and he filled in ten different positions for Villa and missed only 12 League games in seven seasons before retiring in 1955 after 345 League and Cup appearances for the club.

Other players in the 'new' Villa team were Alex Massie, who had played before the war and was soon to take over as team manager, defender Vic Potts, a former Aston schoolboy who came to Villa Park via Spurs and Doncaster Rovers, and George Edwards, an inside-forward who signed from Norwich City in 1938 and who, during the war, had scored 95 goals for Villa, despite guesting for a number of other clubs as well. He went on to score 41 goals in 152 peacetime games for Villa.

There were also stalwarts like 'Mush' Callaghan, who in September 1942, as a police reservist, had been awarded the BEM for his bravery during the blitz on Birmingham. And Frank Broome and Eric Houghton were also still in place as Villa went to runners-up place in the League South, attracting an average home attendance of 32,822.

In the strangely-structured FA Cup of 1945-46, Villa beat Coventry City, Millwall and Chelsea on aggregate to reach the quarter-finals, having

disposed of Millwall 9-1 at Villa Park in their second-leg tie, with Frank Broome scoring a hat-trick.

Then Villa faced Derby County in the last eight and the first leg was played at Villa Park. The war had left Derby with a great side. At inside-forward they had two legendary players, Raich Carter and Peter Doherty, whilst Sammy Crooks and 'Dally' Duncan sped down their wings. Yet with five minutes of the first leg remaining, Villa were leading 3-2.

It already looked only a slender advantage to take to the Baseball Ground, but when Duncan centred the ball high over the Villa defence, Doherty jumped to head the equaliser. Before Villa could settle down, Crooks nipped in for the winner. When the sides met at the Baseball Ground, Broome put Villa in front again but Carter levelled the scores and so put Derby in front on aggregate. The Rams went on to win the FA Cup, although without Sammy Crooks who never recovered from a clattering he received from Callaghan after 30 minutes of the second leg.

The attendance at Villa Park for the first game against Derby was a remarkable 76,588, still the record attendance for the ground and now, of course, one that will never be beaten.

For the remainder of the 1940s, Villa never got beyond the fourth round of the competition, losing to Burnley (in the third round of 1946-47); Manchester United (third round, 1947-48); Cardiff City (fourth round, 1948-49) and Middlesbrough (third round, 1949-50 after two replays). In the First Division they finished no higher than sixth (in 1947-48) and no lower than 12th (1949-50).

Yet there was a new generation of Aston Villa footballer arriving on the scene. Villa's first game in the First Division for seven years was on 31 August 1946, when 50,572 spectators saw them play Middlesbrough with a team that included only Cummings, Callaghan and Broome of the side which played in the previous First Division fixture, against Derby County on 2 September 1939.

Within days of the opening of the 1946-47 season, Broome was transferred to Derby and enjoyed three

Dickie Dorsett, joined Villa from Wolves in 1946 and went on to make over 270 appearances.

good years at the Baseball Ground.

Before long, though, there would be more new arrivals. In September 1946, Dickie Dorsett came from Wolverhampton Wanderers as a skilful wing-half or inside-forward; Johnny Dixon, a former Newcastle United amateur, was in the side that lost to Middlesbrough; and fiery Welsh centre-forward Trevor Ford came from Swansea Town for £12,000 in January 1947; England international winger Leslie Smith had already signed from Brentford, in May 1945 for £7,500; Ivor Powell, the talented Welsh international inside-forward, came from Queen's Park Rangers in December 1948, after 11 seasons at Loftus Road.

The name Frank Moss was also a regular at centre-half, although he was the son of the great pre-war player of the same name. Frank junior signed for Villa from Wolves in 1938, for £2,000, and, after active service in the Royal Navy, took his place in the first post-war season. He was to make 313 League and Cup appearances before injury ended his career in 1955.

A goal from Middlesbrough's Wilf Mannion settled the issue in a rather dull game to herald the start of

Chelsea goalkeeper Bill Robertson watches as George Edwards scores at Stamford Bridge in November 1946.

peacetime League football at Villa Park in August 1946, and at the end of the season Villa were in eighth place. In the FA Cup, they were hammered 5-1 in the third round by Burnley, the eventual runners-up.

The Villa team was settling down. Goalkeeper Joe Rutherford, who had been transferred from Southport for £2,500 in February 1939, returned from wartime service with the RASC and missed only one match in 1946-47. Potts and Cummings were now the regular full-back pairing. Moss was at centre-half with Eddie Lowe, a former 'Bevin Boy' from Halesowen, at left-half; and Bob Iverson was right-half, although Moss' younger brother, Amos, also had a few games in the number-four shirt.

Harry Parkes had replaced Alex Massie at right-half for the opening game of the season but eventually he settled, if that is the right word, to a roving commission, appearing at left-half, centre-half and in four different forward positions.

One star flashing briefly across the sky was John Martin, an inside-forward who had joined Villa from Hednesford Town in January 1935. During the war, Martin had played

DIVISION 1 1946-47											
	P	W	D	L	F	A	W	D	L	F	A	Pts
Liverpool	42	13	3	5	42	24	12	4	5	42	28	57
Manchester U	42	17	3	1	61	19	5	9	7	34	35	56
Wolves	42	15	1	5	66	31	10	5	6	32	25	56
Stoke C	42	14	5	2	52	21	10	2	9	38	32	55
Blackpool	42	14	1	6	38	32	8	5	8	33	38	50
Sheffield U	42	12	4	5	51	32	9	3	9	38	43	49
Preston NE	42	10	7	4	45	27	8	4	9	31	47	47
Aston Villa	42	9	6	6	39	24	9	3	9	28	29	45
Sunderland	42	11	3	7	33	27	7	5	9	32	39	44
Everton	42	13	5	3	40	24	4	4	13	22	43	43
Middlesbrough	42	11	3	7	46	32	6	5	10	27	36	42
Portsmouth	42	11	3	7	42	27	5	6	10	24	33	41
Arsenal	42	9	5	7	43	33	7	4	10	29	37	41
Derby Co	42	13	2	6	44	28	5	3	13	29	51	41
Chelsea	42	9	3	9	33	39	7	4	10	36	45	39
Grimsby T	42	9	6	6	37	35	4	6	11	24	47	38
Blackburn R	42	6	5	10	23	27	8	3	10	22	26	36
Bolton W	42	8	5	8	30	28	5	3	13	27	41	34
Charlton A	42	6	6	9	34	32	5	6	10	23	39	34
Huddersfield T	42	11	4	6	34	24	2	3	16	19	55	33
Brentford	42	5	5	11	19	35	4	2	15	26	53	25
Leeds U	42	6	5	10	30	30	0	1	20	15	60	18

for England against Wales and Scotland and represented the Football League and an All British XI. In 1946-47 he scored eight goals in 29 League games but in 1949, he retired to concentrate on a career as a schoolteacher.

Two matches stand out in this period of Aston Villa's story. In the third round of the 1947-48 FA Cup, Villa were drawn at home to Manchester United and after 13 seconds, George Edwards completed a four-man Villa move to give them a sensational lead without a United player having touched the ball.

But United fought back and after 30 minutes they led 3-1 through Jack Rowley, Johnny Morris and Rowley again. At half-time Morris and Jimmy Delaney had made it 5-1 and Villa looked to be on their way out of the Cup.

But when United goalkeeper Jack Crompton failed to gather Edward's corner, Villa were back in the game and with 20 minutes to go, Smith made it 5-3. Nine minutes from time Dorsett scored and with Villa looking for what would have been a sensational equaliser, United stole up field (although not before Ford had hit the

DIVISION 1 1947-48											
	P	W	D	L	F	A	W	D	L	F	A	Pts
Arsenal	42	15	3	3	56	15	8	10	3	25	17	59
Manchester U	42	11	7	3	50	27	8	7	6	31	21	52
Burnley	42	12	5	4	31	12	8	7	6	25	31	52
Derby Co	42	11	6	4	38	24	8	6	7	39	33	50
Wolves	42	12	4	5	45	29	7	5	9	38	41	47
Aston Villa	42	13	5	3	42	22	6	4	11	23	35	47
Preston NE	42	13	4	4	43	35	7	3	11	24	33	47
Portsmouth	42	13	5	3	44	17	6	2	13	24	33	45
Blackpool	42	13	4	4	37	14	4	6	11	20	27	44
Manchester C	42	13	4	4	43	35	7	3	11	24	33	47
Liverpool	42	9	8	4	39	23	7	2	12	26	38	42
Sheffield U	42	13	4	4	44	24	3	6	12	21	46	42
Charlton A	42	8	4	9	33	29	9	2	10	24	40	40
Everton	42	10	2	9	30	26	7	4	10	22	40	40
Stoke C	42	9	5	7	29	23	5	5	11	12	32	38
Middlesbrough	42	8	7	6	37	27	6	2	13	34	46	37
Bolton W	42	11	2	8	29	25	5	3	13	17	33	37
Chelsea	42	11	6	4	38	27	3	3	15	15	44	37
Huddersfield T	42	7	6	8	25	24	5	6	10	26	36	36
Sunderland	42	11	4	6	33	18	2	6	13	23	49	36
Blackburn R	42	8	5	8	35	30	3	5	13	19	42	32
Grimsby T	42	5	5	11	20	35	3	1	17	25	76	22

Villa's Joe Rutherford collects the ball at a snow-covered Valley in February 1947. The season was extended until June because of bad weather. Moss and Potts are the other Villa players.

Aston Villa in 1947-48. This season Villa, under former player Alex Massie, Villa finished sixth in Division One and were knocked out of the FA Cup after a remarkable game against Manchester United.

DIVISION 1 1948-49

	P	W	D	L	F	A	W	D	L	F	A	Pts
Portsmouth	42	18	3	0	52	12	7	5	9	32	30	58
Manchester U	42	11	7	3	40	20	10	4	7	37	24	53
Derby Co	42	17	2	2	48	22	5	7	9	26	33	53
Newcastle U	42	12	5	4	35	29	8	7	6	35	27	52
Arsenal	42	13	5	3	51	18	5	8	8	23	26	49
Wolves	42	13	5	3	48	19	4	7	10	31	47	46
Manchester C	42	10	8	3	28	21	5	7	9	19	30	45
Sunderland	42	8	10	3	27	19	5	7	9	22	39	43
Charlton A	42	10	5	6	38	31	5	7	9	25	36	42
Aston Villa	**42**	**10**	**6**	**5**	**40**	**36**	**6**	**4**	**11**	**20**	**40**	**42**
Stoke C	42	14	3	4	43	24	2	6	13	23	44	41
Liverpool	42	5	10	6	25	18	8	4	9	28	25	40
Chelsea	42	10	6	5	43	27	2	8	11	26	41	38
Bolton W	42	10	4	7	43	32	4	6	11	16	36	38
Burnley	42	10	6	5	27	19	2	8	11	16	31	38
Blackpool	42	8	8	5	24	25	3	8	10	30	42	38
Birmingham C	42	9	7	5	19	10	2	8	11	17	28	37
Everton	42	12	5	4	33	25	1	6	14	8	38	37
Middlesbrough	42	10	6	5	37	23	1	6	14	9	34	34
Huddersfield T	42	6	7	8	19	24	6	3	12	11	45	34
Preston NE	42	8	6	7	36	36	3	5	13	26	39	33
Sheffield U	42	8	9	4	32	25	3	2	16	25	53	33

bar) and from a corner Stan Pearson made it 6-4. Ten goals had been scored in a superb game of soccer. It was a magnificent performance by both sides.

The other truly outstanding match was in the 1948-49 season. On New Year's Day, Villa were bottom of the First Division with only 16 points from 25 games, having lost 5-2 at home to Blackpool. There followed a difficult third-round FA Cup match with Bolton, and Villa managed a 1-1 draw at Villa Park, followed by a goalless draw on a dreadful Burnden Park pitch. The second replay was at Villa Park, where Villa won 2-1.

Although they lost at home to Cardiff in the next round, Villa had turned the corner. From the moment they had beaten Bolton, their League form changed and they took 26 points from their remaining 17 games, including wins over Arsenal, Huddersfield, Manchester United, Sheffield United, Manchester City, Everton, Preston, Charlton, Stoke and Birmingham to finish in tenth position. Much of the credit for the revival went to Ivor Powell, who had signed the previous December and who had a tremendous impact on the Villa team.

The 1940s were great days for football attendances all over the country and Villa Park was packing them in during 1948-49 with an average home gate of 47,168. A crowd of 63,572 saw Trevor Ford score four as Wolves were beaten 5-1 just after Christmas; there were 64,190 for the visit of Arsenal in late January, when Billy Goffin's goal won the points for Villa; and 68,354 saw the 2-1 win

Trevor Ford, the fiery Welsh forward who joined Aston Villa from Swansea Town in January 1947. He scored 62 goals for Villa.

Aston Villa, 1949-50. Back row (left to right): H.Bourne (trainer), Gibson, Harrison, Rutherford, Parkes, Moss, Martin. Front row: Goffin, Ford, Powell, Dorsett, Smith.

over Manchester United in mid-February.

However, all these massive crowds were eclipsed when Cardiff visited Villa Park for the fourth round of the FA Cup, one week after the win over Arsenal. Some 70,718 people watched Cardiff's new signing Stan Montgomery hold Villa's fiery Welshman Trevor Ford in check and Ken Hollyman and Billy Rees score the Welshmen's goals.

In September 1948, Villa had signed a quite remarkable footballer when Con Martin joined them from Leeds United. An Irish international who hailed from Dublin, Martin was remarkable in that he was, in the main, a superb performer at centre-half, yet also made 26 appearances in goal for Villa in 1951-52. Indeed, some of his 36 caps (30 for the Republic of Ireland and six for Northern Ireland) were won as a goalkeeper and, in all, he played in five different positions in international football.

Ambrose Mulraney, whose career ended in 1948-49 after only 12 games for Villa.

In February 1949, manager Alex Massie paid £17,000 for Newcastle United outside-right Colin Gibson, who had played so well against Villa that season. Gibson had been with Newcastle for only seven months after joining them from Cardiff City, but he stayed at Villa Park until 1956, scoring 26 goals in 167 League and Cup appearances before being transferred to Lincoln City.

One player whose career ended in 1948-49 was winger Ambrose Mulraney, a Scot despite his Irish-sounding name. Mulraney, a former Celtic, Ipswich Town and Birmingham City player, joined Villa via Shrewsbury Town and Kidderminster Harriers in September 1948 but after he had made only 12 League appearances for Villa he injured an Achilles tendon and had to retire from League football.

In 1949-50, Villa finished 12th in Division One after losing their last game of the season, 5-1 at Portsmouth, who had retained the League championship.

Left: **Chelsea's Roy Bentley causes the Villa defence a few problems in October 1949.** *Right:* **Villa again find Bentley in attacking mood. The Villa number-six is Frank Moss.**

DIVISION 1	1949-50											
	P	W	D	L	F	A	W	D	L	F	A	Pts
Portsmouth	42	12	7	2	44	15	10	2	9	30	23	53
Wolves	42	11	8	2	47	21	9	5	7	29	28	53
Sunderland	42	14	6	1	50	23	7	4	10	33	39	52
Manchester U	42	11	5	5	42	20	7	9	5	27	24	50
Newcastle U	42	14	4	3	49	23	5	8	8	28	32	50
Arsenal	42	12	4	5	48	24	7	7	7	31	31	49
Blackpool	42	10	8	3	29	14	7	7	7	17	21	49
Liverpool	42	10	7	4	37	23	7	7	7	27	31	48
Middlesbrough	42	14	2	5	37	18	6	5	10	22	30	47
Burnley	42	9	7	5	23	17	7	6	8	17	23	45
Derby Co	42	11	5	5	46	26	6	5	10	23	35	44
Aston Villa	**42**	**10**	**7**	**4**	**31**	**19**	**5**	**5**	**11**	**30**	**42**	**42**
Chelsea	42	7	7	7	31	30	5	9	7	27	35	40
WBA	42	9	7	5	28	16	5	5	11	19	37	40
Huddersfield T	42	11	4	6	34	22	3	5	13	18	51	37
Bolton W	42	10	5	6	34	22	0	9	12	11	37	34
Fulham	42	8	6	7	24	19	2	8	11	17	35	34
Everton	42	6	8	7	24	20	4	6	11	18	46	34
Stoke C	42	10	4	7	27	28	1	8	12	18	47	34
Charlton A	42	7	5	9	33	35	6	1	14	20	30	32
Manchester C	42	7	8	6	27	24	1	5	15	9	44	29
Birmingham C	42	6	8	7	19	24	1	6	14	12	43	28

Villa outside-right Johnny Dixon checks to see where the ball is. Arsenal goalkeeper Ted Platt seems to have lost it.

Con Martin, Villa's star centre-half who could also play in goal and did so for his country.

In the FA Cup, Villa played three matches but got no further than the first hurdle. A 2-2 draw at home to Middlesbrough was followed by a goalless draw at Villa Park before 'Boro won 3-0 at Elland Road with the help of a goal from Wilf Mannion.

Aston Villa, though, faced the 1950s with renewed confidence and it was to be a decade in which more famous names came to Villa Park and the club's supporters found themselves donning claret and blue favours for a return trip to Wembley. There were, however, some dark clouds on the distant horizon.

League Struggle
— But Cup Glory

BEFORE the 1950-51 season had even started there was a shock for Aston Villa fans when it was announced that manager Alex Massie had resigned. It was three months before Villa named Massie's successor — former Everton inside-forward George Martin, who came to Villa Park from Newcastle United where he had been team boss.

Martin had been at St James' Park since 1947 and he had also played for Hamilton Academical, Hull City, Middlesbrough and Luton Town. By the time Martin was installed at Villa Park it was clear that the club already

had no hope of the League championship and they did well to finish 15th in the table. The season was also marked by the departure of one fine player and the arrival of another.

On the outgoing scene, Trevor Ford left for Sunderland for the then record fee of £30,000. Ford had scored over 50 goals for Villa but in October 1950 his goal touch seemed to have eluded him and it was decided that a change of club would benefit both the fiery Welshman and Aston Villa.

Coming into Villa Park was a young Irishman from Belfast, Danny Blanchflower. The quietly-spoken

former RAF man, who had studied of St Andrew's University, had first played for Glentoran before signing for Barnsley. Now he was a Villa player.

Another player making his mark with Villa in the 1950-51 season was Stan Lynn, a hard-tackling full-back who had joined the club in March 1950. Just before Christmas, Villa bought a man to replace Ford, when Dave Walsh, West Brom's Republic of Ireland centre-forward, made the short journey across the Black Country. Walsh had scored 100 goals for the Throstles but he was never a

Villa Park pictured in 1951. Note that floodlights have yet to be installed. Indeed, they were not in use until 1958.

prolific scorer for Villa — 40 goals in 114 senior games before a move to Walsall in 1955.

Villa already had one excellent new forward on the books after Tommy Thompson was transferred from Newcastle United for £12,500 in September 1950. He repaid the fee with 76 goals in 165 League and Cup games before moving to Preston for £25,000 in June 1955.

Villa — with their youngest team since the war — struggled for survival for much of the season, hovering dangerously near the relegation zone for much of the time.

Yet the season had begun in quite dramatic style with wins over West Brom and Sunderland. But after that

Above: Aston Villa inside-forward Tommy Thompson battles it out with Bolton defenders Higgins and Edwards at Villa Park in December 1951.
Frank Moss tackles Bolton's Nat Lofthouse. Villa drew the game 1-1 with a goal from Billy Goffin.

DIVISION 1 1950-51												
	P	W	D	L	F	A	W	D	L	F	A	Pts
Tottenham H	42	17	2	2	54	21	8	8	5	28	23	60
Manchester U	42	14	4	3	42	16	10	4	7	32	24	56
Blackpool	42	12	6	3	43	19	8	4	9	36	34	50
Newcastle U	42	10	6	5	36	22	8	7	6	26	31	49
Arsenal	42	11	5	5	47	28	8	4	9	26	28	47
Middlesbrough	42	12	7	2	51	25	6	4	11	25	40	47
Portsmouth	42	8	10	3	39	30	8	5	8	32	38	47
Bolton W	42	11	2	8	31	20	8	5	8	33	41	45
Liverpool	42	11	5	5	28	25	5	6	10	25	34	43
Burnley	42	9	7	5	27	16	5	7	9	21	27	42
Derby Co	42	10	5	6	53	33	6	3	12	28	42	40
Sunderland	42	8	9	4	30	21	4	7	10	33	52	40
Stoke C	42	10	5	6	28	19	3	9	9	22	40	40
Wolves	42	9	3	9	44	30	6	5	10	30	31	38
Aston Villa	42	9	6	6	39	29	3	7	11	27	39	37
WBA	42	7	4	10	30	27	6	7	8	23	34	37
Charlton A	42	9	4	8	35	31	5	5	11	28	49	37
Fulham	42	8	5	8	35	37	5	6	10	17	31	37
Huddersfield T	42	8	4	9	40	40	7	2	12	24	52	36
Chelsea	42	9	4	8	31	25	3	4	14	22	40	32
Sheffield W	42	9	6	6	43	32	3	2	16	21	51	32
Everton	42	7	5	9	26	35	5	3	13	22	51	32

bright start, successes were few and far between. By the end of September, Villa had only eight points and although they beat Newcastle 3-0, they had to wait another month for their next win, when they defeated Chelsea 4-2 at Villa Park.

Until Easter, Villa were always in danger of going down. Then they beat Wolves twice — the second match at Villa Park drawing a crowd of over 48,000. On the same day, West Brom beat Huddersfield, who were also contenders for the drop, and Villa then faced vital matches, against Sheffield Wednesday, Chelsea and Everton — all of them likely to fall from grace.

It was up to Villa to gain their own salvation and they did well enough. They beat Wednesday and high-flying Newcastle and earned a point from Stamford Bridge. But still the danger was not past and when Portsmouth drew 3-3 at Villa Park, there were still worries.

Above: **Danny Blanchflower joined Villa from Barnsley in March 1951 for £15,000.** *Opposite:* **Blanchflower in the boot room at Villa Park.**

Then Villa beat Everton 2-1 at Goodison Park and on the very last day of the season they managed a fine 6-2 win over Stoke City at Villa Park. It was Everton and Sheffield Wednesday who went down whilst Villa climbed to a healthy 15th place, although only five points separated them from the 21st team, Wednesday.

In the third round of the Cup, Villa had beaten Burnley 2-0 at Villa Park but in the next round they went down 3-1 to Wolves at Molineux. Nevertheless, it had been a satisfactory season, considering the awful consequences which seemed likely for much of the time. George Martin had begun to settle his Aston Villa side down and Villa fans were looking forward to a big improvement in their club's fortunes.

After their improved form in the second half of the 1950-51 campaign Villa suffered a setback when, after a good start to the following season,

they lost four games in succession, culminating in a 2-0 defeat at White Hart Lane by the previous season's League champions, Tottenham Hotspur.

DIVISION 1 1951-52											
	P	W	D	L	F	A	W	D	L	F	A	Pts
Manchester U	42	15	3	3	55	21	8	8	5	40	31	57
Tottenham H	42	16	1	4	45	20	6	8	7	31	31	53
Arsenal	42	13	7	1	54	30	8	4	9	26	31	53
Portsmouth	42	13	3	5	42	25	7	5	9	26	33	48
Bolton W	42	11	7	3	35	26	8	3	10	30	35	48
Aston Villa	42	13	3	5	49	28	6	6	9	30	42	47
Preston NE	42	10	5	6	39	22	7	7	7	35	32	46
Newcastle U	42	12	4	5	62	28	6	5	10	36	45	45
Blackpool	42	12	5	4	40	27	6	4	11	24	37	45
Charlton A	42	12	5	4	41	24	5	5	11	27	39	44
Liverpool	42	6	11	4	31	25	6	8	7	26	36	43
Sunderland	42	8	6	7	41	28	7	6	8	29	33	42
WBA	42	8	9	4	38	29	6	4	11	36	48	41
Burnley	42	9	6	6	32	19	6	4	11	24	44	40
Manchester C	42	7	5	9	29	28	6	8	7	29	33	39
Wolves	42	8	6	7	40	33	4	8	9	33	40	38
Derby Co	42	10	4	7	43	37	5	3	13	20	43	37
Middlesbrough	42	12	4	5	37	25	3	2	16	27	63	36
Chelsea	42	10	3	8	31	29	4	5	12	21	43	36
Stoke C	42	8	6	7	34	32	4	1	16	15	56	31
Huddersfield T	42	9	3	9	32	35	1	5	15	17	47	28
Fulham	42	5	7	9	38	31	3	4	14	20	46	27

At this stage it seemed to Villa's supporters that they would have to endure another year of uncertainty as their club again tried to stave off relegation.

But there were better times on the way and Villa began to recover and to recapture the form which had seen them safely through 1950-51. By the end of 1951-52, Villa had climbed up to sixth place and were only ten points behind the champions Manchester United when the programme was completed.

Indeed, Villa players almost qualified for talent money and only one point separated them from Portsmouth and Bolton, the fourth and fifth-placed clubs. This drastic improvement had been achieved without a single big-money signing

In February 1952, *Picture Post* photographer George Douglas visited Villa Park to watch the club training.

— the first time since the war that no star player had pulled on a claret and blue shirt for the first time. But there were younger players who were gaining a recognised place in the Villa First Division side.

Stan Lynn held his place at full-back and partnered Harry Parkes, while behind the Villa back line, Con Martin played in goal for a time when Jones was injured. Martin had joined Villa as a full-back but he had played in goal for his native Eire in 1946 during an injury crisis. Peter Aldis came through from Bourneville, and Derek Pace from Bloxwich Scouts. A gritty centre-forward, Pace made up for his lack of inches by being a rare battler in the penalty area.

Villa had one of their best-ever half-back lines during this period with the artistic Danny Blanchflower wearing the number-four shirt in complete contrast to the powerful Dickie Dorsett on the other flank. Later in his illustrious career, Blanchflower was to form a similar combination with Dave Mackay.

At centre-half in the Villa team of 1951-52, Frank Moss was now becom-

ing as good a player as his father, who had also given Villa yeoman service.

Villa did have their problems at centre-forward where Dave Walsh failed to produce the form that had induced Villa to spend money on his transfer from West Brom; in the final analysis, this let in Johnny Dixon and he responded with 26 goals in the League, together with two in the FA Cup.

Villa had some checkered results in this season. Manchester United beat them 5-2 at Villa Park, despite a brilliant display by Moss, and they also lost 5-2 at Bolton and 6-1 at Newcastle. On the credit side, one can look at a superb 7-1 win over Chelsea at Villa Park during the latter half of the season when Villa's forwards rattled up the club's highest score for some years, Goffin scoring a hat-trick.

Blackpool, Burnley, Derby and Fulham also felt the full weight of an on-song Aston Villa forward line as each of those clubs conceded four goals at Villa Park, although perhaps one of Villa's best performances of

the season was a 3-0 win at Blackpool.

The steadying of the Villa defence meant that they finished the season with 70 goals against — 16 of which had been conceded in only three games, which gives a better overall picture of the true improvement.

In the FA Cup, Villa fans were in for a disappointment. Newcastle United were on their way to Wembley to win the trophy and they started their run in the third round by beating Aston Villa at St James' Park. United won 4-2 but Villa were not disgraced. Johnny Dixon played well against his former team and he had the consolation of scoring both Villa's goals on his old hunting ground.

Disastrous starts were by now a common feature of Aston Villa's story and the 1952-53 season was no exception. In their first ten games, Villa managed only two victories, although it must be said that the club suffered a crop of injuries during that period when both Dixon and Thompson missed games. Dixon strained a ligament and then Thompson was out with a cartilage injury.

Villa goalkeeper Keith Jones grabs the ball from Chelsea's Roy Bentley at Stamford Bridge in September 1952. Villa finished 11th in Division One that season.

DIVISION 1 1952-53												
	P	W	D	L	F	A	W	D	L	F	A	Pts
Arsenal	42	15	3	3	60	30	6	9	6	37	34	54
Preston NE	42	15	3	3	46	25	6	9	6	39	35	54
Wolves	42	13	5	3	54	27	6	8	7	32	36	51
WBA	42	13	3	5	35	19	8	5	8	31	41	50
Charlton A	42	12	8	1	47	22	7	3	11	30	41	49
Burnley	42	11	6	4	36	20	7	6	8	31	32	48
Blackpool	42	13	5	3	45	22	6	4	11	26	48	47
Manchester U	42	11	5	5	35	30	7	5	9	34	42	46
Sunderland	42	11	9	1	42	27	4	4	13	26	55	43
Tottenham H	42	11	6	4	55	37	4	5	12	23	32	41
Aston Villa	42	9	7	5	36	23	5	6	10	27	38	41
Cardiff C	42	7	8	6	32	17	7	4	10	22	29	40
Middlesbrough	42	12	5	4	46	27	2	6	13	24	50	39
Bolton W	42	9	4	8	39	35	6	5	10	22	34	39
Portsmouth	42	10	6	5	44	34	4	4	13	30	49	38
Newcastle U	42	9	5	7	34	33	5	4	12	25	37	37
Liverpool	42	10	6	5	36	28	4	2	15	25	54	36
Sheffield W	42	8	6	7	35	32	4	5	12	27	40	35
Chelsea	42	10	4	7	35	24	2	7	12	21	42	35
Manchester C	42	12	2	7	45	28	2	5	14	27	59	35
Stoke C	42	10	4	7	35	26	2	6	13	18	40	34
Derby Co	42	9	6	6	41	29	2	4	15	18	45	32

team was Ken Roberts, who made his debut on the right wing and gave some displays which Villa found most reassuring after they had pinned their faith in the youngster from Crewe.

Making his League debut against Wolves in September was Irish outside-left Peter McParland, who had been signed the previous month from Dundalk for £3,880. McParland played only once that season but was to win a regular place on Villa's left wing in 1953-54 and play a prominent part in them winning the FA Cup in 1957, although the incident surrounding his challenge on Ray Wood was one of the less happy facets of the game. Nevertheless, the youngster from Belfast was one of the most exciting players to watch in the entire Football League.

An older face in a new role was that of Danny Blanchflower, who played several games at inside-forward when Villa were struggling through that injury crisis.

Although Blackpool gained revenge for Villa's win at Bloomfield Road the previous season, by winning 5-1 at Villa Park, Villa also had their moments of goalscoring glory. When Portsmouth made the journey from the south they were soundly whipped 6-0; and Liverpool, too, came a cropper at Villa Park when they went down 4-0.

There was less joy for Villa at Charlton Athletic's sweeping Valley Ground where Charlton won 5-1; Manchester City also scored four goals against Villa at Maine Road. And so while Arsenal took the League championship on goal-average from Preston North End,

Again Villa survived and although they finished lower than the previous season, they went to the sixth round of the FA Cup. As usual, one of the stalwarts of this revival was Harry Parkes. Parkes played his 400th League game for the club in October 1952 and missed only two games all season. The rest of the defence rallied round and Villa conceded nine goals fewer than the previous campaign.

There were a few changes in personnel early in the season when Villa signed Norman Lockhart, the Irish international outside-left from Coventry City, and Derek Parsons, Wolves reserve-team goalkeeper. Another new face to the Villa first

Johnny Dixon
— Star of the Fifties

WHEN Aston Villa began the first post-war season of 1946-47 with a home match against Middlesbrough, they inevitably fielded many new faces from the side which had last fulfilled a League game for the club.

One of those new players was a 22-year-old inside-right from Hebburn, County Durham, called Johnny Dixon. He was in and out of the side in that first season, playing 17 times, either at inside-right or on the right wing, and scoring six goals. Inside a decade, though, he would be making history as the latest Villa skipper to hold aloft the FA Cup.

Dixon had begun his career with Hebburn Boys' Club and represented Durham County Boys before signing for Spennymoor United in 1940. Newcastle United spotted him and he was an amateur trialist at St James' Park, also guesting for Sunderland, Middlesbrough and Hull City during the war.

Newcastle, though, lost track of him and it was Aston Villa who took him on as an amateur in August 1944 before signing him on full-time professional forms in January 1946. When Villa finished runners-up in the Football League South that season — as football was getting back to normal — Dixon played five times and scored three goals, one of them coming on his senior debut, in a 4-1 win over Derby County at Villa Park in April.

He finally established himself as a regular midway through the 1948-49 season, playing in 25 League games which included the last 19. Still at inside-forward, although now wearing the number-ten shirt, he scored seven times.

In 1950-51 he was Villa's leading scorer with 15 League goals and the following season he again topped the charts, this time with 26. Thirteen goals in 1952-53 saw Dixon complete three consecutive seasons as Villa's leading scorer, then Tommy Thompson took over as the club's top marksman, although Dixon was still finding the net regularly and in 1955-56 he top-scored again with 16 goals.

Thereafter he began to play a deeper role for Villa and, inded, eventually reverted to the half-back line. In 1956-57, though, he was still scoring vital goals, none more so than in the FA Cup.

Dixon scored in Villa's three opening games in the Cup, a draw and a win over Luton Town and then victory over Middlesbrough. He gave them the lead at Kenilworth Road and scored both their goals in the Luton game at Villa Park. At Ayresome Park it was Dixon who hit the winner after Villa had trailed 2-1.

He was on target again in the quarter-final replay win over Burnley, but, as important, he was proving to be a magnificent captain.

In his *Aston Villa — The First 100 Years,* Peter Morris writes that the board's belief in the club was projected through the manager and on to the field through the captain.

'It was Dixon's job to generate that spirit among his team mates. Dixon did just this and he was the one man who sustained it right to the finish by his own personal example. Johnny Dixon, of the wry Geordie grin and engaging friendliness for everyone, may not have been the Villa's most dominant captain, nor was he their most talented player. But no footballer can have worn the club's claret and blue colours with more pride or dignity.'

When Villa beat Manchester United at Wembley, it was Dixon who led them to the Royal Box to receive the trophy, and after they had been relegated he helped them back to Division One in 1959. Altogether he made 430 senior appearances and scored 144 goals before retiring in May 1961. Even then he was not lost to the club, working on the coaching staff for another six years. Villa have had no greater servant.

Aston Villa in 1952-53. Back row (left to right): H.Bourne (trainer), Blanchflower, Parkes, Parsons, F.Moss, Aldis. Front row: Roberts, Thompson, Dorsett, Walsh, Dixon, Goffin.

Peter Aldis and Brentford's Tommy Lawton in action during the FA Cup fourth-round replay at Griffin Park in March 1953.

Villa had to be content with the mid-table place that their early season lapses had brought.

In the FA Cup it was a slightly different story and for part of the Cup programme, Villa fans entertained thoughts of Wembley. In the third round they saw Villa beat Middlesbrough 3-1 at Villa Park; after a goalless draw at home to Brentford in the next round, Walsh and Thompson gave Villa a 2-1 win in the replay; and in the fifth round it was the turn of Second Division Rotherham United to provide Villa with their passage into the next stage.

Rotherham had never got that far in the Cup and almost 20,000 fans squeezed into their Millmoor Ground to see Villa win 3-1. Dave Walsh scored twice and Billy Goffin once as Villa negotiated an icy pitch.

Goffin was one of the heroes of Villa Park. A quick and direct player, he endeared himself to the hearts of Villa fans.

The sixth round brought Everton

Dennis Parsons, the Villa goalkeeper, blocks a shot by Tottenham Hotspur's Sid MacClellan at White Hart Lane in April 1953.

Aston Villa outside-right Colin Gibson (7) is airborne in the third-round FA Cup game at Highbury in January 1954.

to Villa Park and the Merseysiders were supported by a large following who swelled the attendance to 60,658.

The only goal of a rousing Cup tie was scored by Everton's fiery centre-forward Dave Hickson. Hickson enjoyed a similar reputation to that of Villa's former star Trevor Ford, and his goal which put Everton into the semi-finals — where they lost 4-3 to Bolton Wanderers — was

rapturously received by his many fans at Villa Park that day.

We have already seen that disastrous starts were part of the Villa trade mark during the early 1950s. Boardroom upheavals also seem to trace a thread through the club's history and at the start of the 1953-54 season, Villa lost manager George Martin following background unrest.

In September 1953, Villa appoin-

ted a successor to Martin and their choice was received with unanimous approval. The club went to Notts County and prised their former star, Eric Houghton, back to Villa Park. Houghton had always been a firm favourite at Villa and he had done a good enough job at Meadow Lane to win the confidence of players, supporters and directors alike when he returned to Aston.

Yet the 1953-54 season turned out to be a poor one as far as Villa were concerned. With Wolverhampton Wanderers winning the League championship and West Bromwich Albion taking the FA Cup at Wembley against Preston North End, Villa were pushed out of the West Midland's moment of soccer glory and they had to content themselves with 13th place in the table, having just failed to average a point a game from their 42 League matches.

Villa's one truly memorable moment this season came in April, when West Brom came to Villa Park looking for two points which would keep them in the race for the First Division title and the coveted League and Cup double, last performed by Villa themselves during the 19th century.

On the day there was no doubting who were the better side as Villa not only prevented their close rivals from taking any points from Villa Park, but also did it to the convincing tune of 6-1.

Villa's young attack scored 70 goals this season — there were four players — McParland, Ken Roberts, Joe Tyrrell and Derek Pace, all under 22 years of age when Villa scored that big win over West Brom — and Thompson led the scoring with 21 goals, followed by Johnny Dixon and Dave Walsh.

Ken Jones was now back in the Villa goal and the defence still featured Harry Parkes, who played another great season at full-back with Peter Aldis alongside him for much of the time. Villa conceded 68 goals and there were two big defeats away from home — 6-1 at Liverpool and 4-0 at Huddersfield.

DIVISION 1 1953-54

	P	W	D	L	F	A	W	D	L	F	A	Pts
Wolves	42	16	1	4	61	25	9	6	6	35	31	57
WBA	42	13	5	3	51	24	9	4	8	35	39	53
Huddersfield T	42	13	6	2	45	24	7	5	9	33	37	51
Manchester U	52	11	6	4	41	27	7	6	8	32	31	48
Bolton W	42	14	6	1	45	20	4	6	11	30	40	48
Blackpool	42	13	6	2	43	19	6	4	11	37	50	48
Burnley	42	16	2	3	51	23	5	2	14	27	44	46
Chelsea	42	12	3	6	45	26	4	9	8	29	42	44
Charlton A	42	14	4	3	51	26	5	2	14	24	51	44
Cardiff C	42	12	4	5	32	27	6	4	11	19	44	44
Preston NE	42	12	2	7	43	24	7	3	11	44	34	43
Arsenal	42	8	8	5	42	37	7	5	9	33	36	43
Aston Villa	42	12	5	4	50	28	4	4	13	20	40	41
Portsmouth	42	13	5	3	53	31	1	6	14	28	58	39
Newcastle U	42	9	2	10	43	40	5	8	8	29	37	38
Tottenham H	42	11	3	7	38	33	5	2	14	27	43	37
Manchester C	42	10	4	7	35	31	4	5	12	27	46	37
Sunderland	42	11	4	6	50	37	3	4	14	31	52	36
Sheffield W	42	12	4	5	43	30	3	2	16	27	61	36
Sheffield U	42	9	5	7	43	38	2	6	13	26	52	33
Middlesbrough	42	6	6	9	29	35	4	4	13	31	56	30
Liverpool	42	7	8	6	49	38	2	2	17	19	59	28

In the FA Cup, Villa went to Highbury for the third round but lost 5-1 to the Gunners, who were in rampant form. The result capped a mediocre season for Villa fans and as soon as the Cup was out of the way, they went along to Villa Park knowing that their side had nothing to play for except a mid-table position.

But Eric Houghton was preparing

his plans for the future and, given the amount of time he had at his disposal in his first season as Villa team boss, he had done as well as anyone could have expected.

And in 1954-55, Villa supporters could forget the bad starts of previous seasons. This season was marked by one of the most sensational finishes to any Aston Villa season since the club was formed in 1874. In their last 15 matches Villa won 23 points — including 11 clear-cut victories — and lifted themselves up the table into sixth position, only five points behind the surprise champions, Chelsea. It was championship form and if Villa had started their amazing run-in just four matches earlier, then they would probably have been the First Division's new title-holders.

Yet if Villa had lifted the championship, they would have been even bigger pretenders than the Stamford Bridge club, for they had no real style and their magnificent late burst was as much due to endeavour and the run of the ball as to outright skill.

Villa finished the season with a defensive record of 73 goals against, which was their worst for some years. Sheffield Wednesday and Charlton each managed to score six goals against Villa away from Villa Park and Newcastle and Leicester (at Villa Park) hit them for five.

But the darkest parts of the season involved the departure of two fine players in Danny Blanchflower and Tommy Thompson, although Thompson's transfer did not take place until the close season when he joined Preston North End for £25,000.

His departure was a great loss to Villa but once he had seen Blanchflower seek new pastures, there was no holding the Scot.

Blanchflower had asked for a move before the New Year, feeling that Villa were not going in the same direction that he would have wished for himself. The board debated and at last decided that there was no point in keeping an unhappy player on the books.

As soon as he went on sale, Blanchflower was the target of several clubs but chiefly the north London rivals Spurs and Arsenal. The Gunners hung back a little and wanted Villa to drop the asking price of £30,000; Spurs had no such reservations and readily agreed to part with the cash. So Blanchflower became a Spurs player and Arsenal — and Villa, of course — lived to regret the day.

There had been backroom changes, too, as Villa brought back Jimmy Hogan to help out with the coaching. Hogan was now well past the age when most soccer coaches retire but he still had enough knowledge and skill in imparting it to make him a valuable addition to the staff where he helped the younger players with his immense fund of knowledge.

In March 1955, Villa's chairman Mr F.H.Normansell died and his place was taken by the former Villa player Chris Buckley.

Changing faces in the dressing-room also brought Vic Crowe from local soccer, Roy Chapman, another junior who found the occasional first-team spot, and Tommy Southern who was signed from West Ham on Christmas Eve 1954 for £12,000. Former Wolves full-back Roy Pritchard signed that winter but veterans Frank Moss and Harry Parkes retired from the game to end a Villa era.

In the FA Cup of 1954-55, Villa played seven matches but got only

DIVISION 1 1954-55											
	P	W	D	L	F	A	W	D	L	F	A	Pts
Chelsea	42	11	5	5	43	29	9	7	5	38	28	52
Wolves	42	13	5	3	58	30	6	5	10	31	40	48
Portsmouth	42	13	5	3	44	21	5	7	9	30	41	48
Sunderland	42	8	11	2	39	27	7	7	7	25	27	48
Manchester U	42	12	4	5	44	30	8	3	10	40	44	47
Aston Villa	42	11	3	7	38	31	9	4	8	34	42	47
Manchester C	42	11	5	5	45	36	7	5	9	31	33	46
Newcastle U	42	12	5	4	53	27	5	4	12	36	50	43
Arsenal	42	12	3	6	44	25	5	6	10	25	38	43
Burnley	42	11	3	7	29	19	6	6	9	22	29	43
Everton	42	9	6	6	32	24	7	4	10	30	44	42
Huddersfield T	42	10	4	7	28	23	4	9	8	35	45	41
Sheffield U	42	10	3	8	41	34	7	4	10	29	52	41
Preston NE	42	8	5	8	47	33	8	3	10	36	31	40
Charlton A	42	8	6	7	43	34	7	4	10	33	41	40
Tottenham H	42	9	4	8	42	35	7	4	10	30	38	40
WBA	42	11	5	5	44	33	5	3	13	32	63	40
Bolton W	42	11	6	4	45	29	2	7	12	17	40	39
Blackpool	42	8	6	7	33	26	6	4	11	27	38	38
Cardiff C	42	9	4	8	41	38	4	7	10	21	38	37
Leicester C	42	9	6	6	43	32	3	5	13	31	54	35
Sheffield W	42	7	7	7	42	38	1	3	17	21	62	26

as far as the fourth round. After drawing 2-2 with Brighton at the Goldstone Ground, they beat the Seagulls 4-2 at Villa Park in the third-round replay. There followed no less than five games against Doncaster Rovers — then a lowly Second Division side — before Rovers finally won the fourth replay 3-1 at The Hawthorns. The sides had played 540 minutes of football before they eventually resolved the matter. Villa would have earned an away draw with Birmingham City had they won. As it was, Doncaster went to St Andrew's and lost 2-1

There were to be no sensational doings towards the end of the following season which ended with Aston Villa missing relegation by the narrowest of margins. Things went from bad to worse each week and every Saturday plunged Villa Park further into the gloomy realisation that Second Division football was just around the corner.

One of the more surprising aspects of this fall from grace was that Villa had dipped into their coffers and

DIVISION 1 1955-56											
	P	W	D	L	F	A	W	D	L	F	A	Pts
Manchester U	42	18	3	0	51	20	7	7	7	32	31	60
Blackpool	42	13	4	4	56	27	7	5	9	30	35	49
Wolves	42	15	2	4	51	27	5	7	9	38	38	49
Manchester C	42	11	5	5	40	27	7	5	9	42	42	46
Arsenal	42	13	4	4	38	22	5	6	10	22	39	46
Birmingham C	42	12	4	5	51	26	6	5	10	24	31	45
Burnley	42	11	3	7	37	20	7	5	9	27	34	44
Bolton W	42	13	3	5	50	24	5	4	12	21	34	43
Sunderland	42	10	8	3	44	36	7	1	13	36	59	43
Luton T	42	12	4	5	44	27	5	4	12	22	37	42
Newcastle U	42	12	4	5	49	24	5	3	13	36	46	41
Portsmouth	42	9	8	4	46	38	7	1	13	32	47	41
WBA	42	13	3	5	37	25	5	2	14	21	45	41
Charlton A	42	13	2	6	47	26	4	4	13	28	55	40
Everton	42	11	5	5	37	29	4	5	12	18	40	40
Chelsea	42	10	4	7	32	26	4	7	10	32	51	39
Cardiff C	42	11	4	6	36	32	4	5	12	19	37	39
Tottenham H	42	9	4	8	37	33	6	3	12	24	38	37
Preston NE	42	6	5	10	32	36	8	3	10	41	36	36
Aston Villa	42	9	6	6	32	29	2	7	12	20	40	35
Huddersfield T	42	9	4	8	32	30	5	3	13	22	53	35
Sheffield U	42	8	6	7	31	35	4	3	14	32	42	33

bought five expensive players in a bid to fight their way back up the First Division table. Some were successful signings; some were most definitely not.

Dave Hickson — the man who had knocked Villa out of the cup a few seasons earlier — came from Everton but within a short time he was moving on to Huddersfield Town, having failed quite dramatically to make any impact at Villa Park.

Sheffield Wednesday's Jackie Sewell was signed in December 1955, for £20,000. Sewell was the man for whom Wednesday had paid Notts County a British record fee of £34,500 in 1951.

In February 1956, Villa signed

Jimmy Dugdale, signed from West Brom for £25,000.

West Brom centre-half Jimmy Dugdale for £25,000, together with winger Leslie Smith from Wolves, also for £25,000. One month later, Smith's Wolves teammate, goalkeeper Nigel Sims, was also on his way to Villa Park.

A sixth new player came to the club when Millwall's young wing-half Pat Saward was signed from the London club for £7,000.

Dugdale had already won an FA Cup winners' medal with West Brom in 1954 and Smith was a Wolves regular, whilst Sims was to develop

Pat Saward was yet another new Villa player. He came from Millwall for £7,000.

into one of the finest goalkeepers ever to wear a Villa jersey.

A native of the Burton upon Trent area, Sims had to understudy the great Bert Williams at Wolves and he grabbed his Villa opportunity with two safe hands. Together with Saward, Houghton's latest signing would form the nucleus of the team which would win the FA Cup the following season.

In the First Division of 1955-56, however, Villa had a job to survive and it was only due to a spell of 11 games towards the end of the season in which they picked up 15 points. Even then, they had to wait until the last day of the season before scraping home.

When the last day came, Villa had won only ten matches all season and were in 21st place. Sheffield United were already doomed and the final Second Division place rested between

Jackie Sewell, who joined Villa from Sheffield Wednesday for £20,000. They paid a British record fee of £34,500 when signing Sewell from Notts County in 1951.

Villa and Huddersfield Town, who were two points better off than Villa.

Villa faced their old rivals West Brom at Villa Park in a game they had to win — and win by a wide margin — in order to survive. Earlier in the season, Albion had beaten Villa 1-0 at The Hawthorns and Villa fans were not at all certain that their side would pull off a win.

In fact, Villa won by the margin of three goals to nil, which was just good enough to save them, Huddersfield going down with a goal-average only 0.2 worse than that of Villa.

In the FA Cup, Villa had struggled to dispose of Hull City after the Tigers earned a 1-1 draw at Villa Park. Villa won the replay at Booth-ferry Park 2-1 but in the fourth round their old Cup adversaries, Arsenal, trounced them 4-1 at Highbury and put another blot on the Villa season.

Villa Park fans had little to which to look forward in the summer of 1956 — yet if only they could have

seen into the immediate future, their hearts would have been lifted. Villa were going to Wembley again and they would take the FA Cup once more — for the first time in the lives of many of their supporters.

Aston Villa achieved two things in 1956-57 — they won the FA Cup and, perhaps more important, pulled themselves up the First Division table to finish in tenth place. And whilst in no way wishing to diminish the FA Cup win, which was all-important to Villa Park fans, one ventures to suggest that First Division survival was more significant, although that would only be temporary.

But it is the Cup for which the season will be remembered. Villa began their run in January and a visit to Luton Town's Kenilworth Road, where the Hatters held Villa to a 2-2 draw. In the replay some 28,000 fans saw Leslie Smith cross for Johnny Dixon to head Villa in front; and then

the same two players exchange passes before Dixon scored his second and put Villa through 2-0.

In the fourth round, Villa made the long journey to the North-East and Middlesbrough's Ayresome Park. Brian Clough and Bill Harris gave 'Boro a 2-1 half-time lead, Smith having scored for Villa. Then Pace equalised and Dixon scored the winner when Middlesbrough's goal-keeper Peter Taylor was late in moving for the Villa player's shot.

Second Division Bristol City were Villa's fifth-round opponents and they went down 2-1 at Villa Park. A crowd of 63,099 saw Pace put Villa in front, John Atyeo equalise and then Jackie Sewell score the winner with a fantastic goal of cool individual skill.

Villa's jubilation was tempered when they learned that they had to travel to their 'bogey' ground — Burnley's Turf Moor. And it looked as though Villa's run of bad results

Nigel Sims ends up in the back of the net after tipping over an Arsenal centre at Highbury in November 1956. Steaming in is the Gunners' Vic Groves, who scored two first-half goals to earn Arsenal both points.

Keith Jones and Jimmy Dugdale are determined to keep out Tottenham centre-forward Bobby Smith at White Hart Lane in January 1957. But Smith got on the scoresheet as Villa went down 3-0.

Peter McParland
— The Flying Irishman

DURING the 1950s, there was one man, above all others, who could win matches for Aston Villa. Opposing managers knew that if they stopped Peter McParland, then they had a good chance of stopping the Villa.

Yet for all his success at Villa Park, and the fact that his name was almost synonymous with that of the club, McParland was a rarity, for Villa had never really trawled Irish waters for their footballers. Indeed, before McParland was first capped at full level for Northern Ireland, against Wales in the 1953-4 season, one had to go back to 1910-11, when Billy Renneville played against Wales, for the last time a Villa winger had worn the emerald green shirt. Indeed, at the time he was only the fourth Villa player to be capped for Ireland, Con Martin and Danny Blanchflower being the others.

McParland, who was born in Newry in April 1934, was an apprentice coppersmith, playing part-time for Dundalk in the League of Ireland club when he joined Villa for a £3,880 fee in August 1952. He soon made his League debut in the most daunting circumstances, playing in a 1-0 defeat by Wolves before a crowd of 56,653.

That was McParland's only senior appearance that season and he had to wait 15 months for his next outing, again against Wolves and this time at Molineux on Christmas Eve 1953. This time it was Villa who triumphed and McParland marked his second appearance with his first goal for the club. Peter McParland had arrived and he stayed in the side until the end of the season.

He was in the Northern Ireland side before his 20th birthday and marked his international debut with two goals against the Welsh. Altogether, McParland won 33 caps for his country and was a star when Wales reached the quarter-finals of the World Cup in Sweden in 1958. In the play-off game against Czechoslovakia, playing at centre-forward, he gave the Irish lead and then hit an extra-time winner after the Czechs had drawn level.

That World Cup experience came a year after McParland made national headlines in the 1957 FA Cup Final. In the semi-final, against West Brom, he had twice saved his side with equalising goals and at Wembley he netted the two which beat Manchester United, a header from Dixon's cross and a shot after Billy Mysercough's earlier effort had come back off the crossbar.

Those goals were scored against stand-in 'keeper Jackie Blanchflower, for in only the sixth minute of the game, McParland had put in a challenge on United's Ray Wood which saw the goalkeeper leave the field with a fractured cheek-bone. Today,

McParland would probably have been sent off, but in the 1950s, trying to bundle the 'keeper over the line was all part and parcel of the game. Whatever, the 1957 Cup Final will always be remembered as Peter McParland's match.

In 1959, it was another two brilliant goals from McParland that put Villa into yet another FA Cup semi-final, and the following season he scored 22 goals, playing brilliantly week after week as Villa returned to Division One as champions. In November 1959, Villa hammered Charlton 11-1 with Gerry Hitchins scoring five times. McParland hit two goals and had a hand in all the other nine. That was the measure of his influence.

Although at his most memorable as a flying left winger, so direct, so dangerous, McParland also gave some performances at centre-forward and wherever he played he had a remarkable eye for goal. In 340 League and Cup games for Aston Villa, he scored 120 times before moving to Wolves for £30,000 in January 1962. He ended his League career with Plymouth and Peterborough but is still remembered as the man who lit up Villa Park in the 1950s.

Villa's first-team squad in 1957. Back row (left to right): Aldis, Lynn, Crowther, Sims, Dugdale, Pace, Birch. Front row: Eric Houghton (manager), Smith, Sewell, Myercough, Dixon, McParland, Bill Moore (trainer). On ground: Saward.

at Turf Moor would continue when Peter Aldis put through his own goal, but Peter McParland managed an equaliser and the clubs withdrew for a replay at Villa Park, where Dixon and McParland helped Villa to a 2-0 win. Over 46,000 fans roared Villa into the semi-finals and a game against West Bromwich Albion.

The FA chose Wolves' Molineux for the semi-final — Birmingham City were playing Manchester United at Hillsborough in the other semi-final — and on 23 March 1957 Villa's Cup run looked to be over when West Brom led with only five minutes to play.

But just as McParland scored Villa's first equaliser, so the Irishman

DIVISION 1 1956-57											
	P	W	D	L	F	A	W	D	L	F	A	Pts
Manchester U	42	14	4	3	55	25	14	4	3	48	29	64
Tottenham H	42	15	4	2	70	24	7	8	6	34	32	56
Preston NE	42	15	4	2	50	19	8	6	7	34	37	56
Blackpool	42	14	3	4	55	26	8	6	7	38	39	53
Arsenal	42	12	5	4	45	21	9	3	9	40	48	50
Wolves	42	17	2	2	70	29	3	6	12	24	41	48
Burnley	42	14	5	2	41	21	4	5	12	15	29	46
Leeds U	42	10	8	3	42	18	5	6	10	30	45	44
Bolton W	42	13	6	2	42	23	3	6	12	23	42	44
Aston Villa	42	10	8	3	45	25	4	7	10	20	30	43
WBA	42	8	8	5	31	25	6	6	9	28	36	42
Birmingham C	42	12	5	4	52	25	3	4	14	17	44	*39
Chelsea	42	7	8	6	43	36	6	5	10	30	37	*39
Sheffield W	42	12	3	4	55	29	2	3	16	27	59	38
Everton	42	10	5	6	34	28	4	5	12	27	51	38
Luton T	42	10	4	7	32	26	4	5	12	26	50	37
Newcastle U	42	10	5	6	43	31	4	3	14	24	56	36
Manchester C	42	10	2	9	48	42	3	7	11	30	46	35
Portsmouth	42	8	6	7	37	35	2	7	12	25	57	33
Sunderland	42	9	5	7	40	30	3	3	15	27	58	32
Cardiff C	42	7	6	8	35	34	3	3	15	18	54	29
Charlton A	42	7	3	11	31	44	2	1	18	31	76	22
*Birmingham City & Chelsea finished in equal 12th position											

netted another and earned Villa yet another replay.

A crowd of 55,549 saw the first

game at Wolves and 58,067 were at St Andrew's for the second match.

When Albion's Ronnie Allen was injured with less than 20 minutes gone, Villa took command and in the 38th minute Billy Myerscough headed the only goal of the game.

Although Albion hit a post and came near on other occasions, Villa hung on to go back to Wembley for the first time since before the war.

They met Manchester United, earlier on the road to a treble of FA Cup, First Division title and European Cup, although by Cup Final day they had been knocked out of Europe, but had won the League championship.

In the sixth minute of the Final,

Peter McParland and Ray Wood lie injured after their collision in the sixth minute of the 1957 FA Cup Final.

McParland scores his second goal past stand-in 'keeper Jackie Blanchflower.

Above (left): Blanchflower can only watch this effort from McParland. *Above (right):* More trouble for United's defence. *Right:* McParland heads goalwards. *Far right:* Sims gathers the ball for Villa. *Below:* General view of the 1957 Cup Final.

Villa parade the Cup through Birmingham.

McParland clashed with United goalkeeper Ray Wood, who was forced to go off with a fractured cheekbone. The incident would not have gone unpunished today, but in 1957 it was permissible to clatter the goalkeeper provided he had both feet on the ground.

With centre-half Jackie Blanchflower in goal and with no substitute to call upon, United did well but they were already on the way to being beaten.

Two goals within five minutes of each other in the second half — both scored by McParland — finished United off and although Tommy Taylor pulled back a goal, and although a groggy Wood eventually returned to goal, it was all over. The shame was that Villa's finest hour for years had been marred by the McParland-Wood incident. But Villa were FA Cup holders.

Skipper Johnny Dixon receives a pat on the head after leaving the Royal Box with the FA Cup. Jackie Sewell is the player behind him, clutching the trophy's plinth.

Down and Up Again

MANCHESTER United, beaten by Aston Villa in the 1957 FA Cup Final, did not have to wait long for their revenge. As League champions, United met Cup holders Villa in the FA Charity Shield at the beginning of the 1957-58 season and won 4-0 with a hat-trick from Tommy Taylor and a goal from Johnny Berry.

It was the sign for which Villa should have been searching. Average teams occasionally win the FA Cup and Villa were, at the very best, a mediocre side, despite those famous names. Certainly, the Wembley victory did not herald a march to even greater heights. Indeed, Villa's grip on the Cup was soon loosened.

Although it took them three games to do it, Stoke City knocked the Cup holders out at the very first hurdle. Stoke were then in the Second Division but they twice held Villa to a draw — 1-1 at the Victoria Ground and 3-3 at Villa Park — before winning 2-0 in the second replay at Molineux. Former Wolves player Dennis Wilshaw played a big part in his new club's victory on his former club's ground.

But by the time Villa were knocked out of the Cup, it was already obvious that the team needed major changes. In the end they were lucky to maintain 14th position in the First Division and the defence had let in the rather ominous total of 86 goals, whilst 19 matches were lost, including six-goal defeats at Leicester and Tottenham. Complacency, it seemed, was the name of the game at Villa Park.

Throughout the season there were team changes and players coming and going, including Stan Crowther moving to Manchester United after they were stricken by the Munich air crash. Crowther went on to play in his second successive FA Cup Final and thus made a little piece of Cup

history by being the only player ever to have played in the competition for two clubs in the same season after the FA waived the qualification rules to help United out.

Derek Pace had already gone to Sheffield United and Billy Myerscough was also sadly out of form. The one bright spot was Vic Crowe, who reverted to right-half in place of Crowther and played exceptionally well. Johnny Dixon, struggling to find form, was left out and Villa missed his flair in the attack, although the following season he came back into the side at right-half, ironically when Saward was left out and Crowe moved over to replace him.

Eventually, Villa went into the transfer market in December 1957 and signed Gerry Hitchens from Cardiff City. Hitchens was doing his National Service but was in fact a Cannock Chase lad and had made his name in the Southern League with Kidderminster Harriers. Villa paid £22,500 for the player who had already won representative honours with England Under-23s, the FA team and the powerful British Army side.

Even with Nigel Sims performing well in goal behind a defence of Stan Lynn and Peter Aldis at full-back and

Vic Crowe, who switched to right-half and proved a rare bright spot in a gloomy season.

	P	W	D	L	F	A	W	D	L	F	A	Pts
DIVISION 1 1957-58												
Wolves	42	17	3	1	60	21	11	5	5	43	26	64
Preston NE	42	18	2	1	63	14	8	5	8	37	37	59
Tottenham H	42	13	4	4	58	33	8	5	8	35	44	51
WBA	42	14	4	3	59	29	4	10	7	33	41	50
Manchester C	42	14	4	3	58	33	8	1	12	46	67	49
Burnley	42	16	2	3	52	21	5	3	13	28	53	47
Blackpool	42	11	2	8	47	35	8	4	9	33	32	44
Luton T	42	13	3	5	45	22	6	3	12	24	41	44
Manchester U	42	10	4	7	45	31	6	7	8	40	44	43
Nottingham F	42	10	4	7	41	27	6	6	9	28	36	42
Chelsea	42	10	5	6	47	34	5	7	9	36	45	42
Arsenal	42	10	4	7	48	39	6	3	12	25	46	39
Birmingham C	42	8	6	7	43	37	6	5	10	33	52	39
Aston Villa	42	12	4	5	46	26	4	3	14	27	60	39
Bolton W	42	9	5	7	38	35	5	5	11	27	52	38
Everton	42	5	9	7	34	35	8	2	11	31	40	37
Leeds U	42	10	6	5	33	23	4	3	14	18	40	37
Leicester C	42	11	4	6	59	41	3	1	17	32	71	33
Newcastle U	42	6	4	11	38	42	6	4	11	35	39	32
Portsmouth	42	10	6	5	45	34	2	2	17	28	54	32
Sunderland	42	7	7	7	32	33	3	5	13	22	64	32
Sheffield W	42	12	2	7	45	40	0	5	16	24	52	31

Jackie Sewell (8) leaps between Dodgin and Wills but Arsenal's Jack Kelsey saves his header at Highbury in December 1958.

Jimmy Dugdale at centre-half, Villa's plight was obvious, although not perhaps to many actually at the club. It was certain that a general shake-up of the Villa Park structure was needed before they could come bouncing back in the best traditions of the club. It would, however, be some time before that shake-up was implemented — by which time Villa would be in the Second Division.

The 1958-59 season was a black campaign for Aston Villa and in April they tumbled into the Second Division for only the second time in their long history. It was a doubly bitter pill for Villa fans to swallow since this same season saw Villa reach a record 16th FA Cup semi-final, where a 1-0 defeat at the hands of Nottingham Forest saved them from the bizarre distinction of becoming the first club ever to have played at Wembley in an FA Cup Final and been relegated in the same season.

There was another off-the-field row at the start of the season when

— against the background of a team in bottom place in the First Division after five successive defeats — Villa's Shareholders' Association tried to unseat two directors in favour of its own men. The bid failed and the directors, Joe Broughton and Bruce Normansell, retained their place on the Villa board.

Villa began their season with a 1-1 draw against Birmingham City at Villa Park and on the Monday following this opener, Portsmouth also visited Villa Park and lost 3-2. With three points from their first two matches, Villa could be forgiven for thinking that things were ticking over nicely. But there was that complacency again. The second Saturday of the season saw Villa go to Upton Park to meet newly-promoted West Ham United. The Hammers ran rings around Villa and won 7-2. The writing was on the wall.

Then Portsmouth won 5-2 against Villa at Fratton Park and Nottingham Forest came to Villa Park and beat the Claret and Blues 3-2;

Wolves beat Villa quite convincingly in a midweek game and then Villa won their first point in a month when they managed to draw 1-1 with Blackpool, who lost centre-forward Dave Charnley, injured during the match.

Wins over Blackburn and Newcastle gave Villa hope but then West Brom won 4-1 at Villa Park and, to compound the problems, McParland asked for a transfer. Although he managed to change McParland's mind, Houghton was on the brink of resignation and his last signing was Ron Wylie from Notts County, for £9,250 in November 1958.

The little Scottish forward came to Villa Park; and Houghton left, following a bleak autumn which had seen Villa scrape only five points out of a possible 16.

On Christmas Eve 1958, Villa were bottom of the First Division, with only 17 points from 23 games. At that point the club announced that they had engaged Joe Mercer as their

Joe Mercer, who took over the reins at Villa Park in place of
Eric Houghton.

Pat Saward in action against West Ham.

manager in succession to Eric Houghton.

Mercer, the former captain of Everton, Arsenal and England, came from Sheffield United where he had been team boss.

Over Christmas, Mercer saw the magnitude of his task. Manchester United won 2-1 at Old Trafford and 2-0 at Villa Park and then West Ham won 2-1, also at Villa Park. Mercer's first signing was Doug Winton, the Burnley full-back who had played in Scotland's 'B' team, but he came too late to help avoid the drop.

Although a handful of reasonable results gave Villa a little hope, the Easter programme put paid to them. On Good Friday, they lost 3-2 at White Hart Lane; on Easter Saturday, they went down 2-1 at Everton; and on Easter Monday, Spurs took a point in a 1-1 draw. When Leicester won 2-1 at Villa Park on 4 April, Villa knew they were virtually doomed.

When the last day of the season arrived, Villa had to beat West Brom, while Manchester City had to lose to Leicester at Maine Road. City beat

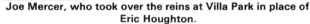

DIVISION 1 1958-59											
	P	W	D	L	F	A	W	D	L	F	A	Pts
Wolves	42	15	3	3	68	19	13	2	6	42	30	61
Manchester U	42	14	4	3	58	27	10	3	8	45	39	55
Arsenal	42	14	3	4	53	29	7	5	9	35	39	50
Bolton W	42	14	3	4	56	30	6	7	8	23	36	50
WBA	42	8	7	6	41	33	10	6	5	47	35	49
West Ham U	42	15	3	3	59	29	6	3	12	26	41	48
Burnley	42	11	4	6	41	29	8	6	7	40	41	48
Blackpool	42	12	7	2	39	13	6	4	11	27	36	47
Birmingham C	42	14	1	6	54	35	6	5	10	30	33	46
Blackburn R	42	12	3	6	48	28	5	7	9	28	42	44
Newcastle U	42	11	3	7	40	29	6	4	11	40	51	41
Preston NE	42	9	3	9	40	39	8	4	9	30	38	41
Nottingham F	42	9	4	8	37	32	8	2	11	34	42	40
Chelsea	42	13	2	6	52	37	5	2	14	25	61	40
Leeds U	42	8	7	6	28	27	7	2	12	29	47	39
Everton	42	11	3	7	39	38	6	1	14	32	49	38
Luton T	42	11	6	4	50	26	1	7	13	18	45	37
Tottenham H	42	10	3	8	56	42	3	7	11	29	53	36
Leicester C	42	7	6	8	34	36	4	4	13	33	62	32
Manchester C	42	8	7	6	40	32	3	2	16	24	63	31
Aston Villa	42	8	5	8	31	33	3	3	15	27	54	30
Portsmouth	42	5	4	12	38	47	1	5	15	26	65	21

Leicester 3-1 at Maine Road, but even then, Villa were winning 1-0 with two minutes to go and they would have stayed up had not Ronnie Allen scored a last-gasp equaliser. They were relegated.

In 1959-60, however, Aston Villa bounced straight back. At the first attempt they stormed away with the Second Division championship, winning 25 of their matches and losing only eight, as well as reaching the semi-finals of the FA Cup before

losing to Wolves in a close and thrilling Cup tie.

During the 1959-60 season, several players made their debuts for the club. Harry Burrows, a junior from the Wigan area who had signed as an amateur in 1956 and was taken on to the professional staff two years later, played one game at inside-left. And Alan Deakin, from Balsall Heath, was another junior who made his first appearance this season.

Jimmy McEwan had joined Villa from Raith Rovers for £8,000 just before the start of the season, in July. A fragile-looking winger, he played 28 games in the championship season. Full-back John Neal was transferred from Swindon Town for £6,000, also in July. Neal came into the side for the second game of the season and did not miss a game thereafter.

Inside-forward Bobby Thomson perhaps made the biggest impact of the new men. Signed from Wolves for £8,000 in June 1959, he scored 20 League goals, second only to McParland in the Villa list.

Nigel Sims takes the ball during the fourth-round FA cup game at Stamford Bridge in January 1959.

Bobby Thomson, who joined Villa from Wolves and made an immediate impact.

Another new face was inside-forward, Mike Tindall, who came through from the junior staff and made two appearances, although like the others he was to serve Villa well in the days to come.

Villa lost only one game at home this season and their defensive record of 43 goals was not bettered by any club in the Football League.

In addition, the presence of Aston Villa on some of the smaller grounds in the League proved to be of immense value to the home clubs and Lincoln City (13,850), Rotherham United (20,545) and Scunthorpe United (13,084) each enjoyed best of the season attendance figures when Villa were the visitors. They attracted 54,769 to Ninian Park to see Cardiff City, promoted one point behind Villa, win 1-0.

At Villa Park, the average League attendance was 34,711 with a highest 'gate' of 54,763 to see the home game against Cardiff, which Villa won 2-0.

Villa began their Second Division programme with a 2-1 win at Brighton where Sewell grabbed the winner near the end of the match in a not-too-impressive Villa performance. In midweek Villa lost 1-0 at Roker Park but that was to be their last defeat for 15 matches.

One week after Liverpool — who eventually finished third — won 2-1 at Anfield on 7 November before a crowd of 49,981, Villa confirmed they were too good for the Second Division with a staggering 11-1 win over Charlton Athletic at Villa Park. It was their biggest win at Villa Park and their biggest League victory since Accrington were beaten 12-2 at Perry Barr in March 1892.

Gerry Hitchens scored five of the first six goals against a Charlton side which, it must be said, lost goalkeeper Duff with an arm injury, although by then Villa were already 6-1 ahead. McParland (two) Thomson (two), Wylie and MacEwan completed the rout.

DIVISION 2 1959-60												
	P	W	D	L	F	A	W	D	L	F	A	Pts
Aston Villa	42	17	3	1	62	19	8	6	7	27	24	59
Cardiff C	42	15	2	4	55	36	8	10	3	35	26	58
Liverpool	42	15	3	3	59	28	5	7	9	31	38	50
Sheffield U	42	12	5	4	43	22	7	7	7	25	29	50
Middlesbrough	42	14	5	2	56	21	5	5	11	34	43	48
Huddersfield T	42	13	3	5	44	20	6	6	9	29	32	47
Charlton A	42	12	7	2	55	28	5	6	10	35	59	47
Rotherham U	42	9	9	3	31	23	8	4	9	30	37	47
Bristol R	42	12	6	3	42	28	6	5	10	30	50	47
Leyton O	42	12	4	5	47	25	3	10	8	29	36	44
Ipswich T	42	12	5	4	48	24	7	1	13	30	44	44
Swansea T	42	12	6	3	54	32	3	4	14	28	52	40
Lincoln C	42	11	3	7	41	25	5	4	12	34	53	39
Brighton & HA	42	7	8	6	35	32	6	4	11	32	44	38
Scunthorpe U	42	9	7	5	38	26	4	3	14	19	45	36
Sunderland	42	8	6	7	35	29	4	6	11	17	36	36
Stoke C	42	8	3	10	40	38	6	4	11	26	45	35
Derby Co	42	9	4	8	31	28	5	3	13	30	49	35
Plymouth A	42	10	6	5	42	36	3	3	15	19	53	35
Portsmouth	42	6	6	9	36	36	4	6	11	23	41	32
Hull C	42	7	6	8	27	30	3	4	14	21	46	30
Bristol C	42	8	3	10	27	31	3	2	16	33	66	27

Villa followed up this sensational win with 5-0 victories over Bristol City and Scunthorpe United and from then on there never looked to be any other Second Division winners but Aston Villa, although lowly Plymouth spoiled the end-of-season party when they inflicted Villa's heaviest defeat of the season — 3-0 at Home Park — on the very last day of the season, by which time Villa were already assured of the title.

The FA Cup also provided Villa Park fans with some exciting moments in 1959-60. In the third round Villa beat Leeds United 2-1 at home. Although Leeds took the lead, Villa soon equalised through McParland and then Wylie scored the winner in front of a crowd of 43,474.

In the fourth round, Villa travelled to Stamford Bridge and 66,671 fans saw the Midlanders win 2-1 with the goals coming from McParland and Thomson. Villa had also won at Stamford Bridge at the same stage of the Cup exactly 12 months earlier.

At Port Vale's ground in the fifth round, 48,749 somehow jammed themselves in to see the Potteries side give Villa quite a game. Vale scored first from a penalty and although Hitchens equalised early in the second half, Villa had to wait until six minutes from time before McEwan crossed and Thomson headed the winner.

In the quarter-finals Villa were drawn at home to Preston North End. Nearly 70,000 fans saw Tom Finney play his last big game at Villa Park and Hitchens gave Villa and lead after 15 minutes. Near the end, McParland made it 2-0 and Villa were into yet another semi-final.

They met Wolverhampton Wanderers at The Hawthorns where 55,596 managed to fit into a stadium for a game which could have attracted twice as many fans. In the 31st minute, Wolves scored the only goal of the game when Sims could not hold a fierce Murray drive and Deeley followed up to poke the ball home.

Both sides had chances after that and near the end, Wolves goalkeeper Malcolm Finlayson did well to save what would have been Villa's equaliser. Wolves were the better side, but all that really mattered was that Villa were on target for First Division soccer once again.

While Joe Mercer spent much of 1960-61, rebuilding the Villa side with youth — the season's only signing was in February when Wolves reserve goalkeeper Geoff Sidebottom came to Villa Park — the club's first season after promotion was a more than satisfactory one and they reached the surprisingly high place of ninth in the First Division, got as far as the fifth round of the FA Cup, and became the first side to win the newly-inaugurated Football League Cup.

In fact, the season's only real black spot came at its conclusion when Gerry Hitchens, who scored League 29 goals that season — and 42 overall — was transferred to Inter-Milan for £85,000.

Villa started the season by beating Chelsea 3-2 at home, but then West Ham beat them 5-2 at Upton Park and Blackpool won 5-3 at Bloomfield Road. Mercer, though, soon got the club back on the rails and Villa won four of the next six games including a 3-1 victory over Manchester United at Villa Park, but then met Spurs at White Hart Lane.

This was the Spurs side which was racing to the double, last achieved by Villa, and after storming into a 4-0 half-time lead, Tottenham finished 6-2 winners in front of a 61,000 attendance. It was their tenth successive win from the start of the season, in a run which ultimately saw them victorious in 11 consecutive First Division games to set a record.

Then Leicester City won 3-1 at Villa Park the following week and after a 2-0 home win over Newcastle, Villa were beaten 2-1 at Highbury.

In matches against neighbouring West Midlands sides Villa fared well, however. A crowd of over 46,000 saw them beat Birmingham City 6-2 at Villa Park, where Hitchins scored a hat-trick, and West Brom were beaten 2-0 at The Hawthorns, although Albion snatched both points in the

Villa defenders try to keep out Arsenal's Vic Groves at Highbury in October 1960.

return game and Wolves did the double over Villa.

Nevertheless, ninth place was good and a placing that Villa fans would gladly have settled for at the start of the season. Vic Crowe, who had assumed the Villa captaincy, played a total of 55 matches in all competitions.

Former skipper Pat Saward had played his last game in a Villa shirt, however. He made only 11 appearances in the League before dropping out of the side altogether in October, and the following March he was transferred to Huddersfield Town after a career total of 169 senior appearances for Villa, with whom he had also been capped 13 times by the Republic of Ireland.

One player making an initial mark was former England Schoolboys centre-half Johnny Sleeuwenhoek, the son of a Dutch Army paratrooper. A Villa junior, he signed professional forms in February 1961 and made his League debut in a 4-0 win at home to Bolton Wanderers in April.

DIVISION 1 1960-61	P	W	D	L	F	A	W	D	L	F	A	Pts
Tottenham H	42	15	3	3	65	28	16	1	4	50	27	66
Sheffield W	42	15	4	2	45	17	8	8	5	33	30	58
Wolves	42	17	2	2	61	32	8	5	8	42	43	57
Burnley	42	11	4	6	58	40	11	3	7	44	37	51
Everton	42	13	4	4	47	23	9	2	10	40	46	50
Leicester C	42	12	4	5	54	31	6	5	10	33	39	45
Manchester U	42	14	5	2	58	20	4	4	13	30	56	45
Blackburn R	42	12	3	6	48	34	3	10	8	29	42	43
Aston Villa	42	13	3	5	48	28	4	6	11	30	49	43
WBA	42	10	3	8	43	32	8	2	11	24	39	41
Arsenal	42	12	3	6	44	35	3	8	10	33	50	41
Chelsea	42	10	5	6	61	48	5	2	14	37	52	37
Manchester C	42	10	5	6	41	30	3	6	12	38	60	37
Nottingham F	42	8	7	6	34	33	6	2	13	28	45	37
Cardiff C	42	11	5	5	34	26	2	6	13	26	59	37
West Ham U	42	12	4	5	53	31	1	6	14	24	57	36
Fulham	42	8	8	5	39	39	6	0	15	33	56	36
Bolton W	42	9	5	7	38	29	3	6	12	20	44	35
Birmingham C	42	10	4	7	35	31	4	2	15	27	53	34
Blackpool	42	9	3	9	44	34	3	6	12	24	39	33
Newcastle U	42	7	7	7	51	49	4	3	14	35	60	32
Preston NE	42	7	6	8	28	25	3	4	14	15	46	30

Sleeuwenhoek would make a total of 260 senior appearances for Villa before moving to Birmingham City in November 1967. He was only 45 when he died, after a heart attack, in 1989.

In the 1960-61 FA Cup, Villa were eventually knocked out by Tottenham as the Spurs drove on relentlessly to Wembley and the double.

In the third round of the competition Villa were drawn away

to Bristol Rovers, who held on for a 1-1 draw at Eastville before being comprehensively beaten 4-0 at Villa Park. The fourth round gave Villa an awkward tie against Peterborough United at London Road. Posh were the team of the moment. After dominating the Midland League for so long, they were storming away with the Fourth Division championship, in doing so, beating Villa's record number of goals in a season.

Villa were fortunate to leave with a 1-1 draw and the replay drew over 64,000 to Villa Park where home advantage saw Villa home 2-1 with Peter McParland scoring both goals, although Peterborough were again unlucky and caused Villa plenty of anxious moments.

And so to the fifth round and mighty Spurs at Villa Park. One week before the teams met in the Cup, they had played a First Division game at Villa Park which Spurs won 2-1. Thus fortified by a morale-boosting win — if, indeed, runaway Spurs needed their morale boosting —

Peter Bonetti's dive is in vain as Jimmy MacEwan (not in picture) puts Villa ahead at Stamford Bridge in December 1960.

Tottenham duly won the Cup tie.

A crowd of 69,672 saw Villa never get out of second gear. John Neal gave them the worst possible start by putting through his own goal and Cliff Jones added a second for Tottenham. Spurs then sat back, content to control the game without going in search of a big win. They returned to Villa Park for the semi-final, when some 70,000 saw them beat Burnley.

Aston Villa were not one of the First Division clubs which shunned the first Football League Cup competition. The result was that Villa took the trophy, although the Final was held over until the following season.

Huddersfield, Preston, Plymouth and Wrexham were removed on the way to the semi-finals, although it took Villa two games to dispose of Preston and three to get rid of Plymouth. In the two-legged semi-final, neither Villa nor Burnley could resolve the tie and that, too, went to a replay before Villa won 2-1 at Old Trafford.

At the start of the following season Villa lost 2-0 in the first leg at Rotherham and then won 2-0 before 30,765 fans — then easily their biggest attendance in the competition — at Villa Park to level the aggregate. The first goal did not come until the 67th minute, when O'Neill took Deakin's pass to beat Ironside in the Rotherham goal, and four minutes later Burrows smashed home the equaliser.

The game went into extra-time and in the 19th minute of the extra period, McParland scored a third goal to ensure that Villa's name was the first on the new trophy.

A Sixties Slump

IN JULY 1961, Joe Mercer signed Derek Dougan from Blackburn Rovers. The Irish international centre-forward was to become a high-profile name in the players' union, but at the start of this season Villa fans were only interested in the possibility of the big Irishman proving a worthy deputy for Gerry Hitchens who had gone off to seek his fortune in Italy.

Unfortunately, Dougan was to miss much of the season after sustaining injuries in a car accident but, before that, Villa Park fans sensed that he was something special.

Players who left the club before the start of the season included forward Jimmy Adam (to Stoke City), full-back Doug Winton (to Rochdale), and winger Mike Kenning and defender Terry Morrall (both to Shrewsbury).

Young Villa players making their way into the first team included Harry Burrows, who scored 13 goals in 34 League games, John Sleeuwen-hoek, now established with 35 appearances at centre-half, Alan Baker, a hard-working midfielder and former England Schoolboy international from Tipton, and Charlie Aitken, who was good enough to win a place in the Scotland Under-23

team this season.

Aitken, a full-back, had been signed from Edinburgh Thistle in August 1959 and he made his League debut in April 1961, at Hillsborough. It was to be the start of a remarkable career in which Aitken amassed 561 League appearances for Villa — 83 more than the legendary Billy Walker who had previously held the club record — and in all games he played 659 times.

After they had won the League Cup against Rotherham early in September, Villa lost the services of Dougan after he and Bobby Thomson were involved in a car crash.

Aston Villa before the start of the 1960-61 season. Back row (left to right): O'Neill, Lynn, Dugdale, Sims, Dougan, Lee, McParland. Front row: Joe Mercer (manager), Wylie, Neal, Crowe, MacEwan, Thomson, Ray Shaw (trainer). On ground: Burrows, Deakin.

Derek Dougan, signed from Blackburn Rovers in July 1961, he missed much of his first season at Villa Park due to injuries received in a car accident.

Dougan suffered head injuries which kept him out of the side until December, but Thomson was back in action rather earlier.

To fill the gap left by Dougan's absence, Peter McParland was switched to centre-forward, where he gave his usual competitive performance, including scoring a hat-trick at home to Blackpool in late September. At the end of the season, McParland's 11 goals gave him third spot in the scoring charts behind Burrows' 13 and Thomson's 12.

Villa climbed further up the First Division to finish in seventh place and there were some memorable League games to recall. At Highbury in March, Villa and Arsenal were drawing 4-4 with the seconds ticking away in a thrilling match when

Geoff Sidebottom, the Villa goalkeeper, looks in a tangle as Spurs' Cliff Jones tries a spectacular kick. Les Allen (10) is the other Tottenham player.

Tommy Ewing, the diminutive former Scotland winger who Villa had signed from Partick Thistle for £20,000 a month earlier, popped up to crack home a last-gasp equaliser.

When Blackpool came to Villa Park they were hammered 5-0 with Peter McParland seemingly in at every kill.

And over Easter, Villa scored 13 goals in two games against Leicester City and Nottingham Forest.

On Easter Saturday, Leicester came to Villa Park and even the great Gordon Banks could not prevent them from going down 8-3 with Thomson scoring a fine hat-trick. On Easter Monday, Harry Burrows scored the first goal against Forest at Villa Park before the game was two minutes old and Villa won 5-1.

The one drawback to the League season was when Birmingham City, struggling manfully to avoid relegation to the Second Division, won 3-1 at Villa Park.

Strangely, Villa were also involved in another match which decided the double hopes of another club. Burnley were going on to win the FA Cup and they also vied with Alf Ramsey's Ipswich Town for the First Division title. Ipswich needed to win their final home match, which was against Villa, and this they duly did to prevent Burnley from becoming the

DIVISION 1 1961-62											
	P	W	D	L	F	A	W	D	L	F	A	Pts
Ipswich T	42	17	2	2	58	28	7	6	8	35	39	56
Burnley	42	14	4	3	57	26	7	7	7	44	41	53
Tottenham H	42	14	4	3	59	34	7	6	8	29	35	52
Everton	42	17	2	2	64	21	3	9	9	24	33	51
Sheffield U	42	13	5	3	37	23	6	4	11	24	46	47
Sheffield W	42	14	4	3	47	23	6	2	13	25	35	46
Aston Villa	42	13	5	3	45	20	5	3	13	20	36	44
West Ham U	42	11	6	4	49	37	6	4	11	27	45	44
WBA	42	10	7	4	50	23	5	6	10	33	44	43
Arsenal	42	9	6	6	39	31	7	5	9	32	41	43
Bolton W	42	11	7	3	35	22	5	3	13	27	44	42
Manchester C	42	11	3	7	46	38	6	4	11	32	43	41
Blackpool	42	10	4	7	41	30	5	7	9	29	45	41
Leicester C	42	12	2	7	38	27	5	4	12	34	44	40
Manchester U	42	10	3	8	44	31	5	6	10	28	44	39
Blackburn R	42	10	6	5	33	22	4	5	12	17	36	39
Birmingham C	42	9	6	6	37	35	4	4	12	28	46	38
Wolves	42	8	7	6	38	34	5	3	13	35	52	36
Nottingham F	42	12	4	5	39	23	1	6	14	24	56	36
Fulham	42	8	3	10	38	34	5	4	12	28	40	33
Cardiff C	42	6	9	6	30	33	3	5	13	20	48	32
Chelsea	42	7	7	7	34	29	2	3	16	29	65	28

Johnny Sleeuwenhoek, son of a former Dutch paratrooper. Sleeuwenhoek gave Villa great service as a centre-half.

Celebrations – but not for Aston Villa. Ipswich fans are ecstatic as Villa concede the first goal of the match between the sides in April 1962. The Suffolk club went on to take the League championship under Sir Alf Ramsey. Villa could finish only seventh.

second successive team to win both major trophies in the same season.

Aston Villa's hopes of retaining the Football League Cup were dashed as early as the third round. After beating West Ham at Upton Park, Villa lost to Ipswich at Villa Park.

Villa fought through to the sixth round of the FA Cup, although they might well have gone out as early as the third round when Third Division Crystal Palace ran them close at Villa Park.

Palace twice took the lead and it was only a hopeful shot-cum-centre from Burrows which found the winning goal and send Villa through 4-3. After Huddersfield and Charlton, Villa faced Spurs and lost 2-0. Perhaps the happiest man at Villa Park in 1961-62 was Burrows who finished as leading scorer with 20 goals in all competitions.

The 1962-63 season was disrupted by the blanket of snow and ice that held Britain in its grip for over three

months and the enforced mid-season break meant that Villa would never regain the splendid motion which had carried them to the beginning of December in such fine style.

The result was that Villa fell down the First Division and finished in 15th place, although they also reached their second Football League Cup Final — a feat which was tempered by the fact that they lost to Birmingham City in the two-legged Final.

When the season opened in glorious sunshine, there was no sign of the dreadful winter to follow and Villa's young team scored a superb 3-1 home win over West Ham United to give their fans great hope for the coming campaign.

In midweek, Derek Dougan scored both the goals which sunk Spurs 2-1, also at Villa Park, and Villa followed this up by beating Manchester City 2-0 at Maine Road. Even when Spurs won 4-2 at White Hart

Lane, Villa came back, drawing 1-1 with Blackpool and beating Arsenal 2-1 at Highbury.

By the middle of November, Villa were seventh in the table and they continued their good run, signing winger Phil Woosnam from West Ham for £27,000. Bolton were beaten 5-0 just before Christmas and that proved to be the watershed in Villa's First Division programme.

Villa did not play a match between 19 January and 13 February, when they lost 4-0 at Anfield, and even then their League programme did not get under way in earnest until 9 March. When they did begin to feel their way again, the form which had taken them to the fringes of the championship race escaped them.

At one stage, after a string of defeats, Villa had stumbled down to 18th position and were in danger of making a relatively swift return to the Second Division. The penultimate League match of the season was

Charlie Aitken
— A Remarkable Servant

WHEN Charlie Aitken made his League debut for Aston Villa, against Sheffield Wednesday at Villa Park on the last day of the 1960-61 season, it was a fairly unremarkable occasion. Villa won 4-1 to finish ninth in the First Division and the attendance numbered 26,034, none of whom could have imagined that they were witnessing the start of a remarkable career which was to set a club record unlikely ever to be beaten.

Yet Charlie Aitken, a full-back who was born in Edinburgh in May 1942 and who joined Villa as a youngster from Edinburgh Thistle in August 1959, was embarking on the first of 659 appearances in a Villa first-team shirt, which eclipsed the previous club record — 531, held by the great Billy Walker — by a mile.

And during his 16-year career, Aitken gained a League Cup winners' prize, played in two others Finals, was a major force when Villa won the Third Division title and helped them back into the First Division. He also gained three Under-23 caps for Scotland and was voted the Villa supporters Player of the Year and was also the Midlands Footballer of the Year.

Sheffield Wednesday always seemed to figure in his highlights, for besides making his League debut against the Owls, Aitken also scored his first senior goal against them, in March 1964, and when he made his 200th appearance for Villa in August 1966, it was against Wednesday yet again.

Aitken won a regular place in the first team in 1961-62, when he took over the left-back position from John Neal, and after coming into the side in mid-September, he missed only two game near the end of a season in which Villa finished seventh in Division One. The following year he was ever-present and played in both legs of the Football League Cup Final, which Villa lost 3-1 on aggregate to Birmingham.

He missed precious few games after that, although he was now playing in a Villa side which was struggling to hold its place in the top flight. In 1966-67 they were relegated and three years later went down again. Still Aitken was one of the few consistencies in the side and as Villa began their climb back he played in another League Cup Final, when Third Division Villa won their way to Wembley after a famous semi-final win over Manchester United.

When they went up as champions in 1971-72, he was absent on three times, and in 1975, he reached his third League Cup Final and this time gained a winners' tankard when Villa beat Norwich 1-0. That was a great season for player and club, for Villa also regained their First Division status and Aitken played in every game.

In December 1973, he had passed Walker's record for League appearances, almost 40 years after Walker had retired, and just seemed to go on and on.

Eventually, Aitken decided to call it a day and his wonderful career came to an end on 31 January 1976, in a 2-0 home defeat by Queen's Park Rangers, in many ways as unremarkable as his first appearance all those years before.

In May 1976, Aitken signed for the New York Cosmos and played in 17 NASL games that year and in eight the following year, lining up in some games with the legendary Pelé.

He had a spell back in England with Worcester City and opened a jewellery and antiques business in Birmingham, still finding time to play for the Villa All Stars XI in charity games.

If Charlie Aitken did not play in one of the more auspicious periods of Aston Villa's history, he still shared in some glorious moments and there has never been a player who gave such long and commited service. He is one of the club's all-time greats.

Derek Dougan is beaten to the ball by West Ham centre-half Ken Brown at Upton Park in December 1962.

against Liverpool at Villa Park and Joe Mercer gave a debut to a young player called George Graham.

Graham scored a goal on his first appearance in senior football, Liverpool were beaten 2-0 and Villa were safe after drawing their last game, 1-1 at Ipswich.

It seems incredible that Graham was subsequently sold to Chelsea for only £5,000.

Villa were soon to part with Derek Dougan, who was transferred to Peterborough United in June for £21,000. Dougan, of course, returned to big-time football with Leicester City and Wolves.

One Villa player who went straight to Molineux was Peter McParland, who joined Wolves for £30,000.

Lew Chatterley, a utility defender who had won England Youth honours, signed full-time professional forms on his 17th birthday in February 1962 and at the end of the following season he made the first of 164 senior appearances for Villa.

In the FA Cup of 1962-63, Villa again had to contend with the weather. They were drawn away to

DIVISION 1 1962-63	P	W	D	L	F	A	W	D	L	F	A	Pts
Everton	42	14	7	0	48	17	11	4	6	36	25	61
Tottenham H	42	14	6	1	72	28	9	3	9	39	34	55
Burnley	42	14	4	3	41	17	8	6	7	37	40	54
Leicester C	42	14	6	1	53	23	6	6	9	26	30	52
Wolves	42	11	6	4	51	25	9	4	8	42	40	50
Sheffield W	42	10	5	6	38	26	9	5	7	39	37	48
Arsenal	42	11	4	6	44	33	7	6	8	42	44	46
Liverpool	42	13	3	5	45	22	4	7	10	26	37	44
Nottingham F	42	12	4	5	39	28	5	6	10	28	41	44
Sheffield U	42	11	7	3	33	20	5	5	11	25	40	44
Blackburn R	42	11	4	6	55	34	4	8	9	24	37	42
West Ham U	42	8	6	7	39	34	6	6	9	34	35	40
Blackpool	42	8	7	6	34	27	5	7	9	24	37	40
WBA	42	11	1	9	40	37	5	6	10	31	42	39
Aston Villa	42	12	2	7	38	23	3	6	12	24	45	38
Fulham	42	8	6	7	28	30	6	4	11	22	41	38
Ipswich T	42	5	8	8	34	39	7	3	11	25	39	35
Bolton W	42	13	3	5	35	18	2	2	17	20	57	35
Manchester U	42	6	6	9	36	38	6	4	11	31	43	34
Birmingham C	42	6	8	7	40	40	4	5	12	23	50	33
Manchester C	42	7	5	9	30	45	3	6	12	28	57	31
Leyton O	42	4	5	12	22	37	2	4	15	15	44	21

Bristol City in the third round and drew 1-1, before winning the replay 3-2 — seven weeks later — and then going down 1-0 at Old Trafford. Manchester United — like the four winners of the Cup immediately before them — had to beat Villa on their way to take the trophy.

It was the Football League Cup which brought Aston Villa most hope of glory in 1962-63. They crushed Peterborough 6-1 at Villa Park, where Dougan scored a hat-trick, beat Stoke 3-1, and then hammered another six

Mike Tindall, who came up through the ranks and made 136 senior appearances for Aston Villa.

Phil Woosnam, the winger who joined Villa from West Ham from £27,000. Woosnam was later a leading light in the North American Soccer League.

Bobby Thomson, who was transferred to Birmingham City in September 1963 after hitting 70 goals in 172 games for Villa.

goals past Preston North End to reach the quarter-finals where they disposed of Norwich 4-1.

In a two-legged semi-final, Villa won 3-1 at Sunderland after a goalless draw at Villa Park.

They had only to travel across the city to St Andrew's for the first-leg of the Final but the Blues won 3-1 and then held Villa 0-0 at Villa Park.

It was a repeat, in reverse, of Villa's semi-final score-line against Sunderland, and Birmingham fully deserved their win, for Villa never turned on the form which had got them to the Final.

Villa's season can be strictly divided into two halves — before the ice age and after. And the interceding lull cost them dearly.

The following campaign of 1963-64 was a black season for Aston Villa. They slumped to 19th place in the First Division, missed relegation by the skin of their teeth and were knocked out of both the FA Cup and the Football League Cup in the earliest stages, with the FA Cup exit proving particularly humiliating at the hands of humble Aldershot.

In July 1963, Villa paid £23,000 for Notts County's giant centre-forward Tony Hateley. Twenty-two-year-old Hateley was born in Derby and had a fearsome reputation as a striker. He was, Villa felt, just the man to succeed Derek Dougan, the man who had never hit it off at Villa Park.

The season was also the last at Villa Park for manager Joe Mercer, whose illness led to him resigning from the job. By the time Villa had been

bundled out of the FA Cup Villa's fans were in no mood to tolerate any more unpleasant shocks and, as is often the case in football, the manager's head had to roll.

With considerable structural alterations giving Villa Park a new look, the team kicked-off the season, hoping to emulate the previous season's run which had taken them to the First Division top-ten before winter struck.

Hateley was joined in the Villa first team by several other new faces including former apprentice Mick Wright who came into the defence to begin a career which would span 316 senior appearances before he was forced to retire through injury ten years later.

Hateley scored 17 goals in the League and with Burrows weighing in with 16, the pair looked to have hit it off. But before the season was a couple of months old, Villa had allowed Bobby Thomson to leave for Birmingham and Villa fans complained that their club was too fond of letting good players go. They pointed to Dougan and to Derek Pace.

Ron Wylie tries to back head the ball against West Ham in October 1963. Villa lost this League Cup tie 2-0.

DIVISION 1 1963-64											
	P	W	D	L	F	A	W	D	L	F	A	Pts
Liverpool	42	16	0	5	60	18	10	5	6	32	27	57
Manchester U	42	15	3	3	54	19	8	4	9	36	43	53
Everton	42	14	4	3	53	26	7	6	8	31	38	52
Tottenham H	42	13	3	5	54	31	9	4	8	43	50	51
Chelsea	42	12	3	6	36	24	8	7	6	36	32	50
Sheffield W	42	15	3	3	50	24	4	8	9	34	43	49
Blackburn R	42	10	4	7	44	28	8	6	7	45	37	46
Arsenal	42	10	7	4	56	37	7	4	10	34	45	45
Burnley	42	14	3	4	46	23	3	7	11	25	41	44
WBA	42	9	6	6	43	35	7	5	9	27	26	43
Leicester C	42	9	4	8	33	27	7	7	7	28	31	43
Sheffield U	42	10	6	5	35	22	6	5	10	26	42	43
Nottingham F	42	9	5	7	34	24	7	4	10	30	44	41
West Ham U	42	8	7	6	45	38	6	5	10	24	36	40
Fulham	42	11	8	2	45	23	2	5	14	13	42	39
Wolves	42	6	9	6	36	34	6	6	9	34	46	39
Stoke C	42	9	6	6	49	33	5	4	12	28	45	38
Blackpool	42	8	6	7	26	29	5	3	13	26	44	35
Aston Villa	**42**	**8**	**6**	**7**	**35**	**29**	**3**	**6**	**12**	**27**	**42**	**34**
Birmingham C	42	7	7	7	33	32	4	0	17	21	60	29
Bolton W	42	6	5	10	30	35	4	3	14	18	45	28
Ipswich T	42	9	3	9	38	45	0	4	17	18	76	25

Pace was a prime example because since leaving Villa Park he had been Sheffield United's leading scorer for six consecutive seasons. And when United won 1-0 at Villa Park that season, it was Pace who knocked home the winner to rub salt into Villa's wounds.

In the Football League Cup, Villa beat Barnsley and were rewarded with another home draw against West Ham United. This time, however, Villa were beaten 2-0 and shortly after the game, Mercer went into the transfer market and bought Shrews-bury Town's David Pountney for £20,000. Pountney was a useful signing. He was a powerfully-built wing-half who had made over 200 appearances for the Gay Meadow club.

But it was an easy-looking third round FA Cup tie which altered the shape of things at Villa Park. In the first match — played on Villa's home ground — Fourth Division Aldershot, with luck and a brilliant goalkeeping performance, managed a goalless draw. When Villa went down to Hampshire for the replay they were beaten by the tiny Recreation Ground's cramped atmosphere and Aldershot won 2-1. It was a terrible fate to befall such a mighty Cup-fighting club as Villa.

The result also saw the end of Joe Mercer as Villa's manager. He had been overworking and the additional burden of Villa's poor performances and strokes of ill-luck, like Phil Woosnam being taken ill, meant that his health gave way. One morning Mercer was polishing his car when he felt unwell. The doctor called it 'hypertension' and every football manager in the country knew just

Alan Deakin. One of the most talented of Villa's teenage team of the early 1960s, he went on to make 270 appearances for the club.

how Joe Mercer felt. It was left to his assistant, Dick Taylor, to bring Villa away from relegation. He managed it — but only just.

Dick was the official manager of Aston Villa as the club began the 1964-65 season. Taylor, a native of the Black Country, began his career with a brief spell at Wolverhampton Wanderers before spending most of his playing days with Grimsby Town and Scunthorpe United. He had then served Scunthorpe United and Sheffield United (under Mercer) as trainer-coach before following his

Charlie Aitken and Liverpool's Roger Hunt in a heading battle at Anfield during a First Division match in September 1964.

Jimmy MacEwan, the veteran who was given a free transfer to Walsall after 181 games for Villa.

old boss to Villa Park, where he had been for six years.

The first game of this season gave Taylor little comfort as Villa lost 2-1 at home to Leeds United who had just been promoted to the First Division under their new manager, Don Revie. By the middle of September, Villa had lost four games out of the opening six and had conceded 15 goals.

During that spell they made their first signing under Taylor's regime when Arsenal's Scottish international winger Johnny MacLeod came to Villa Park for £29,500, which was a record for Villa at that time.

Villa gained their first victory by beating Sunderland 2-1 at home, but by the end of September they were bottom of the table, one point worse off than Wolves.

A 2-0 win over Sheffield Wednesday raised them to last-but-one position but after a surprise League Cup win at Leeds, Villa came back to earth with a resounding bump when they travelled to Old Trafford and were soundly thrashed 7-0 by Manchester United. Dennis Law scored four goals, in direct contrast to the fortunes of Villa's Hateley, who was carried off with an injury.

Taylor continued to make signings. Barry Stobart, the former Wolves forward, returned to the West Midlands from Manchester City for £30,000 and Villa also brought goalkeeper Colin Withers to Villa Park for £18,000. Other players to join Villa during this season were Willie Hamilton, the Hibs inside-forward, John Woodward from Stoke City and Tony Scott from West Ham.

Full-back Keith Bradley, a former Villa apprentice, made his League debut in a 1-0 win at Birmingham City in February. Although Bradley had to battle for a place with the likes of Charlie Aitken, Mick Wright and Gordon Lee, he managed 122 senior appearances and won some honours before being transferred to Peterborough United in November 1972.

Out of Villa Park went the veteran Jimmy MacEwan, given a free

DIVISION 1 1964-65											
	P	W	D	L	F	A	W	D	L	F	A	Pts
Manchester U	42	16	4	1	52	13	10	5	6	37	26	61
Leeds U	42	16	3	2	53	23	10	6	5	30	29	61
Chelsea	42	15	2	4	48	19	9	6	6	41	35	56
Everton	42	9	10	2	37	22	8	5	8	32	38	49
Nottingham F	42	10	7	4	45	33	7	6	8	26	34	47
Tottenham H	42	18	3	0	65	20	1	4	16	22	51	45
Liverpool	42	12	5	4	42	33	5	5	11	25	40	44
Sheffield W	42	13	5	3	37	15	3	6	12	20	40	43
West Ham U	42	14	2	5	48	25	5	2	14	34	46	42
Blackburn R	42	12	2	7	46	33	4	8	9	37	46	42
Stoke C	42	11	4	6	40	27	5	6	10	27	39	42
Burnley	42	9	9	3	39	26	7	1	13	31	44	42
Arsenal	42	11	5	5	42	31	6	2	13	27	44	41
WBA	42	10	5	6	45	25	3	8	10	25	40	39
Sunderland	42	12	6	3	45	26	2	3	16	19	48	37
Aston Villa	42	14	1	6	36	24	2	4	15	21	58	37
Blackpool	42	9	7	5	41	28	3	4	14	26	50	35
Leicester C	42	9	6	6	43	36	2	7	12	26	49	35
Sheffield U	42	7	5	9	30	29	5	6	10	20	35	35
Fulham	42	10	5	6	44	32	1	7	13	16	46	34
Wolves	42	8	2	11	33	36	5	2	14	26	53	30
Birmingham C	42	6	8	7	36	40	2	3	16	28	56	27

Willie Hamilton, played 54 times for Villa after joining them from Hibernian for £25,000 in August 1965. Sadly, his career was marred by injury and illness.

transfer to Walsall; Harry Burrows to Stoke City for £30,000; Ron Wylie to Notts County; and Bill Atkins to Stockport.

Villa spent the whole season in the bottom four of the First Division and at the end of it they were fortunate to maintain 16th place and missed relegation by only six points. The defence had conceded 82 goals.

In the FA Cup, Villa started brightly with a 3-0 home third-round win over Coventry. Phil Woosnam spurred Villa on before over 47,000, about half of them from Coventry. In the fourth round Villa beat Sheffield United 2-0 at Bramall Lane and that brought them into confrontation with Wolves at Villa Park.

Hateley scored for Villa as the sides drew 1-1 and withdrew to fight again at Molineux. Over 52,000 fans had seen the first match and nearly 48,000 crammed the Wolves ground for the replay which resulted in a goalless draw. The second replay was at The Hawthorns and this time Villa fell as Wolves snapped at their heels relentlessly all evening to win 3-1.

Just as Villa had been the FA Cup side of their day, so they were gaining a reputation in the Football League Cup and in 1964-65 they went back to their third semi-final. Victories over Luton Town, Leeds United, Reading and Bradford City (by 7-1 with Hateley scoring four times) gave Villa a semi-final against Chelsea.

The first leg was played at Villa

Tony Hateley, the big centre-forward who scored 86 goals in only 148 appearances for Villa.

Park and when Chelsea won 3-2, Villa knew that their task for the return at Stamford Bridge would be a hard one. They were right. They could only draw 1-1 and it was Chelsea who went through to the Final whilst Villa were left to strive

for First Division survival as best they could.

It is to the eternal credit of Dick Taylor that he managed to keep Villa in the First Division during this period and although football fans will always cry for the blood of a manager when things are not going well, it is doubtful whether Villa supporters realised the full extent of the traumas that Taylor was enduring, particularly as his side was plagued for much of his reign by injuries and illness which often robbed him of his key players at the most crucial times.

In 1965-66, Villa managed to stay afloat and in fact pulled away from the relegation zone to the extent that when the season ended, they had climbed to 16th position. So, twice in consecutive seasons, Taylor had breathed enough life into Villa to give them a final placing some way from the relegated clubs. In the previous campaign, it had been Birmingham and Wolves who went down to complete a disastrous season for the West Midlands; this time Northampton and Blackburn were the unlucky pair.

Whereas Villa had finished in the same position as the previous season, in 1964-65 they had missed the drop by seven points — in 1965-66 the gap had been a mere three, although in the previous season they had won only one more point.

There were some shocking results this season. Relegated Northampton Town had beaten Villa twice — they won only ten games all season — and Manchester United had thrashed Villa 6-1 at Old Trafford, although Villa had themselves scored six goals against fellow relegation strugglers Fulham at Craven Cottage.

In addition, Villa also managed five goals at White Hart Lane, only on that occasion Spurs also completed a nap hand and the result was a rare 5-5 draw.

Villa had conceded 80 goals and it was obvious that unless some major surgery was carried out quickly, then they would not remain in the First Division for very much longer. Off the field, the club's transfer dealings totted up to a debit of over £21,000, which was quite a lot of money in the mid-1960s. To add to the prob-

lem, the dealings had probably resulted in Villa having a weaker side when they should have been building a stronger one.

In the FA Cup, Leicester City came to Villa Park in early January and won 2-1 to complete an unhappy post-Christmas period for Villa fans. Only the Football League Cup looked a likely source of glory and Villa managed two good wins in the second and third rounds.

First they won an awkward tie at Swansea 3-2, then travelled to Roker Park and won 2-1 — always a feat to win on Wearside. In the fourth round Villa forced a 1-1 draw at Fulham before winning the Villa Park replay 2-0.

There the Cup run ended. In the fifth round, West Brom took full advantage of their home advantage at The Hawthorns and won 3-1. For yet another season, Villa's only involvement as the programme was drawing to a close was to survive for another 12 months in the First Division. Soon, there would be no escape.

The 1966-67 season started with Villa losing two of their best-known players; it ended with the club at last bowing to the inevitable and going down to the Second Division.

In many ways, Villa's relegation was almost a kindness because the club had battled so long against the drop with ever-failing resources. Of all the seasons which Dick Taylor had to endure, this was his worst, with several of his team again sidelined at critical times.

September saw the departure of Welsh international winger Phil Woosnam. He had been a familiar figure in the Villa Park set-up, with his crew-cut hairstyle and speedy runs down the wing. He left England altogether and flew to the United States where he became involved in the bid to establish soccer in America. Woosnam at first went to play for Atlanta but quickly rose to the top of the American soccer hierarchy.

The following month saw Tony Hateley leave Villa Park. The big centre-forward was off on another ride on his multi-thousand pound merry-go-round which eventually took him to such clubs as far apart as Chelsea and Liverpool. This time

DIVISION 1 1965-66											
	P	W	D	L	F	A	W	D	L	F	A	Pts
Liverpool	42	17	2	2	52	15	9	7	5	27	19	61
Leeds U	42	14	4	3	49	15	9	5	7	30	23	55
Burnley	42	15	3	3	45	20	9	4	8	34	27	55
Manchester U	42	12	8	1	50	20	6	7	8	34	39	51
Chelsea	42	11	4	6	30	21	11	3	7	35	32	51
WBA	42	11	6	4	58	34	8	6	7	33	35	50
Leicester C	42	12	4	5	40	28	9	3	9	40	37	49
Tottenham H	42	11	6	4	55	37	5	6	10	20	29	44
Sheffield U	42	11	6	4	37	25	5	5	11	19	34	43
Stoke C	42	12	6	3	42	22	3	6	12	23	42	42
Everton	42	12	6	3	39	19	3	5	13	17	43	41
West Ham U	42	12	5	4	46	33	3	4	14	24	50	39
Blackpool	42	9	5	7	36	29	5	4	12	19	36	37
Arsenal	42	8	8	5	36	31	4	5	12	26	44	37
Newcastle U	42	10	5	6	26	20	4	4	13	24	43	37
Aston Villa	42	10	3	8	39	34	5	3	13	30	46	36
Sheffield W	42	11	6	4	35	18	3	2	16	21	48	36
Nottingham F	42	11	3	7	31	26	3	5	13	25	46	36
Sunderland	42	13	2	6	36	28	1	6	14	15	44	36
Fulham	42	9	4	8	34	37	5	3	13	33	48	35
Northampton T	42	8	6	7	31	32	2	7	12	24	60	33
Blackburn R	42	6	1	14	30	36	2	3	16	27	52	20

Colin Withers blocks a shot by Ian St John at Anfield in February 1967. Villa lost 1-0 on their way to relegation.

Withers in action again but this time he is helpless to stop Martin Peters' goal for West Ham at Upton Park in March 1967.

Peter Broadbent, the former Wolves star upon whom Aston Villa pinned some of their hopes of avoiding relegation. Alas, Broadbent's best days were behind him and Villa went down.

it was to Stamford Bridge that Hateley was bound, having asked for a transfer one day and being sold for £100,000 the next.

In some ways, that figure seemed more significant than the multimillion pound transfers of today. In 1966, we were still not used to massive inflation. Hateley had scored 86 goals in 148 first-team appearances for Villa. It was a fine record.

The pre-Christmas period saw Villa go into the transfer market themselves and Dick Taylor pinned much of his hopes on Peter Broadbent, Wolves' veteran forward. Broadbent's best days were over but he did contribute something to a Villa side full of young and relatively inexperienced players.

There were more awful results — a 6-2 home defeat by Chelsea in September was followed a week later by a 5-0 hammering at Leicester. And in early December, Villa went down 6-1 at Stoke, a week after beating Manchester United 2-1 at Villa Park. A week later, they scored an important 3-0 win at Newcastle.

Yet, as New Year's Day dawned, Villa faced 1967 in extreme difficulty with much less than a point a game after 24 matches.

In the FA Cup there was a little ray of hope when Villa beat Preston North End 1-0 at Deepdale; but in the fourth round they went to Anfield and lost 1-0. Earlier in the season West Brom had inflicted a crushing blow to Villa's morale by winning 6-1 at The Hawthorns in the second round of the Football League Cup.

With the Cups out of the way, there was only the League on which to concentrate and Villa began to slide deeper and deeper into the mire of relegation, despite another signing in the shape of winger Willie Anderson, who had understudied George Best at Manchester United. Anderson came to Villa Park for £20,000 and made his debut two days after signing, in a 3-1 defeat at Stamford Bridge.

In early April, Fulham came to Villa Park with Johnny Haynes — the first £100 per week footballer in Britain — making his 500th League appearance for the Cottagers. At that time Villa stood in 21st place, level on points with West Brom. Blackpool were already beyond rescue.

Fulham drew 1-1 and when Nottingham Forest beat Villa 3-0 at the City Ground, relegation looked certain.

Villa took only one point from the next four matches and in the last game of the season, Southampton hammered the final nail into Villa's coffin by winning 6-2 at The Dell. Villa were down again and this time their fans realised that they had no right to a permanent place in the top drawer of soccer. Aston Villa were a Second Division club.

DIVISION 1 1966-67	P	W	D	L	F	A	W	D	L	F	A	Pts
Manchester U	42	17	4	0	51	13	7	8	6	33	32	60
Nottingham F	42	16	4	1	41	13	7	6	8	23	28	56
Tottenham H	42	15	3	3	44	21	9	5	7	27	27	56
Leeds U	42	15	4	2	41	17	7	7	7	21	25	55
Liverpool	42	12	7	2	36	17	7	6	8	28	30	51
Everton	42	11	4	6	39	22	8	6	7	26	24	48
Arsenal	42	11	6	4	32	20	5	8	8	26	27	46
Leicester C	42	12	4	5	47	28	6	4	11	31	43	44
Chelsea	42	7	9	5	33	29	8	5	8	34	33	44
Sheffield U	42	11	5	5	34	22	5	5	11	18	37	42
Sheffield W	42	9	7	5	39	19	5	6	10	17	28	41
Stoke C	42	11	5	5	40	21	6	2	13	23	37	41
WBA	42	11	1	9	40	28	5	6	10	37	45	39
Burnley	42	11	4	6	43	28	4	5	12	23	48	39
Manchester C	42	8	9	4	27	25	4	6	11	16	27	39
West Ham U	42	8	6	7	40	31	6	2	13	40	53	36
Sunderland	42	12	3	6	39	26	2	5	14	19	46	36
Fulham	42	8	7	6	49	34	3	5	13	22	49	34
Southampton	42	10	3	8	49	41	4	3	14	25	51	34
Newcastle U	42	9	5	7	24	27	3	4	14	15	54	33
Aston Villa	42	7	5	9	30	33	4	2	15	24	52	29
Blackpool	42	1	5	15	18	36	5	4	12	23	40	21

From Third to First Again

NOT unnaturally, Aston Villa started the season with a new manager — the former Burnley centre-half Tommy Cummings, who had been managing Mansfield Town. In fact, Villa had been managerless since before the last game of the previous season when Dick Taylor and his entire coaching staff were axed.

Taylor, along with his assistants and former Villa players Bill Baxter and Johnny Dixon, was out of a job even before that 6-2 humiliation at The Dell.

Cummings came to Villa Park full of optimism and hope that he could steer Villa back into Division One at the first attempt. After all, although the club had been twice before relegated, they had always bounced back within a season or two at the most. Yet for much of the 1967-68 season, Villa fans feared that their team might actually go down to the Third Division.

At the beginning of October, Villa were in the bottom four of the Second Division and deep in trouble once again. Morale was low in the players' camp and Colin Withers, John Sleeuwenhoek, and Mick Wright had each asked for a transfer, wanting out of Villa Park as soon as possible. Sleeuwenhoek and Wright were granted their requests straight away.

Sleeuwenhoek was sold to Birmingham City for £45,000 in November, but Wright remained with Villa until he was forced to retire through injury six years later. Withers, too, remained a Villa player, until his move to Lincoln in 1969.

Cummings also bought in new players and of these, Brian Godfrey ended the season as Villa's top scorer with 13 goals. Two others, Brian Greenhalgh and Tommy Mitchinson — who Cummings had bought from Mansfield — scored a combined total of 21 goals and so the Villa boss could be pleased with his signings.

Godfrey, a former Everton and Scunthorpe midfielder, joined Villa

Aston Villa at the start of 1967-68, ready to begin their battle out of Division Two. Alas, it was a battle they lost. Back row (left to right): Aitken, Sleeuwenhoek, Woodward, Withers, Chatterley, Pountey, Deakin. Middle row: Tommy Cummings (manager), Anderson, Parker, Stobart, Tindall, Broadbent, MacLeod, W.Baxter (trainer). On ground: Bradley, Scott, Wright.

Brian Godfrey joined Villa in September 1967 and went on to make 160 senior appearances for the club, scoring 25 goals.

Tommy Cummings, the Villa boss who could not get the club back into the top flight and eventually paid with his job.

from Preston North End in September 1967, along with forward Greenhalgh in a double deal with the Deepdale club, worth some £55,000.

Cummings also introduced defender Fred Turnbull, a former Villa trialist who had turned full-time professional in September 1966, whilst Mike Tindall, whose career had been threatened by a serious injury sustained at White Hart Lane, in November 1964, had a few games. Aitken and, despite their transfer requests, Withers and Wright were performing heroically week after week.

With these new players, and with some of the staff that he had inherited, Cummings set about rescuing Villa. At the end of the season, Cummings had done a good enough job and Villa were safe — although

16th place in the Second Division was not the kind of position that the club's fans could get used to.

There were unfamiliar trips to Plymouth, Rotherham and Carlisle, all Second Division outposts, and Villa fans missed the bubble and excitement of Old Trafford and Highbury.

Another cause for concern was that Villa's average attendance had fallen to 19,745. Within many supporters' living memories, it had been over 40,000, although one has to say, of course, that attendances everywhere were dwindling at this time.

Third Division Northampton Town beat Villa 3-1 at Northampton in the second round of the Football League Cup, and after beating Millwall 3-0 in the FA Cup, Villa were dumped 1-0 at home to Rotherham.

Cummings enlisted the aid of former West Ham star Malcolm Musgrove as his coach and he gave the first-team captaincy to Lew Chatterley. He also signed another Mansfield player in defender Dick Edwards, and by the end of the season had blooded several young Villa players. Difficult years still lay ahead for Aston Villa Football Club and the signs were there as the club went into the transfer market, not for established stars, but for Third Division

DIVISION 2 1967-68											
	P	W	D	L	F	A	W	D	L	F	A	Pts
Ipswich T	42	12	7	2	45	20	10	8	3	34	24	59
QPR	42	18	2	1	45	9	7	6	8	22	27	58
Blackpool	42	12	6	3	33	16	12	4	5	38	27	58
Birmingham C	42	12	6	3	54	21	7	8	6	29	30	52
Portsmouth	42	13	6	2	43	18	5	7	9	25	37	49
Middlesbrough	42	10	7	4	39	19	7	5	9	21	35	46
Millwall	42	9	10	2	35	16	5	7	9	27	34	45
Blackburn R	42	13	5	3	34	16	3	6	12	22	33	43
Norwich C	42	12	4	5	40	30	4	7	10	20	35	43
Carlisle U	42	9	9	3	38	22	5	4	12	20	30	41
Crystal P	42	11	4	6	34	19	3	7	11	22	37	39
Bolton W	42	8	6	7	37	28	5	7	9	23	35	39
Cardiff C	42	9	6	6	35	29	4	6	11	25	37	38
Huddersfield T	42	10	6	5	29	23	3	6	12	17	38	38
Charlton A	42	10	6	5	43	25	2	7	12	20	43	37
Aston Villa	42	10	3	8	35	30	5	4	12	19	34	37
Hull C	42	6	8	7	25	23	6	5	10	33	50	37
Derby Co	42	8	5	8	40	35	5	5	11	31	43	36
Bristol C	42	7	7	7	26	25	6	3	12	22	37	36
Preston NE	42	8	7	6	29	24	4	4	13	14	41	35
Rotherham U	42	7	4	10	22	32	3	7	11	20	44	31
Plymouth A	42	5	4	12	26	36	4	5	12	12	36	27

Defender Fred Turnbull, joined Villa from the junior ranks and helped the club back from Division Three and on to Wembley. He eventually totalled 183 appearances for the club.

Barry Hole, Tommy Cummings' last signing for Villa, who walked out after a bust-up with caretaker boss Arthur Cox.

footballers who would 'do a job' for the club. There were dark days ahead, even though the club had made a substantial profit — some £78,000 in 1967, thanks to World Cup receipts in the summer of 1966 and the sale of Tony Hateley.

What a season the 1968-69 campaign turned out to be. Third Division football stared Villa in the face, mounted police kept back angry fans, there were boardroom takeover bids (including one from the United States), public protest meetings, and a fantastic end-of-season run in which Villa escaped relegation under one of the most colourful and controversial managers that the game has ever seen.

Matters boiled over in November of this season when Villa were stranded at the foot of the Second

Division after three defeats in a row and with only 11 points from their first 19 games. On the day that Preston North End beat Villa 1-0 at Villa Park, the Villa fans called for the heads of the board and the management; policemen on horseback had to move irate Villa supporters from jostling outside the ground after the game.

Heads did, indeed, roll but they were not those of the directors, but those of manager Tommy Cummings and his colleague Malcolm Musgrove. Earlier in the season, Cummings had appointed Arthur Cox as his new trainer and it was Cox who took over as caretaker manager now that Cummings had been fired.

There followed a mass protest meeting at Digbeth Civic Hall when

the board were given an ultimatum by the fans — 'Get it straight — or get out!' Meanwhile, Cox was having his own problems as Villa's Welsh international wing-half, Barry Hole, who was Cummings' last signing for Villa, walked out after a bust-up.

There came threats to the board's survival from all manner of quarters — from Phil Woosnam's Atlanta Chiefs in America, from a faction headed by Sir Frank Price, the former Lord Mayor of Birmingham, from Ron Harrison, the chairman of Walsall FC.

Eventually, in December 1968, the entire Villa board, an elderly crew with one of the highest averages ages of any League club board and headed by chairman Norman Smith (60), resigned and a new set of directors, led by Douglas Ellis, a Birmingham travel agent, and Pat Matthews, a financier, took control.

Doug Ellis was to become a great name in the affairs of Aston Villa but when he became chairman he quickly discovered the extent of the club's financial problems. Towards the end of 1968, Villa were some £200,000 adrift of their debts and other commitments. Attendances were still falling and the Villa Park needed a great deal of repair and maintenance. That Ellis overcame these problems and today Villa are a rich club with one of the finest grounds in the world is a tribute to his drive and business acumen.

The new board also included former Villa player Harry Parkes. Immediately they were installed, the new Villa board named former Preston, Arsenal and Scotland wing-half, Tommy Docherty, as their new manager.

Docherty had just half a season to prevent Villa going into the Third Division for the first time in the club's history. He went back to one of his old clubs, Rotherham United, to buy Brian Tiler, a tough and experienced half-back. He also switched Dick Edwards from wing-half to centre-half — a move which paid immediate dividends — and when Tiler scored on his debut as Villa beat Cardiff City 2-0 at Villa Park, Docherty's faith had been repaid twice over.

Villa won five successive games in the first month of the New Year, during which time they had moved from bottom place to fifth-from-bottom. Docherty also inspired the Villa public to come flocking back. On 7 December, Villa had attracted an all-time low for a Saturday afternoon League game when only 12,747 fans turned up to see Charlton force a goalless draw at Villa Park as the Claret and Blues grovelled around the Second Division basement with the likes of Fulham, Bristol City, Oxford United and Bury.

Six weeks later, however, the crowds were pouring back as Docherty not only saved Villa from relegation but also steered them to the fifth round of the FA Cup. Against Southampton in a fourth-round replay, Villa won 2-1 in front of over 59,000 fans. Only in the last 16 did they fall, when Spurs beat them 3-2 at White Hart Lane.

Before the season ended, Docherty made another signing — Arsenal's Dave Simmons — and by the end of the Easter programme, Villa were out of danger. It had been one of the most traumatic seasons in the history of Aston Villa Football Club and for weeks the club had been headline

Brian Tiler, the former Rotherham United defender who was signed for Villa by Tommy Docherty and played a leading role in their League Cup Final appearance.

DIVISION 2 1968-69											
	P	W	D	L	F	A	W	D	L	F	A	Pts
Derby Co	42	16	4	1	43	16	10	7	4	22	16	63
Crystal P	42	14	4	3	45	24	8	8	5	25	23	56
Charlton A	42	11	8	2	39	21	7	6	8	22	31	50
Middlesbrough	42	13	7	1	36	13	6	4	11	22	36	49
Cardiff C	42	13	3	5	38	19	7	4	10	29	35	47
Huddersfield T	42	13	6	2	37	14	4	6	11	16	32	46
Birmingham C	42	13	3	5	52	24	5	5	11	21	35	44
Blackpool	42	9	8	4	33	20	5	7	9	18	21	43
Sheffield U	42	14	4	3	41	15	2	7	12	20	35	43
Millwall	42	10	5	6	33	23	7	4	10	24	26	43
Hull C	42	10	7	4	38	20	3	9	9	21	32	42
Carlisle U	42	10	5	6	25	17	6	5	10	21	32	42
Norwich C	42	7	6	8	24	25	8	4	9	29	31	40
Preston NE	42	8	8	5	23	19	4	7	10	15	25	39
Portsmouth	42	11	5	5	39	22	1	9	11	19	36	38
Bristol C	42	9	9	3	30	15	2	7	12	16	38	38
Bolton W	42	8	7	6	29	26	4	7	10	26	41	38
Aston Villa	**42**	**10**	**8**	**3**	**22**	**11**	**2**	**6**	**13**	**15**	**37**	**38**
Blackburn R	42	9	6	6	30	24	4	5	12	22	39	37
Oxford U	42	8	5	8	21	23	4	4	13	13	32	33
Bury	42	8	4	9	35	33	3	4	14	16	47	30
Fulham	42	6	7	8	20	28	1	4	16	20	53	25

news — for all the wrong reasons. The fans felt that their club had turned a corner. Alas, it had not.

Of all the dark days that Aston Villa had endured in the 1950s and 1960s, the 1969-70 season was surely the darkest of them all. When it ended, Villa were in 21st place in the Second Division, two points adrift of the next club, Charlton Athletic, and heading towards the Third Division for the very first time in their history.

It seemed an incredible prospect, not only for the thousands of Villa supporters, but for the masses who

New Villa boss Tommy Docherty pictured with three of his signings. From left to right are Bruce Rioch, 'Chico' Hamilton and Neil Rioch. The trio cost a total of around £150,000, most of it for Bruce Rioch who was the Third Division's first six-figure transfer whe he moved to Villa Park from Luton.

DIVISION 2 1969-70												
	P	W	D	L	F	A	W	D	L	F	A	Pts
Huddersfield T	42	14	6	1	36	10	10	6	5	32	27	60
Blackpool	42	10	9	2	25	16	10	4	7	31	29	53
Leicester C	42	12	6	3	37	22	7	7	7	27	28	51
Middlesbrough	42	15	4	2	36	14	5	6	10	19	31	50
Swindon T	42	13	7	1	35	17	4	9	8	22	30	50
Sheffield U	42	16	2	3	50	10	6	3	12	23	28	49
Cardiff C	42	12	7	2	38	14	6	6	9	23	27	49
Blackburn R	42	15	2	4	42	19	5	5	11	12	31	47
QPR	42	13	5	3	47	24	4	6	11	19	33	45
Millwall	42	14	4	3	38	18	1	10	10	18	38	44
Norwich C	42	13	5	3	37	14	3	6	12	12	32	43
Carlisle U	42	10	6	5	39	28	4	7	10	19	28	41
Hull C	42	11	6	4	43	28	4	5	12	29	42	41
Bristol C	42	11	7	3	37	13	2	6	13	17	37	39
Oxford U	42	9	9	3	23	13	3	6	12	12	29	39
Bolton W	42	9	6	6	31	23	3	6	12	23	38	36
Portsmouth	42	8	4	9	39	35	5	5	11	27	45	35
Birmingham C	42	9	7	5	33	22	2	4	15	18	56	33
Watford	42	6	8	7	26	21	3	5	13	18	36	31
Charlton A	42	7	8	6	23	28	0	9	12	12	48	31
Aston Villa	**42**	**7**	**8**	**6**	**23**	**21**	**1**	**5**	**15**	**13**	**41**	**29**
Preston NE	42	7	6	8	31	28	1	6	14	12	35	28

followed football in general. In the Cups, Villa also crashed, losing to Charlton in the third round of the FA Cup and to West Brom in the second round of the League Cup.

When the season opened, work was in hand to modernise part of Villa Park, Villa had been on a close season tour to America, and new signings had been made including Ian 'Chico' Hamilton from Southend United for £40,000, brothers Bruce and Neil Rioch from Luton Town for £100,000, and Pat McMahon, a former Celtic midfielder who came on a free transfer.

Everything looked set for a determined assault on the Second Division title. Yet after half their matches had been played, Villa found themselves at the foot of the table again with only 16 points — well behind the sides at the top. From then on things got even worse and when the final table was drawn up, Villa had won only eight matches and had 29 points. Even worse, they had scored only 36 goals.

Tommy Docherty did not stay around to see the club's final humiliation. After the Cup defeat, Vic Crowe found himself in charge of the team.

Crowe had been in America with Woosnam and Atlanta Chiefs, with whom Peter McParland was also playing, and had then returned to Birmingham before Docherty gave him the chance to coach Aston Villa's Central League team. Now Crowe was given the job of working a soccer miracle and pulling his old club back from the brink.

Villa had started the season badly — beaten 1-0 by Norwich at Villa Park on the opening day — and the pattern had been maintained. There was little that Crowe could do to halt the slide into the Third Division. He had none of Docherty's undoubted flamboyance — which other Football League manager, in those days, would sign a Zambian international called Freddie Mwila? — but Crowe was a first-rate coach and his main problem was a complete lack of time.

He was given the Villa job when the side was already doomed — even

Aston Villa before the start of the 1969-70 season. Back row (left to right): Hamilton, Hole, Turnbull, Lynch, Bradley. Middle row: Martin, Simmonds, Edwards, Dunn, N.Rioch, Aitken, Rudge. Front row: Arthur Cox (coach), Wright, Ferguson, Tiler, B.Rioch, Anderson, Tommy Docherty (manager).

Villa goalkeeper John Dunn holds a shot against QPR at Loftus Road in February 1970. Mick Wright is the other Villa player. At the end of the season Villa were relegated to the Third Division for the first time in their history.

if the statistics pointed out that Villa could fight their way out of the black hole in which they found themselves, there was no realistic way in which the side could turn those games into points.

Between them, Docherty and Crowe called up 30 players to the Villa first team — always a sign of a struggling team; another sure sign was that Bruce Rioch, who played in every Aston Villa game in 1969-70, had the distinction of becoming the club's leading scorer — with only six goals. Pat McMahon and Willie Anderson chipped in with five apiece.

One major signing once the season got under way was that of the former Burnley and Scotland Under-23 forward Andy Lochhead, who cost £30,000 from Leicester City in February. Lochhead could not manage a goal in 12 League games, although he would do rather better in subsequent seasons.

So Aston Villa were Third Division bound. What the ghost of George

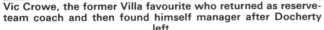

Vic Crowe, the former Villa favourite who returned as reserve-team coach and then found himself manager after Docherty left.

Andy Lochhead, who cost Villa £30,000 when they signed him from Leicester City in February 1970. He repaid them with 44 goals in 154 games.

Ramsey made of it all is anyone's guess. When he brought Villa to greatness, the prospect of even having a Third Division in the Football League was unthinkable. It was a lesson to everyone in football that even the greatest names must occasionally fall and mix with the humblest. Teams like Chesterfield, Halifax Town and Bradford City would be at Villa Park the following season. There was even the prospect of a local derby with Walsall.

Even from the Third Division, Aston Villa gave their fans something to cheer about. Although they missed promotion, Villa marched back to another Football League Cup Final and although that was ultimately lost, there could not have been a Villa supporter who even considered the possibility of Wembley as the season got under way with a League match at Chesterfield.

Even so, Villa took £50,000 in season-ticket sales during the summer of 1970 to underline Tommy Docherty's famous remark: "We'd get five thousand turn up to watch the shirts dry at Villa Park!"

Crowe began his first full season in charge of Villa with a new assistant, as Stuart Williams left for foreign shores, and former Villa star Ron Wylie moved over from St Andrew's to rejoin his old club.

Villa started the season with a 3-2 win at Saltergate and in their first 13 League games they lost only once

Pat McMahon, seen here in action in the 1971 League Cup Final, joined Villa on a free transfer from Celtic in June 1969 and scored 30 goals in 150 appearances for the club.

DIVISION 3 1970-71

	P	W	D	L	F	A	W	D	L	F	A	Pts
Preston NE	46	15	8	0	42	16	7	9	7	21	23	61
Fulham	46	15	6	2	39	12	9	6	8	29	29	60
Halifax T	46	16	2	5	46	22	6	10	7	28	33	56
Aston Villa	46	13	7	3	27	13	6	8	9	27	33	53
Chesterfield	46	13	8	2	45	12	4	9	10	21	26	51
Bristol R	46	11	5	7	38	24	8	8	7	31	26	51
Mansfield T	46	13	7	3	44	28	5	8	10	20	34	51
Rotherham U	46	12	10	1	38	19	5	6	12	26	41	50
Wrexham	46	12	8	3	43	25	6	5	12	29	40	49
Torquay U	46	12	6	5	37	26	7	5	11	17	31	49
Swansea C	46	11	5	7	41	25	4	11	8	18	31	46
Barnsley	46	12	6	5	30	19	5	5	13	19	33	45
Shrewsbury T	46	11	6	6	37	28	5	7	11	21	34	45
Brighton & HA	46	8	10	5	28	20	6	6	11	22	27	44
Plymouth A	46	6	12	5	39	33	6	7	10	24	30	43
Rochdale	46	8	8	7	29	26	6	7	10	32	42	43
Port Vale	46	11	6	6	29	18	4	6	13	23	41	42
Tranmere R	46	8	11	4	27	18	2	11	10	18	37	42
Bradford C	46	7	6	10	23	25	6	8	9	26	37	40
Walsall	46	10	1	12	30	27	4	10	9	21	30	39
Reading	46	10	7	6	32	33	4	4	15	16	52	39
Bury	46	7	9	7	30	23	5	4	14	22	37	37
Doncaster R	46	8	5	10	28	27	5	4	14	17	39	35
Gillingham	46	6	9	8	22	29	4	4	15	20	38	33

— a shock 1-0 home defeat by Mansfield Town.

Indeed, up until their appearance in the Football League Cup Final, Villa looked strong promotion candidates as they fought out the top placings with Preston and Fulham (subsequently promoted), Halifax, Chesterfield and Bristol Rovers. After Wembley, Villa fell away badly and

they won only five points from the six games which followed the Final. The gap between Villa and the top clubs increased rapidly and they left themselves with no chance of catching up and finished in fourth place, seven points short of promotion.

For the first time in their history Villa were obliged to enter the earliest stages of the FA Cup, so far as Football League teams are concerned, and in the first-round match against fellow Third Division side Torquay United on 21 November, Villa lost 3-1 at Plainmoor, their goal coming from Charlie Aitken.

Villa also found themselves in the first round of the League Cup and here they soon accounted for Notts County, beating the Fourth Division champions elect 4-0. It was the start of the Wembley march and Burnley, Northampton, Carlisle and Bristol Rovers all fell in Villa's path, although Northampton and Rovers each forced replays.

Villa fans could hardly wait for the

semi-final draw and when it paired their club with mighty Manchester United, 8,000 of them trekked to Old Trafford for the first leg and were rewarded with a 1-1 win.

Andy Lochhead scored the first after 40 minutes and although Kidd equalised shortly afterwards, the result was good enough.

At Villa Park seven days later, Villa gave United a goal start and then fought back through Lochhead and McMahon to reach Wembley. United were falling from grace but their name was still held in awe and when McMahon's late header put Villa through, all football — outside of Old Trafford — applauded them.

When Tottenham Hotspur won the 1971 Football League Cup, Villa gave a good account of themselves, although it was obvious that even their enthusiasm and drive was no ultimate match for the First Division side.

Even so, Villa had two chances to win the game before Spurs scored late

Villa goalkeeper John Dunn watches the ball sail over his crossbar at Wembley in the 1971 League Cup Final. Other players are (left to right) Kinnear (Spurs), Aitken (Villa), Peters (Spurs) and Turnbull (Villa).

Tottenham's Pat Jennings manages to punch the ball away from the leaping Pat McMahon of Aston Villa. Covering the goalmouth is Cyril Knowles (3).

Martin Chivers steers the second goal wide of John Dunn and Villa's dreams of Wembley glory are almost over.

in the game. Andy Lochhead missed an open goal, allowing Spurs to get back and clear his half-hit shot; and Ian Hamilton clipped the bar with a rasping, rising shot with Jennings well beaten.

Martin Chivers had been well-shackled by Turnbull all afternoon, but twice in the last 12 minutes of the game, he escaped and scored the goals which gave Spurs the trophy. Villa and Vic Crowe had faced a difficult season and they had coped well, however, as Villa fans were again given something about which to cheer.

One player who played a big part in Villa's end to the season but who did not appear at Wembley was Geoff Vowden, the free-scoring forward who had been transferred from Birmingham City for £12,500 in March. Vowden was cup-tied but he scored five goals in 14 League matches to give a taste of things to come.

The 1971-72 season was the campaign when Aston Villa began their return to the top flight. After steadying themselves in the uncharted waters of the Third Division the previous season, Villa knew which way to go and, more important, how to get there without foundering.

With a few new faces in the team, and with the knowledge gained from the previous campaign, Vic Crowe brought Villa through on the first leg of their journey back to the top drawer of English football.

In the close season of 1971, Crowe released one Villa stalwart in exchange for a player who was to help spearhead his plans. Villa's captain, Brian Godfrey, went to Eastville while Bristol Rovers striker Ray Graydon made the opposite journey to Villa Park.

Graydon was to score 14 goals in Villa's push out of the doldrums and although Godfrey's move was to be an unpopular one with the fans, it was the only way that Crowe could secure the signature of Graydon.

Other new faces included Chelsea's goalkeeper, Tommy Hughes, although he was soon replaced by Jim Cumbes, a £36,000 signing from West Bromwich Albion; and from Birmingham City came wing-half Malcolm Beard.

With Godfrey departed, Crowe turned to Harry Gregory to lead Villa. Signed from Charlton Athletic in 1970-71, Gregory took to his new responsibilities well and he was a mainstay of Villa's useful start to the season.

Plymouth came to Villa Park on the first day of 1971-72 and were beaten 3-1. Then followed a 1-1 draw with Walsall — a game which surprisingly attracted only 13,000 — and then a 2-0 win at home to Rochdale before Villa lost their first game, at Bolton.

Brighton were the next visitors to Villa Park and Villa beat their promotion rivals 2-0. By this time

Ian 'Chico' Hamilton, scored 48 goals in 252 appearances for Villa and played in two Wembley Finals for them.

Bruce Rioch took over the Villa captaincy and at the end of October — with Rioch's younger brother, Neil, in the side, Villa beat Blackburn 4-1 with the younger Rioch scoring twice.

Again Villa went out of the FA Cup at the first attempt — this time beaten by Fourth Division promotion seekers, Southend United, but by the turn of the year, wins over Oldham, Bradford City, Bolton and Swansea had eased them up the table until victory over Barnsley in mid-January gave Villa the lead.

On 12 February, the Third Division attendance record was broken when 48,110 saw Villa beat Bournemouth 2-1 at Villa Park.

After netting £35,000 from a match against Brazilian aces Santos — Pelé and all — Villa bought Ian Ross from Liverpool for £70,000 and the midfielder made his debut in the 2-0 win over Port Vale.

Five days after an important 3-0 win over Notts County at Meadow Lane, Crowe went into the transfer market again and paid Luton £75,000 for centre-half Chris Nicholl, with

Willie Anderson jumps over Birmingham City 'keeper Mike Kelly in a pre-season friendly at Villa Park in August 1971. A crowd of 36,711 saw Villa win 2-1, both their goals coming from Anderson.

another £15,000 due if Villa got promoted.

Thus strengthened, Villa forged ahead and although they lost 2-1 to Brighton on 25 March, promotion was gained five points ahead of the Sussex club. On 24 April, Villa clinched promotion by drawing 1-1 at Mansfield.

Five days later, Villa were the champions after a 5-1 home win over Torquay United and when they beat Chesterfield 1-0 on the last day of the

	P	W	D	L	F	A	W	D	L	F	A	Pts
DIVISION 3 1971-72												
Aston Villa	46	20	1	2	45	10	12	5	6	40	22	70
Brighton & HA	46	15	5	3	39	18	12	6	5	43	29	65
Bournemouth	46	16	6	1	43	13	7	10	6	30	24	62
Notts Co	46	16	3	4	42	19	9	9	5	32	25	62
Rotherham U	46	12	8	3	46	25	8	7	8	23	27	55
Bristol R	46	17	2	4	54	26	4	10	9	21	30	54
Bolton W	46	11	8	4	25	13	6	8	9	26	28	50
Plymouth A	46	13	6	4	43	26	7	4	12	31	38	50
Walsall	46	12	8	3	38	16	3	10	10	24	41	48
Blackburn R	46	14	4	5	39	22	5	5	13	15	35	47
Oldham A	46	11	4	8	37	35	6	7	10	22	28	45
Shrewsbury T	46	13	5	5	50	29	4	5	14	23	36	44
Chesterfield	46	10	5	8	25	23	8	3	12	32	34	44
Swansea C	46	10	6	7	27	21	7	4	12	19	38	44
Port Vale	46	10	10	3	27	21	3	5	15	16	38	41
Wrexham	46	10	5	8	33	26	6	3	14	26	37	40
Halifax T	46	11	6	6	31	22	2	6	15	17	39	38
Rochdale	46	11	7	5	35	26	1	6	16	22	57	37
York C	46	8	8	7	32	22	4	4	15	25	44	36
Tranmere R	46	9	7	7	34	30	1	9	13	16	41	36
Mansfield T	46	5	12	6	19	26	3	8	12	22	37	36
Barnsley	46	6	10	7	23	30	3	8	12	9	34	36
Torquay U	46	8	6	9	31	31	2	6	15	10	38	32
Bradford C	46	6	8	9	27	32	5	2	16	18	45	32

Aston Villa at the start of 1971-72. Back row (left to right): Brown, Graydon, Chatterley, Lochhead, Beard, Gibson, Wright. Middle row: Rudge, Martin, Aitken, Crudgington, Turnbull, Hughes, Curtis, B.Rioch, Anderson. Front row: Vic Crowe (manager), Tiler, Gregory, McMahon, Hamilton, N.Rioch, Bradley, Vowden, Ron Wylie (assistant manager).

Villa commercial manager Eric Woodward pictured with the great Pelé before the friendly against Santos at Villa Park in February 1972. A crowd of 54,437 saw Villa win 2-1.

season, Villa had established a new Third Division record of 70 points.

Their average attendance for this Third Division season had been a remarkable 31,952.

Villa also played seven matches in the League Cup but got only as far as the fourth round after replays against Wrexham and Crystal Palace. And the youth side won the FA Youth Cup. But the really important thing was that Villa were no longer a Third Division club.

One youngster had made his first appearance during the season when Brian Little, a former Villa apprentice from County Durham, scored in the 5-1 win over Torquay. It was the first full game in a career which would see Little play over 300 times for Aston Villa.

There is no doubt that Aston Villa's achievement in finishing third in their first season back in the Second Division was a fine one indeed. Although they were 11 points

Andy Lochhead in action against Bournemouth at Villa Park in February 1972. A crowd of 48,110 saw this Third Division game which was featured on BBC TV's *Match of the Day*.

A typical headed goal by Andy Lochhead, against Port Vale in February 1972. Some 32,806 spectators saw a 2-0 Villa win.

This time Pat McMahon heads home against Notts County at Meadow Lane in March 1972 as Villa go nearer to the Third Division title. McMahon scored twice in Villa's 3-0 win watched by over 34,000 fans.

Villa's FA Youth Cup winning team which beat Liverpool 5-2 on aggregate in April 1972. Back row (left to right): Frank Upton (coach), Bobby McDonald, Dougie George, Tony Betts, Roy Stark, Jimmy Brown, Alan Little. Front row: Dave Smith, Brian Melling, John Gidman, Jake Findlay, Brian Little.

Charlie Aitken scores the only goal of the game at Bradford City's Valley Parade in April 1972 and promotion from the Third Division is almost assured. Villa went on to lift the championship.

Aston Villa, Third Division champions in 1971-72. Back row (left to right): Fred Turnbull, Andy Lochhead, Chris Nicholl, Jim Cumbes, Charlie Aitken, Geoff Vowden, Ian Ross. Front row: Mick Wright, Willie Anderson, Bruce Rioch, Ian Hamilton, Ray Graydon.

Villa captain Bruce Rioch receives the Third Division championship trophy from Football League president Len Shipman before the last game of the season, against Chesterfield on 5 May 1972. A crowd of 45,586 saw Villa round off a marvellous season by beating the Derbyshire club 1-0 with a goal from Ian Ross.

Above (left): Villa manager Vic Crowe, stadium manager Bert Bond and chairman Doug Ellis at the opening of the £68,000 Bodymoor Heath training ground in November 1972. *Above (right):* Work begins on the Trinity Road executive boxes at Villa Park in July 1972. *Below:* More ground development in the summer of 1972, this time in the dressing-room area.

behind second club Queen's Park Rangers, it should also be remembered that in subsequent seasons, third place was good enough to bring First Division soccer. In fact, the rules were changed only 12 months after Villa missed out.

Yet before the season had even started there was yet another boardroom battle and public meetings which perhaps served to show what passions Aston Villa arouse, so great a club are they.

This particular battle resulted in Harry Parkes losing his seat to former Test cricketer Alan Smith, although Doug Ellis remained as a director. There was yet another upheaval in October, when Ellis was elected chairman and former Villa player and manager, Eric Houghton, was appointed a director, with Dick Greenhalgh and Bob Mackay losing their seats. Then Harry Kartz, who had resigned because of business commitments, was reinstated and at the end of the season, Sir William Dugdale and Harry Cressman joined the board in the seemingly neverending game of Aston Villa musical chairs.

On the field, Villa also had changes during the close season when Alun Evans, the former Wolves star who became Britain's first £100,000 teenage footballer when he was transferred to Liverpool, joined Villa from Anfield for £75,000.

Charlie Aitken in a tussle with Manchester City's Francis Lee, watched by Ian Ross, Geoff Vowden, Pat McMahon and Rodney Marsh during the 1972 FA Charity Shield match at Villa Park. A crowd of 34,890 saw Villa lose 1-0.

Two wins in their first two matches gave Villa a great start, coupled with a Football League Cup win over Hereford. But then Burnley won 4-1 at Turf Moor and this result brought Villa's thoughts of a quick return to the First Division down to earth.

By the middle of October, Villa were out of the League Cup, beaten 2-0 at Elland Road after drawing 1-1 with Leeds at Villa Park before 46,815 fans.

The FA Cup also brought little cheer, when Everton beat them 3-2 at Goodison Park, although Villa played well enough to merit that tight scoreline.

Just before the Villa-Everton tie, Vic Crowe bought Derby County's young full-back, John Robson, for £90,000. Robson was to give Villa a good few seasons before his career was sadly halted by a serious illness.

The turn of the year was a good time from Villa's point of view — at least so far as the Second Division

Bruce Rioch and Franz Beckenbauer before the start of the friendly between Villa and Bayern Munich at Villa Park in January 1973. The teams drew 1-1 in front of 22,699 spectators.

programme went — and they enjoyed wins over Brighton, Cardiff and Swindon to take them well into February.

However, they were never really in contention for the top two places and the end of the season saw them finish well behind promoted clubs, Burnley and QPR.

Another youngster making his

DIVISION 2 1972-73	P	W	D	L	F	A	W	D	L	F	A	Pts
Burnley	42	13	6	2	44	18	11	8	2	28	17	62
QPR	42	16	4	1	54	13	8	9	4	27	24	61
Aston Villa	42	12	5	4	27	17	6	9	6	24	30	50
Middlesbrough	42	12	6	3	29	15	5	7	9	17	28	47
Bristol C	42	10	7	4	34	18	7	5	9	29	33	46
Sunderland	42	12	6	3	35	17	5	6	10	24	32	46
Blackpool	42	12	6	3	37	17	6	4	11	19	34	46
Oxford U	42	14	2	5	36	18	5	5	11	16	25	45
Fulham	42	11	6	4	32	16	5	6	10	26	33	44
Sheffield W	42	14	4	3	40	20	3	6	12	19	35	44
Millwall	42	12	5	4	33	18	4	5	12	22	29	42
Luton T	42	6	9	6	24	23	9	2	10	20	30	41
Hull C	42	9	7	5	39	22	5	5	11	25	37	40
Nottingham F	42	12	5	4	32	18	2	7	12	15	34	40
Orient	42	11	6	4	33	18	1	6	14	16	35	36
Swindon T	42	8	9	4	28	23	2	7	12	18	37	36
Portsmouth	42	7	6	8	21	22	5	5	11	21	37	35
Carlisle U	42	10	5	6	30	24	1	7	13	10	28	34
Preston NE	42	6	8	7	19	25	5	4	12	18	39	34
Cardiff C	42	11	4	6	32	21	0	7	14	11	37	33
Huddersfield T	42	7	9	5	21	20	1	8	12	15	36	33
Brighton & HA	42	7	8	6	32	31	1	5	15	14	52	29

mark was full-back John Gidman, who had been a leading figure in Villa's 1972 FA Youth Cup win. For one Villa youngster, though, there were harder times ahead. Free-scoring reserve-team forward Keith Leonard, who became a full-time professional in April 1972, suffered a double fracture of his right leg the following December and was out of action for seven months.

Although Aston Villa had lost their ever-consistent goalscorer, Andy Lochhead, who joined Oldham Athletic in August for £15,000, the club really felt that 1973-74 was going to be their season for promotion.

Crowe had made two useful signings in the much-travelled Welsh international Trevor Hockey, a midfielder who came from Norwich City for £38,000, and Irish international striker Sammy Morgan, from Port Vale for £25,000, and at the end of September, Villa were unbeaten and stood nicely placed in fourth spot.

There followed two away defeats

Willie Anderson (left) joined Cardiff City for £60,000 in February 1973. Bruce Rioch (right) moved to Derby County a year later after the Rams boss Dave Mackay offered Villa some £200,000 for his signature.

at the hands of Notts County and Fulham before Villa got back to form with a 5-0 trouncing of Cardiff City at Villa Park. By the middle of November, Villa were in third place, two points behind the second club Orient.

Suddenly, though, they slipped and fell. Five defeats and a draw in six games pushed them right down the table.

The rot started when Hull managed a 1-1 draw at Villa Park and this was followed by defeats at the hands of Swindon, Sunderland, Luton, West Brom and Oxford. Only a 1-1 draw with Notts County gave Villa any profit in that time.

It was 23 February before Villa won another game — when they beat Cardiff 1-0 at Ninian Park. Cardiff were to miss relegation only by goal-average and Villa's win could not be described as a turning point for them.

In 13 games, Villa had scored only five goals and this actually put them into the fringe of the relegation struggle instead of in the heat of the promotion race.

There were several reasons for the

DIVISION 2 1973-74											
	P	W	D	L	F	A	W	D	L	F	A	Pts
Middlesbrough	42	16	4	1	40	8	11	7	3	37	22	65
Luton T	42	12	5	4	42	25	7	7	7	22	26	50
Carlisle U	42	13	5	3	40	17	7	4	10	21	31	49
Orient	42	9	8	4	28	17	6	10	5	27	25	48
Blackpool	42	11	5	5	35	17	6	8	7	22	23	47
Sunderland	42	11	6	4	32	15	8	3	10	26	29	47
Nottingham F	42	12	6	3	40	19	3	9	9	17	24	45
WBA	42	8	9	4	28	24	6	7	8	20	21	44
Hull C	42	9	9	3	25	15	4	8	9	21	32	43
Notts Co	42	8	6	7	30	35	7	7	7	25	25	43
Bolton W	42	12	5	4	30	17	3	7	11	14	23	42
Millwall	42	10	6	5	28	16	4	8	9	23	25	42
Fulham	42	11	4	6	26	20	5	6	10	13	23	42
Aston Villa	42	8	9	4	33	21	5	6	10	15	24	41
Portsmouth	42	9	8	4	26	16	5	4	12	19	46	40
Bristol C	42	9	5	7	25	20	5	5	11	22	34	38
Cardiff C	42	8	7	6	27	20	2	9	10	22	42	36
Oxford U	42	8	8	5	27	21	2	8	11	8	25	36
Sheffield W	42	9	6	6	33	24	3	5	13	18	39	35
Crystal P	42	6	7	8	24	24	5	5	11	19	32	34
Preston NE	42	7	8	6	24	23	2	6	13	16	39	*31
Swindon T	42	6	7	8	22	27	1	4	16	14	45	25

*Preston North End had one point deducted for fielding an ineligible player

demise, not least the failure of some players to produce their true form at the crucial time. Ray Graydon and Bruce Rioch were also suffering from injuries — Rioch moved to Derby for £200,000 in February — and in the final analysis, that awful spell of bad results left Villa a slightly below average Second Division club when the season ended.

York City knocked Villa out of the League Cup, 1-0 at Bootham Crescent, but in the FA Cup, the club had

Goalkeeper Jim Cumbes joined Villa in October 1971, from West Brom. Cumbes also enjoyed a fine career as a Worcestershire cricketer.

Bruce Rioch
— *Pace and Power in Villa's Return*

WHEN Tommy Docherty took over the reins at Villa Park in December 1968, he inherited an Aston Villa side which was struggling in the Second Division. Typically, Docherty was soon busy in the transfer market, but probably the most significant signing he made did not join the club until the following summer when Bruce Rioch, Luton Town's goalscoring midfielder, became the first Third Division player to be transferred for £100,000 when he moved to Aston Villa in July 1969. Rioch's brother, Neil, also joined Villa from Luton at the same time.

Bruce Rioch had scored 24 goals in 44 League games for Luton when they won the Fourth Division championship in 1967-68 and although his first season at Villa Park saw his new club relegated to the Third Division, he played a leading role when Villa were promoted under new manager Vic Crowe at the end of 1971-72, skippering the side and scoring nine goals in his 40 games as Villa stormed to the title.

Of course, Rioch had already tasted glory with Villa. In their first season as a Third Division club, he played in their League Cup Final team at Wembley, although he had missed all but one of the earlier rounds after being injured.

But during the championship season he really came into his own and one of his goals proved particularly vital, the winner at York in early April when Villa were seeking victory at every turn in their bid for promotion.

Rioch was essentially an attacking player, with power, speed and wonderful shooting power. It was inevitable that Villa would not be able to hold on to him and in February 1974 they could hardly refuse Derby County's offer of £200,000.

Derby boss Dave Mackay spent that kind of money because he wanted more goals from midfield — and he could have hardly been better rewarded when, in his first full season at the Baseball Ground, Rioch was the Rams' leading scorer with 15 goals as they won the First Division title for the second time in three years.

His talents also brought him to the notice of the Scottish selectors, for although he was born in Aldershot in September 1967, he qualified for Scotland through his soldier father. He won 24 caps for Scotland and led them in the 1978 World Cup finals, the only English-born player ever to skipper the Scots in full internationals.

In October 1976, Rioch scored four goals in a game against Spurs, but two months later Derby boss Colin Murphy sold him to Everton for £180,000. Within a year, however, Rioch was back at the Baseball Ground

when Tommy Docherty, the man who had signed him for Villa, bought him again.

Alas, his second spell at Derby was not as happy — there was a well-publicised bust-up with Docherty — and after loan spells with Birmingham City and Sheffield United, and a spell in the North American Soccer League with Seattle Sounders, he became player-coach of Fourth Division Torquay United and was later manager at Plainmoor.

As a manager, Bruce Rioch has carved for himself a successful new career. He took Middlesbrough from the point of liquidation in the Third Division to the First, had a spell with Millwall, who had just been relegated to the Second Division, and then brought Bolton Wanderers back to national prominence with an FA Cup run in 1992-93 which saw the Trotters eliminate Liverpool on the way. Under Rioch, Bolton finished that season with promotion to the new First Division, underlining the feeling that he will be one of the more prominent managers of the 1990s.

'Chico' Hamilton heads goalwards in the FA Cup fourth-round tie at Highbury in January 1974. Jeff Blockley (arm raised) and Pat Rise are the Arsenal players. The game ended 1-1 and Villa won the replay 2-0.

a share of glory, including an epic 2-0 win over Arsenal in the fourth round at Villa Park after the sides had drawn 1-1 at Highbury.

In the first game, Morgan was sent off after a challenge on Arsenal goalkeeper, Bob Wilson, and Villa hung on with ten men after having earlier taken the lead through the Irishman.

In the replay, nearly 48,000 fans saw Villa make no mistake. Morgan got his revenge by heading Villa in front before half-time and after the interval, Evans found his goal touch

Aston Villa Celebrate their Centenary

Aston Villa celebrated their Centenary in 1974 and it was fitting that the club should regain their First Division place the following year.

The Centenary celebration took several forms but none more emotive than the gathering together of many former players.

Above: This group contains some members of the team which beat Manchester United in the 1956-57 FA Cup Final at Wembley, when Peter McParland scored twice. From left to right (standing) are Jimmy Dugdale, Peter McParland, Derek Pace, Stan Lynn, Johnny Dixon and Jackie Sewell. Seated left is Leslie Smith.

Opposite: The great 'Pongo' Waring, who scored 167 goals in 226 League and FA Cup games for Aston Villa, including a club record 50 goals from only 40 games in 1930-31. Waring was in his 68th year at the time of the club's 100th anniversary.

Twelve months later, this great club were restored to the top flight of English football.

to make the score 2-0.

Alas, high-flying Burnley put an end to Villa's Wembley hopes in the next round when they won 1-0 at Turf Moor. Villa had hoped that their Centenary Year would be celebrated with a return to First Division football. In the end, they had learned enough lessons to make sure that the celebrations would not be long delayed.

In June 1974, Aston Villa appointed their sixth manager in ten turbulent years. Former Norwich and Manchester City manager, Ron Saunders, became the latest boss at Villa Park in place of Vic Crowe.

Crowe had got Villa out of the Third Division but it appeared that he could not obtain them promotion from the Second, the events of the 1973-74 season had left the Villa board with the feeling that they must look for a new man, and Saunders, a former forward with Portsmouth, and a man who had the reputation of something of a disciplinarian, was that person.

DIVISION 2 1974-75											
	P	W	D	L	F	A	W	D	L	F	A	Pts
Manchester U	42	17	3	1	45	12	9	6	6	21	18	61
Aston Villa	42	16	4	1	47	6	9	4	8	32	26	58
Norwich C	42	14	3	4	34	17	6	10	5	24	20	53
Sunderland	42	14	6	1	41	8	5	7	9	24	27	51
Bristol C	42	14	5	2	31	10	7	3	11	16	23	50
WBA	42	13	4	4	33	15	5	5	11	21	27	45
Blackpool	42	12	6	3	31	17	2	11	8	7	16	45
Hull C	42	12	8	1	25	10	3	6	12	15	43	44
Fulham	42	9	8	4	29	17	4	8	9	15	22	42
Bolton W	42	9	7	5	27	16	6	5	10	18	25	42
Oxford U	42	14	3	4	30	19	1	9	11	11	32	42
Orient	42	8	9	4	17	16	3	11	7	11	23	42
Southampton	42	10	6	5	29	20	5	5	11	24	34	41
Notts Co	42	7	11	3	34	26	5	5	11	15	33	40
York C	42	9	7	5	28	18	5	3	13	23	37	38
Nottingham F	42	7	7	7	24	23	5	7	9	19	32	38
Portsmouth	42	9	7	5	28	20	3	6	12	16	34	37
Oldham A	42	10	7	4	28	16	0	8	13	12	32	35
Bristol R	42	10	4	7	25	23	2	7	12	17	41	35
Millwall	42	8	9	4	31	19	2	3	16	13	37	32
Cardiff C	42	7	8	6	24	21	2	6	13	12	41	32
Sheffield W	42	3	7	11	17	29	2	4	15	12	35	21

Not only did Saunders win Villa back their long-cherished First Division status, he also steered them to the Football League Cup Final at Wembley, where they won the trophy. He also took the club into the fifth round of the FA Cup where they were narrowly beaten at Ipswich.

Manchester United were making an appearance in the Second Division fixture list this season after their manager, the former Villa boss,

New Villa manager Ron Saunders speaks to the players at the club's training ground in the summer of 1974.

Tommy Docherty, had failed to halt their slide from the top.

It was a slide which had begun with Villa beating United in the League Cup semi-final some seasons earlier. Happily, both clubs would be reinstated in the immediate future. When the two sides met in the League in 1974-75, honours were shared with United winning 2-1 at Old Trafford in November, in front of a crowd of 55,615, and Villa triumphing 2-1 at Villa Park in February, when 39,156 were present.

Villa had made one major signing this season when Manchester City midfielder Frank Carrodus joined them for £95,000 in August. Carrodus appeared in 35 games as Villa won promotion and was to play a big part in future.

Also making his first appearance in the first team was midfielder Steve Hunt, who had been at Villa Park since his days as an apprentice. Hunt,

'Chico' Hamilton scores from the penalty spot in the 6-1 League Cup replay hammering of Hartlepools United at Villa Park in November 1974.

Villa line up before the 1975 League Cup Final against Norwich City at Wembley. From left to right are Ross, Hamilton, Nicholl, Graydon, Alun Evans, Cumbes, Leonard, McDonald, Carrodus, Robson, Aitken, Little, Ron Saunders.

Ray Graydon hammers home the rebound after Kevin Keelan had saved his penalty. It was the only goal of a mediocre Final.

John Robson, a £90,000 capture from Derby. Robson enjoyed glory with Villa but sadly had to retire through a serious illness.

though would make little impression in his early days at Villa Park and had a spell away before returning to become one of the successes in a dismal era.

Villa's leading scorer in this successful season was young Brian Little, who netted 20 League goals, one more than Ray Graydon.

Little scored a hat-trick when Oldham were beaten 5-0 at Villa Park towards the end of the season, Graydon had scored all the goals in a 3-0 win over Millwall in September, and Sammy Morgan had also hit three in one match, a 6-0 romp over Hull at Villa Park in the fourth League game of the season.

The average League attendance this season was 27,654 with a high of 57,266 for the last home game, a 2-0 win over Sunderland, who were also chasing promotion. In the last game of the season, Villa beat Norwich, who were also in with a chance of going up, 4-1 at Carrow Road in front of a 35,999 crowd.

At the season's end, Manchester United sat on top of the Second Division table with 61 points, with Villa three points behind on 58. Norwich also went up, in third place with 53. The fourth-placed side were Sunderland with 51 points.

In the Football League Cup, Villa enjoyed a splendid second-round win over Everton after drawing 1-1 at Villa Park, and their 3-0 win at Goodison was one of the shocks of the season.

In the third round, tiny Crewe provided the shock by drawing 2-2 at Gresty Road and losing only 1-0 at Villa Park, and although Hartlepool managed a draw on their home ground, when they came to Villa Park they were hammered 6-1.

A 2-1 win at Colchester brought Villa an unattractive semi-final with Chester and in the first leg, at Sealand Road, Villa twice took the lead, only to lose it in a 2-2 draw.

Chester fought hard at Villa Park but the home side squeezed through

Villa players chair Ian Ross, who holds aloft the League Cup. The others are (left to right) Charlie Aitken, Keith Leonard, Jim Cumbes, John Robson, Chris Nicholl and Bobby McDonald.

Bathtime celebrations at Wembley after Villa's 1975 League Cup Final victory.

Ron Saunders with the League Cup. In successive seasons, Saunders had taken three different clubs to the Final.

Keith Leonard heads a goal against Southampton at Villa Park in March 1975 as the club inch back towards the First Division.

3-2 to ensure that Ron Saunders completed a unique hat-trick in taking three different clubs to the League Cup Final in successive seasons.

It was also third time lucky for Saunders. Against his old club, Norwich City, Ray Graydon scored from a rebound after City's Kevin Keelan had saved the Villa man's penalty kick. It was the only goal of a mediocre Final and came a few minutes from the end. Nevertheless it put the icing on the cake for Aston Villa as they went on to clinch promotion.

Brian Little, Villa's leading scorer with 20 goals as they finished Second Division runners-up.

Scenes at Villa Park after the home game against Sunderland in April 1975 when over 57,000 fans came to celebrate promotion.

Consolidation and the League Cup Again

NOT only had Aston Villa brought First Division football back to their palatial stadium, they had also given Villa fans an entirely new experience in 1975-76 — European football.

Since Manchester United took the first steps in 1956, English clubs had counted European competition as part and parcel of the everyday programme. Yet Villa, this most famous of clubs and the side which had pioneered much of football's early history, had never played a competitive European game at first-team level. Now, as Football League Cup holders, they were entitled to a place in the UEFA Cup.

Unfortunately, Villa's first venture into European competition came to an abrupt end. On 17 September 1975, Aston Villa took to the field against Antwerp of Belgium with this side: Cumbes; Gidman, Aitken,

Ross, Nicholl, Phillips, Graydon, McDonald, Morgan, Hamilton and Carrodus. Robson substituted for McDonald during the match and Hamilton was eventually replaced by Hunt.

Almost at once, Villa found that this was a different game and a hat-trick by Kodat and a further goal by Heyligen, gave Antwerp a 4-1 win.

At Villa Park on the first day of October, Villa tried to pull back that

September 1975 and Ian Ross introduces new boys Andy Gray and John Burridge to John Gidman and John Robson.

Villa's party about to fly out to Antwerp for their debut in European competition in the 1975-76 UEFA Cup.

three-goal lead but Kodat scored again to increase the Belgians' advantage and Villa were dumped out 5-1 on aggregate. It was an inauspicious start to Villa's new-found status.

But the First Division was the most important thing to occupy Villa's attention and immediately after that European exit they drew 0-0 at Middlesbrough to go into eighth place in the table and set the fans

Chris Nicholl clutches his knee as John Burridge grabs the ball from Arsenal's Sammy Nelson at Highbury in January 1976.

thinking about a possible Championship.

Before long, they would be thinking instead about a quick return to the Second Division, however. A succession of mediocre results put Villa into a mid-table position by Christmas and as the season wore on they found themselves stuck in 18th place for the period between mid-March and mid-April.

In October, Villa had signed Andy Gray, the Dundee United striker who cost £110,000 and made his debut in the goalless draw at Ayresome Park before opening his account in the next game, a 1-1 draw with Spurs. For Gray it was the first of 78 goals in 210 senior games for Villa.

In December, Villa went into the transfer market again when they signed Coventry City's experienced midfielder Dennis Mortimer for £175,000. He made his first appearance in a 4-1 home win over West Ham, the start of a glorious career which saw him make over 400 appearances altogether for Villa and share in some of the greatest moments in the club's history.

Other future Villa stars making their first appearances this season included Gordon Cowans and John Deehan, both former apprentices who had great days ahead.

In the last three games of the 1975-76 season Villa picked up five points with wins over Derby and Middlesbrough and a draw at West Ham and those vital points gave them a final position of 16th place. Even with three-up-and-three-down, Villa had avoided relegation by nine points as their neighbours Wolves joined Burnley and Sheffield United in the drop.

In the FA Cup, Southampton had won a third-round replay at Villa Park when Jim McCalliog had scored twice, although the game went to extra-time.

In the Football League Cup, Lou Macari and Steve Coppell gave Manchester United a 2-1 win at Villa Park in the third round.

All in all, the season had been an

DIVISION 1			1975-76									
	P	W	D	L	F	A	W	D	L	F	A	Pts
Liverpool	42	14	5	2	41	21	9	9	3	25	10	60
QPR	42	17	4	0	42	13	7	7	7	25	20	59
Manchester U	42	16	4	1	40	13	7	6	8	28	29	56
Derby Co	42	15	3	3	45	30	6	8	7	30	28	53
Leeds U	42	13	3	5	37	19	8	6	7	28	27	51
Ipswich T	42	11	6	4	36	23	5	8	8	18	25	46
Leicester C	42	9	9	3	29	24	4	10	7	19	27	45
Manchester C	42	14	5	2	46	18	2	6	13	18	28	43
Tottenham H	42	6	10	5	33	32	8	5	8	30	31	43
Norwich C	42	10	5	6	33	26	6	5	10	25	32	42
Everton	42	10	7	4	37	24	5	5	11	23	42	42
Stoke C	42	8	5	8	25	24	7	6	8	23	26	41
Middlesbrough	42	9	7	5	23	11	6	3	12	23	34	40
Coventry C	42	6	9	6	22	22	7	5	9	25	35	40
Newcastle U	42	11	4	6	51	26	4	5	12	20	36	39
Aston Villa	42	11	8	2	32	17	0	9	12	19	42	39
Arsenal	42	11	4	6	33	19	2	6	13	14	34	36
West Ham U	42	10	5	6	26	23	3	5	13	22	48	36
Birmingham C	42	11	5	5	36	26	2	2	17	21	49	33
Wolves	42	7	6	8	27	25	3	4	14	24	43	30
Burnley	42	6	6	9	23	26	3	4	14	20	40	28
Sheffield U	42	4	7	10	19	32	2	3	16	14	50	22

Villa's Leighton Phillips in a mid-air battle with Keith Robson of West Ham at Upton Park in April 1976.

Dennis Mortimer, joined Villa from Coventry for £175,000 and went on to make over 400 appearances for the club.

Andy Gray in typical celebratory pose after scoring yet another goal.

extremely disappointing one from the fans' point of view, although Saunders knew that he had at least settled the side down into the First Division.

That period of consolidation was about to be rewarded and in 1976-77, Villa enjoyed a tremendous season — winners of the Football League Cup, never out of the top dozen placings in the First Division to finally finish in fourth place and so doubly qualify for the UEFA Cup, and also quarter-finalists in the FA Cup.

Villa started off the season with a resounding 4-0 win over West Ham United at Villa Park; they finished it with an equally emphatic 4-0 win over West Bromwich Albion, also at Villa Park, and in between sandwiched all sorts of goodies for their diehard fans.

Although they ultimately failed to finish in the first three in the First Division, Villa were up at the top for

a long time. After beating Arsenal 5-1 at Villa Park on 20 October, they moved into second place and until they drew 0-0 at Bristol City on 2 April, they were never out of the top five.

Andy Gray hit 25 of Villa's 76 League goals and in defence goalkeeper John Burridge and defenders John Gidman, Gordon Smith, Leighton Phillips (an £80,000 signing from Cardiff City in September 1974), Chris Nicholl and Dennis Mortimer kept a tight rein on opposition attacks, conceding only 50 goals in Villa's 42 League matches.

Villa 5 Liverpool 1 at Villa Park in December 1976. Brian Little bends the ball around Ray Clemence and into the net for goal number four – and the game is still only 31 minutes old.

A classic Andy Gray goal against Leicester at Filbert Street in January 1977. It put Villa into the fourth round of the FA Cup.

Gray scores the only goal of the League game at Upton Park in January 1977. A week later Villa beat the Hammers in the FA Cup at Villa Park.

The combined efforts of Ian Gillard, Phil Parkes and Frank McLintock cannot prevent Brian Little scoring at Highbury in February 1977 to help Villa into the League Cup semi-finals after two drawn games against QPR. Little hit all three in Villa's eventual 3-0 win.

DIVISION 1 1976-77											
	P	W	D	L	F	A	W	D	L	F	A	Pts
Liverpool	42	18	3	0	47	11	5	8	8	15	22	57
Manchester C	42	15	5	1	38	13	6	9	6	22	21	56
Ipswich T	42	15	4	2	41	11	7	4	10	25	28	52
Aston Villa	42	17	3	1	55	17	5	4	12	21	33	51
Newcastle U	42	14	6	1	40	15	4	7	10	24	34	49
Manchester U	42	12	6	3	41	22	6	5	10	30	40	47
WBA	42	10	6	5	38	22	6	7	8	24	34	45
Arsenal	42	11	6	4	37	20	5	5	11	27	39	43
Everton	42	9	7	5	35	24	5	7	9	27	40	42
Leeds U	42	8	8	5	28	26	7	4	10	20	25	42
Leicester C	42	8	9	4	30	28	4	9	8	17	32	42
Middlesbrough	42	11	6	4	25	14	3	7	11	15	31	41
Birmingham C	42	10	6	5	38	25	3	6	12	25	36	38
QPR	42	10	7	4	31	21	3	5	13	16	31	38
Derby Co	42	9	9	3	36	18	0	10	11	14	37	37
Norwich C	42	12	4	5	30	23	2	5	14	17	41	37
West Ham U	42	9	6	6	28	23	2	8	11	18	42	36
Bristol C	42	8	7	6	25	19	3	6	12	13	29	35
Coventry C	42	7	9	5	34	26	3	6	12	14	33	35
Sunderland	42	9	5	7	29	16	2	7	12	17	38	34
Stoke C	42	9	8	4	21	16	1	6	14	7	35	34
Tottenham H	42	9	7	5	26	20	3	2	16	22	52	33

thrashed 5-1, and removed Millwall 2-0 to reach the semi-final against Queen's Park Rangers.

Rangers spent £12,000 on a system of hot-air balloons to dry out Loftus Road sufficiently for the first leg to be played and the result was a goalless draw.

At Villa Park, Deehan put the home side ahead but Gerry Francis sent the game into extra-time at 1-1. There were further thrills as Deehan shot Villa in front again, Burridge saved a penalty, and then Queen's Park Rangers substitute Peter Eastoe made it 2-2 in the 115th minute of the game.

At Highbury six days later, the sides tried again and this time Brian Little scored a hat-trick as Villa romped home 3-0.

After the marathon semi-final, it took three games against Everton in the Final before Villa finally lifted the League Cup.

The Wembley game ended goalless and the Hillsborough replay was a 1-1 draw, after extra-time. It was almost a month before the game was replayed for a second time — this one at Old Trafford.

Latchford scored first for Everton, and three goals in four minutes near the end — Nicholl and Little for Villa and Lyons for Everton — made extra-time look a certainty until Little scored the winner with less than a minute to play. Over 210,000 people had watched the three games and Villa were back in Europe for the second time.

One new face this season was Alex Cropley, a left-sided midfield player who came from Arsenal for £125,000 in December.

Undoubtedly Villa's best win of the season was their 5-1 victory over the champions, Liverpool, on 15 December, when Gray and Deehan each scored twice.

In the FA Cup, Villa reached the last eight before Manchester United beat them 2-1 in the seething cauldron of Old Trafford, where the attendance was 57,089.

It was the Football League Cup, however, which provided Villa with their main reason for celebration in 1976-77. Right from the start of the League Cup campaign Villa looked as though they were determined to win the trophy.

They whipped Manchester City 3-0, beat Norwich 2-1, had another big win over Wrexham, who they

Ron Saunders meets HRH Princess Anne before the 1977 League Cup Final first game against Everton at Wembley.

Chris Nicholl (5) stoops to head away from an Everton attack as Andy Gray watches open-mouthed.

Brian Little scores the winning goal in the 1977 League Cup Final second replay at Old Trafford. Said Little afterwards, "I don't miss chances like that!"

Chris Nicholl and Dennis Mortimer holds up the Football League Cup which took Villa ten games to win.

Left: Villa boss Ron Saunders holds aloft the League Cup. *Right:* Cheers! Gordon Smith, the man who came on as subsitute and provided the cross for Little's winning goal.

Aston Villa, the Football League Cup holders, before the start of the 1977-78 season. Back row (left to right): Charlie Young, Jake Findlay, John Burridge, Nigel Spink, Allan Evans, Ivor Linton. Middle row: Roy McLaren (first-team coach), David Evans, Mike Buttress, John Gregory, Andy Gray, Gordon Smith, David Hughes, Gordon Cowans, Peter Downs (physiotherapist). Front row: John Deehan, Alex Cropley, Leighton Phillips, John Gidman, Ron Saunders (manager), John Robson, Brian Little, Dennis Mortimer, Frank Carrodus.

In 1977-78, Villa did much better in their second attempt at a European trophy and reached the quarter-finals of the UEFA Cup with good victories over some of the more famous names in European soccer.

In the First Division too, they did well, although finishing in eighth place and never striking the high spots of the previous season. In fact, eighth place was the highest position that the club managed in the table

all season and they finally achieved it with a fine 6-1 win over Ipswich Town in the penultimate game of the season, and maintained it despite a disappointing 3-1 defeat at Molineux on the last day.

Jimmy Rimmer blocks a shot from Exeter City's Nicky Jennings in the League Cup game at St James' Park in September 1977.

West Ham goalkeeper Mervyn Day can only watch as Ken McNaught opens the scoring with a fine header in October 1977.

John Deehan breaks between Chelsea's Micky Droy and Steve Wicks at Stamford Bridge in November 1977.

Again, Andy Gray was leading scorer, but this time with only 13 goals, and in goal the former Manchester United, Swansea and Arsenal goalkeeper Jimmy Rimmer, signed from Arsenal in August for £65,000, played in every match.

Other major close-season signings were defenders Allan Evans, from Dunfermline Athletic for £30,000 in May, and Ken McNaught, for £200,000 from Everton in July. Evans would go on to play well over 450 games for Villa, McNaught some 260.

The domestic Cups were a disappointment. In the Football League Cup, Villa reached the fourth round via Exeter and Queen's Park Rangers, before Brian Clough's Nottingham Forest beat them 4-2 at the City Ground.

Villa's FA Cup run ended even earlier when Everton gained some crumb of revenge for their League Cup Final defeat by Villa, when they won 4-1 at Goodison Park in the third round.

In the UEFA Cup, Villa did much better. Their first-round match was against the Turkish team, Fenerbahçe, and after Deehan (2), Gray and Little gave Villa a 4-0 start at Villa Park, they had little trouble in adding a further two goals in Turkey.

The first-leg of the second round was also played at Villa Park and this time the Poles of Górnik Zabrze gave away a two-goal deficit and were unable to pull it back in Poland.

So to the third round and the Spaniards, Athletic Bilbao, the side which had once had an epic struggle with Manchester United in the early days of the European Cup. Again Villa were at home first and again they won 2-0.

	P	W	D	L	F	A	W	D	L	F	A	Pts
DIVISION 1 1977-78												
Nottingham F	42	15	6	0	37	8	10	8	3	32	16	64
Liverpool	42	15	4	2	37	11	9	5	7	28	23	57
Everton	42	14	4	3	47	22	8	7	6	29	23	55
Manchester C	42	14	4	3	46	21	6	8	7	28	30	52
Arsenal	42	14	5	2	38	12	7	5	9	22	25	52
WBA	42	13	5	3	35	18	5	9	7	27	35	50
Coventry C	42	13	5	3	48	23	5	7	9	27	39	48
Aston Villa	42	11	4	6	33	18	7	6	8	24	24	46
Leeds U	42	12	4	5	39	21	6	6	9	24	32	46
Manchester U	42	9	6	6	32	23	7	4	10	35	40	42
Birmingham C	42	8	5	8	32	30	8	4	9	23	30	41
Derby Co	42	10	7	4	37	24	4	6	11	17	35	41
Norwich C	42	10	8	3	28	20	1	10	10	24	46	40
Middlesbrough	42	8	8	5	25	19	4	7	10	17	35	39
Wolves	42	7	8	6	30	27	5	4	12	21	37	36
Chelsea	42	7	11	3	28	20	4	3	14	18	49	36
Bristol C	42	9	6	6	37	26	2	7	12	12	27	35
Ipswich T	42	10	5	6	32	24	1	8	12	15	37	35
QPR	42	8	8	5	27	26	1	7	13	20	38	33
West Ham U	42	8	6	7	31	28	4	2	15	21	41	32
Newcastle U	42	4	6	11	26	37	2	4	15	16	41	22
Leicester C	42	4	7	10	16	32	1	5	15	10	38	22

Right: Leighton Phillips and Johann Cruyff exchange pennants before the start of the game against Barcelona in March 1978.
Far right: Villa party in the dug-out at the Nou Camp stadium.
Below: Brian Little scores for Villa but they went down 4-3 on aggregate.

In the Basque port they again managed a 1-1 draw and Villa fans looked forward eagerly to another home first leg, this time against Spanish football's other representatives, CF Barcelona.

This time, however, Villa were unable to gain the advantage and Barcelona took a 2-0 lead through Cruyff, the Dutch master, and Zuvira.

In the 82nd minute, Cruyff limped off to an ovation from the Villa crowd and in the last four minutes, Villa drew level when McNaught and Deehan staged a grandstand finish.

In Barcelona's magnificent Nou Camp stadium, Villa might have won the tie had John Gidman not been sent off in the 23rd minute. Even then they took the lead through

John Deehan powers a header past the West Brom goalkeeper at The Hawthorns in April 1978.

Andy Gray tries a shot against Everton at Villa Park in September 1978.

Gary Shelton is robbed of the ball at Loftus Road in September 1978.

Little, but the strain of playing with ten men soon told and Migueli and Asensi scored the goals which put Barcelona into the hat for the semi-final draw.

In 1978-79, Aston Villa again finished eighth in the First Division to establish themselves as one of English football's better and more consistent sides. Nevertheless, this was a mediocre season in many ways, remembered as much as anything for Villa's short but eventful League Cup run which ended in the fourth round, but which involved five matches and some unpleasant incidents.

Villa's League Cup first-round match against Sheffield United at Villa Park towards the end of August was uneventful enough and young Gary Shelton gave them a 1-0 win.

But there then followed three bruising encounters with Crystal Palace. The first match at Villa Park on 4 October saw Villa draw 1-1 and Shelton was carried off with a bad leg injury.

Manager Ron Saunders declared angrily after the match: "I keep reading about these sides that want to come and play football; but all that happens is that they want to try and kick you off the pitch."

In the replay at Selhurst Park, Villa and Palace fought out a goalless draw

Alan Sunderland opens the scoring for Arsenal at Highbury in October 1978, beating Villa goalkeeper Jimmy Rimmer. Gary Williams (3) can do nothing.

Rimmer is beaten again but this time Williams heads a certain Crystal Palace goal off the line at Selhurst Park later the same month. Villa drew this League Cup replay before winning the third game 3-0 at Coventry. Phillips (10) and Mortimer (6) are the other Villa players.

Allan Evans scores a disputed goal against Chelsea at Stamford Bridge in November 1978 but referee Clive Thomas allows what proved to be the winner.

and Villa defender Allan Evans was sent off.

At the third attempt, Villa won 3-0 with goals from Gray (two) and John Gregory (a £40,000 signing from Northampton Town in June 1977) and at last Second Division Luton Town knew who they would be facing in the next round.

It was struggling Luton who gave football a shock when they won 2-0 at Villa Park to knock out the club which had done so well in the League Cup. Villa had Gray carried off and never recovered.

Villa also had no reason to remember the FA Cup of 1978-79. In the third round they went to the City Ground, Nottingham, where Forest beat them 2-0 and John Deehan was sent off in another futile incident which cost Villa dearly.

In the First Division, Jimmy Rimmer played another full season as Villa coasted to a respectable place behind the leaders. Full-back John Robson had his contract cancelled in November after it was learned that he was suffering from multiple sclerosis in one of the most tragic

Left: **Ken McNaught joined Villa from Everton from £200,000 in July 1977.** *Right:* **Goalkeeper Jimmy Rimmer signed from Arsenal for £65,000 a month after McNaught was transferred to Villa.**

DIVISION 1 1978-79													
Liverpool	42	19	2	0	51	4	11	6	4	34	12	68
Nottingham F	42	11	10	0	34	10	10	8	3	27	16	60
WBA	42	13	5	3	38	15	11	6	4	34	20	59
Everton	42	12	7	2	32	17	5	10	6	20	23	51
Leeds U	42	11	4	6	41	25	7	10	4	29	27	50
Ipswich T	42	11	4	6	34	21	9	5	7	29	28	49
Arsenal	42	11	8	2	37	18	6	6	9	24	30	48
Aston Villa	42	8	9	4	37	26	7	7	7	22	23	46
Manchester U	42	9	7	5	29	25	6	8	7	31	38	45
Coventry C	42	11	7	3	41	29	3	9	9	17	39	44
Tottenham H	42	7	8	6	19	25	6	7	8	29	36	41
Middlesbrough	42	10	5	6	33	21	5	5	11	24	29	40
Bristol C	42	11	6	4	34	19	4	4	13	13	32	40
Southampton	42	9	10	2	35	20	3	6	12	12	33	40
Manchester C	42	9	5	7	34	28	4	8	9	24	28	39
Norwich C	42	7	10	4	29	19	0	13	8	22	38	37
Bolton W	42	10	5	6	36	28	2	6	13	18	47	35
Wolves	42	10	4	7	26	26	3	4	14	18	42	34
Derby Co	42	8	5	8	25	25	2	6	13	19	46	31
QPR	42	4	9	8	24	33	2	4	15	21	40	25
Birmingham C	42	5	9	7	24	25	1	1	19	13	39	22
Chelsea	42	3	5	13	23	42	2	5	14	21	50	20

Ron Saunders, manager of the year in 1975 and still winning honours for Villa as the new decade dawned.

Colin Gibson slides in as Glenn Hoddle of Tottenham tries to get the ball under control.

Frank Stapleton of Arsenal tries a spectacular overhead kick against Villa at Highbury in February 1980. Villa players are Allan Evans (4) and Ken McNaught (4).

Garry Birtles scores for Nottingham Forest at Villa Park in April 1980. The Villa players in a desperate scramble are Jimmy Rimmer, Brendan Ormsby and Allan Evans.

blows suffered by a professional player in recent years. Villa staged a testimonial match for Robson later on, but it was a sad blow, both to the club and to a very fine player. Robson had made 144 League appearances for Villa (three as a substitute) to add to the 171 (plus one as substitute) he had made for Derby County.

Villa ended the season on an indifferent note when they lost two of their last three games, ending up with a 3-2 win over Manchester City at Maine Road.

In December, they had signed Kenny Swain, Chelsea's talented young midfielder, for £100,000 and youngsters like Colin Gibson, Gary Shaw and Gary Williams also made their first appearances.

Villa fans could look back on the 1979-80 season with great satisfaction, especially as it was to precede even more successful days.

Although their famous club did

Midfielder Des Bremner, who joined Villa in September 1979 for £250,000 from Hibernian. Bremner made 226 appearances for the club.

not take any major honours, Villa finished seventh in the First Division and reached the quarter-finals of the FA Cup before going out to the eventual winners, West Ham United.

Before the season started, Saunders went into the transfer market again to buy midfielder Des Bremner from Hibernian for £250,000 plus young Scots forward Joe Ward, and winger Tony Morley from Burnley for £200,000.

In September 1979, Andy Gray was sold to Wolves for a British record fee of £1,469,000.

Yet Villa's season started quietly

DIVISION 1 1979-80											
	P	W	D	L	F	A	W	D	L	F	A	Pts
Liverpool	42	15	6	0	46	8	10	4	7	35	22	60
Manchester U	42	17	3	1	43	8	7	7	7	22	27	58
Ipswich T	42	14	4	3	43	13	8	5	8	25	26	53
Arsenal	42	8	10	3	24	12	10	6	5	28	24	52
Nottingham F	42	16	4	1	44	11	4	4	13	19	32	48
Wolves	42	9	6	6	29	20	10	3	8	29	27	47
Aston Villa	**42**	**11**	**5**	**5**	**29**	**22**	**5**	**9**	**7**	**22**	**28**	**46**
Southampton	42	14	2	5	53	24	4	7	10	12	29	45
Middlesbrough	42	11	7	3	31	14	5	5	11	19	30	44
WBA	42	9	8	4	37	23	2	11	8	17	27	41
Leeds U	42	10	7	4	30	17	3	7	11	16	33	40
Norwich C	42	10	8	3	38	30	3	6	12	20	36	40
Crystal P	42	9	9	3	26	13	3	7	11	15	37	40
Tottenham H	42	11	5	5	30	22	4	5	12	22	40	40
Coventry C	42	12	2	7	34	24	4	5	12	22	42	39
Brighton & HA	42	8	8	5	25	20	3	7	11	22	37	37
Manchester C	42	8	8	5	28	25	4	5	12	15	41	37
Stoke C	42	9	4	8	27	26	4	6	11	17	32	36
Everton	42	7	7	7	28	25	2	10	9	15	26	35
Bristol C	42	6	6	9	22	30	3	7	11	15	36	31
Derby Co	42	9	4	8	36	29	2	4	15	11	38	30
Bolton W	42	5	11	5	19	21	0	4	17	19	52	25

Aston Villa's FA Youth Cup winning team of 1980. It was the first of a series of honours for the club as the League championship, European Cup and Super Cup followed.

Villa first-team skipper Dennis Mortimer with Robert Hopkins, captain of the FA Youth Cup winning side. Hopkins made only a brief appearance in Villa's senior team before enjoying a career with Birmingham City, Manchester City and West Brom.

enough with a 1-1 draw against doomed-to-be-relegated Bolton Wanderers at Burnden Park. They finished it on the last Saturday of the season with a 4-1 hiding at Anfield, where Liverpool clinched the championship which they had been threatening to take all season.

During the season, Villa gave a first outing to goalkeeper Nigel Spink, a former West Ham junior who had joined Villa from Southern League club Chelmsford City.

Threaded in between the League programme there were some high spots for Aston Villa in the Cup, although it has to be said that Villa's progress to the last eight was at the expense of several lowly teams. In fact, Villa did not play a First Division side in the FA Cup.

The club's first Cup challenge came in late August when they beat Colchester United 2-0 at Layer Road in a second-round first-leg of the Football League Cup. It was a result which gave Villa confidence for the return at Villa Park but it was United who did all the running before reversing the scoreline and leaving Villa severely embarrassed before they scraped through on penalties.

In the next round, Everton managed a goalless draw at Villa Park and in the replay it was obvious from early on that Villa had missed their chance. The Merseysiders won 4-1 with Swain getting the lone Villa goal.

In the FA Cup things went better for Villa. After removing Bristol Rovers 2-1 at Eastville in the third round they faced a difficult away game against Second Division Cambridge United and the relative newcomers to the Football League managed a 1-1 draw before going down 4-1 at Villa Park.

Third Division title hopefuls Blackburn Rovers also proved difficult to dislodge, drawing 1-1 at Ewood Park before Evans squeezed Villa through at home.

And so to West Ham. Villa fans must have felt that this was their year for Wembley. Into the quarter-finals, and without a First Division team played, they came up against Second Division Hammers with every reason to be making travelling arrangements to London on 10 May.

But the only bubbles being blown were by West Ham supporters as they saw their team win 1-0 at Upton Park.

There was the usual boardroom battle in 1979-80 and the usual speculation that Brian Clough would be coming to take over, although as Clough reminded everyone: "Villa already have a manager — and a good one. I hope he's there for years!"

Champions of England — and Europe

IN MAY 1980, Ron Saunders dipped into the transfer market once more to sign Newcastle United striker Peter Withe for club record fee of £500,000. Withe could have joined either Leeds United or Everton instead of Villa, but his was a wise choice, for at the end of the season he was Villa's leading scorer in a team which had just carried off the Football League championship, 71 years after they had last won it.

Withe, of course, was just one of a squad of excellent players and from the very first game of the 1980-81 season, Villa looked like a side determined to do well. They began with two victories, a 2-1 win at Elland Road on the first day of the season and a 1-0 home win over Norwich City on the following Wednesday.

Their first defeat came at Portman Road in early September and was then promptly followed by another,

at home to Everton, but then Villa embarked on an unbeaten 12-match run to the end of November, when they lost 2-1 at Anfield, and by then they were sitting on top of the First Division.

The reverse at Liverpool was immediately followed by a home draw against Arsenal and a defeat at Ayresome Park, but this spell proved only a brief interlude in a successful march towards the title.

Villa's Gary Shaw (left) is challenged by a Norwich defender in the game at Villa Park in August 1980. Shaw scored the only goal of the game.

Another long unbeaten spell of ten matches after Christmas put them within sight of the championship and successive wins over Southampton, Leicester City and West Brom in April left them to fight it out with Ipswich Town.

The Suffolk club had to visit Villa Park the week after Withe's goal had given Villa that win over West Brom, and on 14 April they dented the Midlanders' hopes by winning 2-1.

But after beating Nottingham Forest and Middlesbrough at home and drawing with Stoke City, Villa reached the final day of the 1980-81 season needing to draw at Highbury to make certain of their first League championship for over 70 years.

There were an estimated 20,000 Villa fans in the 57,427 crowd and they were jolted when Arsenal, whose own championship aspirations had only just fizzled out, won 2-0 with goals from Young and McDermott.

On the same day, however, Ipswich lost 2-1 at Ayresome Park — making their final game against Southampton irrelevant to the outcome of the title — and so Villa were champions after all, their defeat at Highbury irrelevant. They finished with 60 points, four ahead of Ipswich and seven ahead of third-placed Arsenal.

Withe had top-scored with 20 League goals and close behind him was Gary Shaw, who scored 18. There was also excellent support up from from Tony Morley with ten.

What was remarkable was Villa's consistency when it came to team selection. They used only 14 players all season, there were seven ever-presents and ten players appeared in at least 36 League games each.

Southampton's Yugoslavian goalkeeper Ivan Katalinic is put under pressure by Ken McNaught and Peter Withe at The Dell in October 1980. Malcolm Waldron is the Saints' left-back. Villa won 2-1.

Gary Shaw is grounded against Ipswich Town at Portman Road in January 1981, when Villa went out of the FA Cup at the first hurdle. The Ipswich players are Franz Thyssen (4) and Russell Osman.

Dave Geddis scores Villa's second in the return game against Southampton at Villa Park in March 1981. Saints' Nick Holmes can only admire his effort. Villa won 2-1.

DIVISION 1 1980-81

	P	W	D	L	F	A	W	D	L	F	A	Pts
Aston Villa	42	16	3	2	40	13	10	5	6	32	27	60
Ipswich T	42	15	4	2	45	14	8	6	7	32	29	56
Arsenal	42	13	8	0	36	17	6	7	8	25	28	53
WBA	42	15	4	2	40	15	5	8	8	20	27	52
Liverpool	42	13	5	3	38	15	4	12	5	24	27	51
Southampton	42	15	4	2	47	22	5	6	10	29	34	50
Nottingham F	42	15	3	3	44	20	4	9	8	18	24	50
Manchester U	42	9	11	1	30	14	6	7	8	21	22	48
Leeds U	42	10	5	6	19	19	7	5	9	20	28	44
Tottenham H	42	9	9	3	44	31	5	6	10	26	37	43
Stoke C	42	8	9	4	31	23	4	9	8	20	37	42
Manchester C	42	10	7	4	35	25	4	4	13	21	34	39
Birmingham C	42	11	5	5	32	23	2	7	12	18	38	38
Middlesbrough	42	14	4	3	38	16	2	1	18	15	45	37
Everton	42	8	6	7	32	25	5	4	12	23	33	36
Coventry C	42	9	6	6	31	30	4	4	13	17	38	36
Sunderland	42	10	4	7	32	19	4	3	14	20	34	35
Wolves	42	11	2	8	26	20	2	7	12	17	35	35
Brighton & HA	42	10	3	8	30	26	4	4	13	24	41	35
Norwich C	42	9	7	5	34	25	4	0	17	15	48	33
Leicester C	42	7	5	9	20	23	6	1	14	20	44	32
Crystal P	42	6	4	11	32	37	0	3	18	15	46	19

Dennis Mortimer
— Villa's Champion Captain

WHEN Dennis Mortimer held aloft the Football League championship trophy in 1981, he became the first Aston Villa captain to do so for over 70 years.

And it was particularly appropriate that Mortimer should be the man to collect that honour, for he had proved a marvellous skipper and a great servant to the club he joined from Coventry City midway through the 1975-76 season.

Born at Liverpool in April 1952, Mortimer played for Kirby Boys before Coventry signed him as an apprentice in July 1967. He became a full-time professional in September 1969 and made his debut as a substitute against West Ham the following month. He was still eligible for the FA Youth Cup and led Coventry to the Final, where they lost a four-match battle to a Tottenham side which included Steve Perryman and Graeme Souness.

Mortimer soon established himself in the first team at Highfield Road and blossomed into an attacking midfielder who was one of the few rays of hope in some otherwise dreary times for Coventry.

His sale to Villa, for £175,000 in December 1975, was especially hurtful to the Sky Blues fans. Mortimer had played in 222 senior games for their club, scoring 12 goals.

On the international scene, Mortimer was probably unlucky never to have won a full cap. He made six appearances for the Under-23 side, scoring twice in a 3-1 win over Holland at Highbury in January 1973, and played three times for the 'B' during his days at Villa Park, skippering that England side on a tour of Australia.

With Villa, Mortimer satisfied his hunger for top honours, for besides the League championship success, he led them to the European Cup a year later and then the European Super Cup, adding all this to a League Cup Final triumph in 1977. There was also an appearance in the 1982 World Club Championship game in Tokyo.

His Villa debut also came against West Ham and although he missed a few games through injury, he finished his first season with 14 League appearances.

The following season he was virtually ever-present and played in all ten games in the League Cup, which Villa won after a three-game Final against Everton.

That was the prelude to a period of sustained success for Villa, who were always high in the table before their title win in 1980-81, when Mortimer was one of seven ever-presents.

In February 1984 he reached a remarkable double milestone, completing 600 appearances in top-class football and 300 with Villa alone. After a seven-match loan spell with Sheffield United in December that year, Mortimer was transferred to Brighton in August 1985. He had made 403 full appearances for Villa (plus one as a substitute) and had scored 36 goals.

Twleves months after joining Brighton, Mortimer returned to the West Midlands to sign for Birmingham City and spent his last season in senior soccer as a Blues player. When he retired, Mortimer had made 718 appearances and scored 52 goals in a wonderful career.

In August 1987, he went into non-League football, as a non-contract player with Alan Buckley's Kidderminster Harriers and later moved to Redditch United, where he was player-manager.

In 1990, Dennis Mortimer was appointed Football in the Community Officer with West Bromwich Albion.

Left: Tony Morley gets in a shot against Ipswich in April 1981, but Villa went down 2-1 to their close rivals. *Right:* Gordon Cowans scores from the penalty spot in the 2-0 win over Forest later the same month.

Left: Allan Evans gets the better of Middlesbrough's David Armstrong at Villa Park in late April 1981, when Villa won 3-0. *Right:* Villa fans at Highbury on the last day of the season.

Arsenal goalkeeper Pat Jennings waits for Peter Withe's effort at Highbury on the last day of the 1980-81 season. The other Gunners' players are Kenny Sansom and Willie Young. Arsenal won 2-0 but Villa still finished champions.

Allan Evans
— Striker Turned Defensive Rock

WHEN Allan Evans was making his way in football in his native Scotland, there was no hint that he would one day become one of the best defenders in the British game. And even when he joined Villa, it still seemed that Evans would make his name by scoring goals rather than stopping them.

Born in the village of Polbeth, near Edinburgh, in October 1956, Evans lived with his family in Malta and Cyprus before returning to schools football. Dunfermline Athletic signed him as an apprentice in December 1972 and he became a full-time professional in October 1973. His debut for the Scottish League Cup could not have been more unfortunate, for Evans broke his leg against Rangers.

He quickly recovered, though, and in his last season with Dunfermline scored 15 goals from centre-forward including hat-tricks against both Clyde and Stranraer. Villa were attracted to the free-scoring youngster and in May 1977 they signed him for £30,000.

Evans continued his goalscoring exploits in his early days at Villa Park, including a remarkable double hat-trick against Sheffield United Reserves in a Central League game in February 1978. That hastened his appearance in the first team and the following month, Evans made his League debut as a striker against Leicester City. His first goal for Villa came against Newcastle United on 8 April that year, on his third League appearance, but it did not herald the start of a prolific scorer career at Villa.

Instead, Evans was switched to defence and began ten magnificent years at the heart of Aston Villa's rearguard. Established in the first team, he went on to share in some of the club's greatest moments, winning a League championship medal and a European Cup winners' medal in successive seasons, as well as playing in the side that lifted the European Super Cup in 1983.

In the League championship season he missed only three games and was absent only once in Villa's European Cup campaign. Perhaps not surprisingly, Evans was also amongst the goals, for even as a defender he never lost his passion for scoring. In the championship-winning season he netted seven times, including two against Sunderland in a 4-0 win at Villa Park, and vital goals in 2-1 wins at St Andrew's and Roker Park.

In March 1982, Evans won the first of four full caps for Scotland when he played in a 2-1 victory over Holland at Hampden Park after the Scots had suffered a glut of injuries. He stayed in the side for the next game, a 1-1 draw in Belfast and was back for the big match against England at Hampden, when the Scots lost their 100th meeting with the Auld Enemy, 1-0.

Evans had sufficiently impressed Jock Stein to be included in the party for the 1982 World Cups in Spain and he played in the opening game, a 5-2 romp over New Zealand. That, though, was his last appearance for his country.

During the 1986-87 season, as Villa plunged into the Second Division, the glory days gone if not forgotten, Evans lost his place in the first team. But when they came straight back as runners-up, he started the last 18 games and was a key figure in the vital run-in.

In 1990 he was finally released by the club after making a total of 461 full appearances, which put him fifth in Villa's all-time list. He also scored 60 goals in all competitions. After a spell in Australia, Evans became assistant to another former Villa player, Brian Little, at Leicester.

League champions 1981. Although losing their last match of the season, Villa can celebrate in the Highbury dressing-room after Ipswich failed in their attempt.

Villa fans cram Birmingham city centre to see Villa receive a civic reception after their great triumph.

The League champions atop an open bus on their progress through Birmingham.

Villa manager Ron Saunders shows off the League championship trophy.

The Aston Villa first-team squad, manager Ron Saunders and coaches pictured with the League championship trophy.

The average League attendance at Villa Park was 33,641 with a biggest home 'gate' of 47,988 for the game

The last link with the past disappears as the remaining offices at Villa Park are demolished in July 1981.

against West Brom. The visit of fellow title contenders, Ipswich, the following week had attracted marginally less, some 47,495.

It was Ipswich who had knocked Villa out of the FA Cup, winning 1-0 at Villa Park in the third round, whilst Villa's League Cup progress was also checked in the third round with an embarrassing defeat at Second Division Cambridge United.

The season also saw the retirement of Brian Little, who did not appear at all during the season and retired through injury in May 1981. Mike Pejic, the £225,000 signing from Stoke City in September 1979, had also played his last game for Villa after being injured in his first season, suffering a leg injury against Liverpool in December 1979.

This was no time for sentiment, though, and Villa, the newly-crowned English champions, now looked forward to fresh challenges in the European Cup for 1981-82.

Their League season began with a 1-0 defeat at home to newly-

promoted Notts County, hardly an auspicious start for the defending League champions, and was followed by a 2-1 defeat at Roker Park. Villa never really recovered from that poor start — they won only one of their first nine League games and had a run of six consecutive draws — and eventually finished 11th in the First Division, a massive 30 points behind champions Liverpool in this, the first season when three points were awarded for a win.

In the FA Cup they were beaten 1-0 at White Hart Lane in the fifth round after knocking out Notts County and Bristol City, and in the League Cup they eliminated Wolves, Leicester City and Wigan Athletic before West Brom won a fifth-round tie 1-0 before a crowd of 35,197 at Villa Park.

But it was to Europe — and to a behind-the-scenes row — that all attentions were focussed as the 1981-82 season ran its course.

In the first round of the European Cup, Villa were drawn against Valur,

Above: Peter Withe scores the first of his two goals against FA Cup holders Tottenham Hotspur in the 2-2 FA Charity Shield draw at Wembley in August 1981. **Below:** Withe puts Spurs goalkeeper Ray Clemence under pressure.

the champions of Iceland, and Donovan (two), Withe (two) and Morley gave them a comfortable 5-0 lead to take into the second leg, which they won 2-0 with goals from Gary Shaw.

In the second round the opposition looked a little more difficult with a tie against Dynamo Berlin. Villa did the hard part by winning 2-1 in Berlin, where Morley scored both their goals, and although the East Germans won 1-0 at Villa Park to level the aggregate scores, it was Villa who went into the quarter-finals on the away goals rule.

By the time Villa faced the Soviet champions, Dynamo Kiev, in March, they were fourth from bottom of the First Division and manager Ron Saunders had resigned after some discord with the board. It was his quietly-spoken assistant, Tony Barton, who took charge on a 'caretaker' basis and Villa went through to the European Cup semi-finals, holding the Soviets to a goalless draw in Kiev and winning the return leg 2-0 with goals from Shaw and McNaught.

On 30 March, Villa began a run of four successive League victories with a 2-1 home win over West Brom, on 1 April Tony Barton's position was made 'permanent', and on 7 April, Villa beat Anderlecht of Belgium 1-0 at Villa Park with a Morley goal. Another goalless draw

Jimmy Rimmer is unable to prevent Ipswich Town scoring the only goal of the game at Villa Park in October 1981.

Tony Morley gets up high to head Villa's second goal at Highbury in March 1982, but the Gunners eventually won 4-3. The goalkeeper is George Wood and the other players are Paul Davis and Chris Whyte.

Aston Villa line up in the Feyenoord Stadium, Rotterdam, before the 1982 European Cup Final.

Tony Barton, took over in a crisis and steered Villa to European glory.

in the away leg was sufficient to send Aston Villa into the 1982 European Cup Final.

What was arguably the biggest game in Villa's history took place on a glorious evening in late May 1982, in the Feyenoord Stadium, Rotterdam, where the superb West German side, Bayren Munich, were the opposition.

After only ten minutes, Villa lost goalkeeper Jimmy Rimmer with a neck injury. Rimmer, who had conceded only two goals in eight European ties that season, was replaced by 23-year-old Nigel Spink, who was appearing in only his second major game.

The Germans dominated play for long periods of the first half but Spink responded magnificently, urged on by 10,000 cheering Villa fans. Dennis Mortimer, too, was in sparkling form, driving Villa forward from midfield, but the real hero of the night was Peter Withe.

Some 22 minutes into the second half, Tony Morley took the ball past Augenthaler and then got it into the middle where Withe, ever the opportunist, prodded it into the net off goalkeeper Muller and a post.

There was no doubt that Villa had often been second-best for long periods of the game, but they had the experience to hold on to that lead and when the final whistle sounded, their fans erupted in a sea of claret and blue favours.

Tony Barton, manager of Aston Villa for only seven weeks, could not hold back the tears.

DIVISION 1 1981-2

	P	W	D	L	F	A	W	D	L	F	A	Pts
Liverpool	42	14	3	4	39	14	12	6	3	41	18	87
Ipswich T	42	17	1	3	47	25	9	4	8	28	28	83
Manchester U	42	12	6	3	27	9	10	6	5	32	20	78
Tottenham H	42	12	4	5	41	26	8	7	6	26	22	71
Arsenal	42	13	5	3	27	15	7	6	8	21	22	71
Swansea C	42	13	3	5	34	16	8	3	10	24	35	69
Southampton	42	15	2	4	49	30	4	7	10	23	37	66
Everton	42	11	7	3	33	21	6	6	9	23	29	64
West Ham U	42	9	10	2	42	29	5	6	10	24	28	58
Manchester C	42	9	7	5	32	23	6	6	9	17	27	58
Aston Villa	42	9	6	6	28	24	6	6	9	27	29	57
Nottingham F	42	7	7	7	19	20	8	5	8	23	28	57
Brighton & HA	42	8	7	6	30	24	5	6	10	13	28	52
Coventry C	42	9	4	8	31	24	4	7	10	25	38	50
Notts Co	42	7	5	8	32	33	5	3	13	29	36	47
Birmingham C	42	8	6	7	29	25	2	8	11	24	36	44
WBA	42	6	6	9	24	25	5	5	11	22	32	44
Stoke C	42	9	2	10	27	28	3	6	12	17	35	44
Sunderland	42	6	5	10	19	26	5	6	10	19	32	44
Leeds U	42	6	11	4	23	20	4	1	16	16	41	42
Wolves	42	8	5	8	19	20	2	5	14	13	43	40
Middlesbrough	42	5	9	7	20	24	3	6	12	14	28	39

Left: Peter Withe scores the only goal of the 1982 European Cup Final. *Right:* Withe celebrates his match-winning strike.

Another view of Withe's moment of triumph as the Villa fans behind the goal go wild.

Manager Tony Barton, goalscorer Peter Withe and skipper Dennis Mortimer with the European Cup.

A smiling Tony Barton with his first-team squad show off the European Cup before the start of the 1982-83 season.

Villa return to Birmingham after their glorious night in Rotterdam.

A brass band leads the Villa team coach through the streets of Birmingham for yet another civic reception.

The Downward Spiral

AFTER their European success, Aston Villa began the 1982-83 season in high spirits. Although their defence of the League championship the previous season had been extremely disappointing, their results had picked up under Tony Barton and there was, indeed, some optimism in the Villa camp when they kicked-off the new campaign against Sunderland at Villa Park.

That optimism was dulled when Sunderland won 3-1 and was then dashed altogether as Villa followed up with a 5-0 defeat at Goodison Park and a 1-0 defeat at The Dell.

Yet from their next four matches, Villa took maximum points, beating both Luton Town and Nottingham Forest 4-1 at home, then winning 1-0 at Maine Road and beating Swansea City 2-0 at Villa Park.

And that was how Villa's season developed, indifferent runs followed by some excellent spells. For instance, four straight wins over November and December, against Brighton, Manchester United, Stoke City and West Ham, were followed by a five-match run from which Villa took only one point.

Their defence of the European Cup had begun with a 3-1 aggregate win over the Turkish side, Besiktas, and a 6-2 aggregate hammering of Dinamo Bucharest, which took Villa into the quarter-finals and a plum tie against Juventus.

The Italians won 2-1 at Villa Park, however, and that was enough, for few away sides prosper in Turin, where Villa duly lost the return leg 3-1.

There was activity both on and off the field in 1982-83. On the transfer scene, Barton sold full-back Kenny Swain to Nottingham Forest in

Above and below: Villa Park is practically empty for the Eurropean Cup game against Besiktas which was played behind closed doors following a UEFA ruling.

Andy Blair joined Villa from Coventry City in August 1981, for £300,000, and helped them win the European Super Cup.

Pour the champagne! Doug Ellis returns to Villa Park in December 1982, following another boardroom reshuffle.

October and in March, reserve-teamer Robert Hopkins was allowed to move to Birmingham City, whilst into Villa Park came the Blues' midfielder Alan Curbishley, for Hopkins plus £100,000.

Behind-the-scenes, there was yet another boardroom shuffle and in December, Doug Ellis returned to Villa Park as chairman, seven years after being succeeded by Sir William Dugdale and three years after losing a boardroom battle which saw him resign as a director.

One familiar playing figure whose Villa Park days were drawing to a close was goalkeeper Jimmy Rimmer. When he was replaced by Nigel Spink following three defeats for Villa around Christmas it brought to an end a remarkable run. In all games since he joined Villa, Rimmer had played in 285 out of 286, missing only a 2-1 defeat at Nottingham Forest in December 1979. Thus, his last 146 appearances had been consecutive.

DIVISION 1 1982-83	P	W	D	L	F	A	W	D	L	F	A	Pts
Liverpool	42	16	4	1	55	16	8	6	7	32	21	82
Watford	42	16	2	3	49	20	6	3	12	25	37	71
Manchester U	42	14	7	0	39	10	5	6	10	17	28	70
Tottenham H	42	15	4	2	50	15	5	5	11	15	35	69
Nottingham F	42	12	5	4	34	18	8	4	9	28	32	69
Aston Villa	**42**	**17**	**2**	**2**	**47**	**15**	**4**	**3**	**14**	**15**	**35**	**68**
Everton	42	13	6	2	43	19	5	4	12	23	29	64
West Ham U	42	13	3	5	41	23	7	1	13	27	39	64
Ipswich T	42	11	3	7	39	23	4	10	7	25	27	58
Arsenal	42	11	6	4	36	19	5	4	12	22	37	58
WBA	42	11	5	5	35	20	4	7	10	16	29	57
Southampton	42	11	5	5	36	22	4	7	10	18	36	57
Stoke C	42	13	4	4	34	21	3	5	13	19	43	57
Norwich C	42	10	6	5	30	18	4	6	11	22	40	54
Notts Co	42	12	4	5	37	25	3	3	15	18	46	52
Sunderland	42	7	10	4	30	22	5	4	12	18	39	50
Birmingham C	42	9	7	5	29	24	3	7	11	11	31	50
Luton T	42	7	7	7	34	33	5	6	10	31	51	49
Coventry C	42	10	5	6	29	17	3	4	14	19	42	48
Manchester C	42	9	5	7	26	23	4	3	14	21	47	47
Swansea C	42	10	4	7	32	29	0	7	14	19	40	41
Brighton & HA	42	8	7	6	25	22	1	6	14	13	46	40

Spink came into a side that was see-sawing about in Division One, but he held his place until the end of the season and Villa finished in sixth place, quite satisfactory considering their poor start to the season and the alarming dip in form towards the end of the year.

Their final position was helped by a 1-1 draw at champions Liverpool

Mark Walters, a former Villa junior who was now making his presence felt in the first team.

Top: **Aston Villa pictured before the start of their World Club Championship match against Penarol in December 1982. Back row (left to right): Jimmy Rimmer, Peter Withe, Gary Williams, Terry Bullivant, Nigel Spink, Ken McNaught, Mark Jones, Dennis Mortimer. Front row: Mark Walters, Colin Gibson, Gordon Cowans, Tony Morley, Des Bremner, Allan Evans, Gary Shaw.** *Bottom (left): Jair (9) beats McNaught's challenge to score. Bottom (right):* **Gary Shaw narrowly fails to connect with a right-wing cross.**

in the penultimate game and a 2-1 win over Arsenal on the last day.

Gary Shaw — the only Birmingham-born player in Villa's League championship winning side — and Peter Withe contributed 33 goals between them, Shaw just edging Withe out of top place, and Gordon Cowans, who was the only ever-present, weighed in with ten.

In the League Cup, now called the Milk Cup, Villa's interest ended at the first hurdle when they were beaten 3-1 on aggregate by Notts County, but in the FA Cup they reached the quarter-finals by beating Northampton Town, Wolves and Watford before losing 2-0 at Highbury to goals by Woodcock and Petrovic.

Before the start of the 1983-84 season, Tony Barton made three signings. In May, midfielder Steve McMahon came from Everton for £300,000 and in June, Barton bought Swindon Town striker Paul Rideout for £250,000 and Orient goalkeeper Mervyn Day for £15,000. McMahon missed only five games, Rideout played in about half the matches, and Day came in for the last 11 games of the season following Spinks' injury sustained in a 3-3 draw at Coventry, when he had to leave the field.

Another Villa player to suffer injury problems was striker Gary Shaw, who had struck up such a wonderful partnership with Peter Withe. Shaw hurt his knee early in the season and that signalled an injury problem which resulted in the goalscorer having six operations in a bid to return to full fitness.

The exciting young winger Mark Walters, a former Birmingham Schools winger, was now beginning

Left: Gordon Cowans scores a penalty at the second attempt against Barcelona in the European Super Cup Final second leg at Villa Park in January 1983. *Right:* Gary Shaw scores Villa's first goal against the Spaniards.

Acting captain Ken McNaught scores a superb headed goal to clinch the Super Cup for Aston Villa.

to make his presence felt and there were debuts this season for midfielder Paul Birch, another local lad, and full-back Tony Dorigo, an Australian-born youngster.

Out of Villa Park went Ken McNaught (to West Brom for £12,000) and Jimmy Rimmer (a free transfer to Swansea City) in August and striker Dave Geddis (to Barnsley for £50,000 in September), whilst in December, Barton sold the crowd-pleasing winger Tony Morley to West Brom for £75,000. Morley continued to enjoy a reasonably

Ken McNaught with the European Super Cup after Villa's 3-1 aggregate win over Barcelona.

successful career with Albion, Preston and Burnley, but his best days were undoubtedly spent as a Villa player.

The real blow to Villa's season, though, happened even before it had started when Gordon Cowans suffered a double-fracture of the right

leg during a tour of Spain. Cowans was out for the entire 1983-84 season.

So Villa began the season without one of their star players and they

Left: **Watford's Nigel Callaghan, later to join Aston Villa, and Colin Gibson in action at Villa Park in February 1983.** *Right:* **Ken McNaught is left stranded by Stoke City's Mark Chamberlain at Villa Park in April 1983.**

Left: **Juventus goalkeeper Dino Zoff and teammate Gaetano Scirea in a tangle with Villa's Andy Blair during the 1983 European Cup quarter-final.** *Right:* **Tony Morley is grounded as Zbigniew Boniek makes progress.**

finished it in tenth place in the First Division, also reaching the semi-finals of the Milk Cup, where they lost 2-1 on aggregate to Everton. There were 42,426 at Villa Park for the second leg but although Rideout pulled a goal back for Villa, they could not close the gap that Everton had opened up at Goodison Park.

In contrast, Villa's FA Cup campaign was soon over. Norwich held them to a 1-1 draw at Villa Park and then won the replay 3-0 at Carrow Road.

In the League there were more moments to forget than to remember. In late October, Villa went down 6-2 at home to Arsenal, for whom Tony Woodcock scored five goals to stir memories of the day that the Gunners' Ted Drake hit all seven at Villa Park before the war. One month

DIVISION 1 1983-84											
	P	W	D	L	F	A	W	D	L	F	A	Pts
Liverpool	42	14	5	2	50	12	8	9	4	23	20	80
Southampton	42	15	4	2	44	17	7	7	7	22	21	77
Nottingham F	42	14	4	3	47	17	8	4	9	29	28	74
Manchester U	42	14	3	4	43	18	6	11	4	28	23	74
QPR	42	14	4	3	37	12	8	3	10	30	25	73
Arsenal	42	10	5	6	41	29	8	4	9	33	31	63
Everton	42	9	9	3	21	12	7	5	9	23	30	62
Tottenham H	42	11	4	6	31	24	6	6	9	33	41	61
West Ham U	42	10	4	7	39	24	7	5	9	21	31	60
Aston Villa	42	14	3	4	34	22	3	6	12	25	39	60
Watford	42	9	7	5	36	31	7	2	12	32	46	57
Ipswich T	42	11	4	6	34	23	4	4	13	21	34	53
Sunderland	42	8	9	4	26	18	5	4	12	16	35	52
Norwich C	42	9	8	4	34	20	3	7	11	14	29	51
Leicester C	42	11	5	5	40	30	2	7	12	25	38	51
Luton T	42	7	5	9	30	33	7	4	10	23	33	51
WBA	42	10	4	7	30	25	4	5	12	18	37	51
Stoke C	42	11	4	6	30	23	2	7	12	14	40	50
Coventry C	42	8	5	8	33	33	5	6	10	24	44	50
Birmingham C	42	7	7	7	19	18	5	5	11	20	32	48
Notts Co	42	6	7	8	31	36	4	4	13	19	36	41
Wolves	42	4	8	9	15	28	2	3	16	12	52	29

after this latest humiliation by Arsenal, Notts County beat Villa 5-2 at Meadow Lane. To plug their defence, Barton signed the Brighton centre-half Steve Foster in March, when he joined Villa for £150,000

plus former apprentice Mark Jones. Foster, though, was to have only a brief career at Villa Park, making only 17 League appearances.

Peter Withe ended the season as leading scorer with 16 League goals, well ahead of his nearest rival, Mark Walters, who had eight.

Although memories of that great night of European triumph were still quite fresh in supporters' minds, and despite finishing in the top half of the table and enjoying relative success in domestic Cup competitions, there was no clear indication that the club was heading anywhere but in the wrong direction. And in June 1984, manager Tony Barton paid the price when he was sacked.

Barton was replaced by Graham Turner, the young Shrewsbury Town manager who had apparently

A bagful of goals. Gary Shaw and Peter Withe, Villa's strikers who between them netted 170 for the club.

Peter Withe greets British supporters as bemused Russians look on. Villa drew 2-2 with Spartak Moscow in the first leg of the 1983-84 UEFA Cup.

Tony Morley, ended his Villa career with a £75,000 move to West Brom in December 1983.

achieved something of a soccer miracle by keeping the Shrews in Division Two, despite small attendance and a consequent lack of money to spend on buying players.

Turner made one signing for Villa in his first season in charge, buying the French international winger, Didier Six, from Mulhouse. Six, the first Frenchman to play in Division One, was an interesting character, who had scored 163 goals in 421 appearances for his previous clubs which included Valencia, Lens, Marseilles, RFC Bruges, Strasbourg and Vfb Stuttgart, as well as appearing in the final stages of two World Cups and running his own TV programme in Lille. But he could not settle in the English Midlands and made only 18 appearances (four as

a substitute) before ending his career with Metz, who he joined in June 1985.

One plus for Turner was that Gordon Cowans had recovered from his broken leg and was ready to take his place in the side for the opening game, a 1-0 win over Coventry City at Villa Park where Des Bremner scored the goal. The veteran Bremner was soon on his way, however, being transferred to Birmingham City for £25,000 in September, after making 227 senior appearances for Villa.

Several other players left Villa Park this season as Turner set in motion something of a clear-out. In August, Andy Blair moved to Sheffield Wednesday for £60,000; Steve Foster was sold to Luton in November for £70,000; Alan Curbishley was given a free transfer and moved to Charlton Athletic in December 1984; and the same month, Dennis Mortimer was loaned to Sheffield United and never played again for Villa before moving permanently to Brighton before the start of the following season. In February 1985, Mervyn Day resurrected his career with a move to Leeds United for £30,000.

Villa followed up their opening-day success with 3-1 win at Stoke, but then followed a 3-0 defeat at Newcastle and 5-0 Villa Park hammering at the hands of Nottingham Forest, for whom Trevor Christie scored a hat-trick.

Manager Graham Turner, who began something of a clear-out of players at Villa Park in 1984.

By the end of the season, Turner had managed to take Villa to tenth place — identical to the previous

DIVISION 1 1984-85											
	P	W	D	L	F	A	W	D	L	F	A	Pts
Everton	42	16	3	2	58	17	12	3	6	30	26	90
Liverpool	42	12	4	5	36	19	10	7	4	32	16	77
Tottenham H	42	11	3	7	46	31	12	5	4	32	20	77
Manchester U	42	13	6	2	47	13	9	4	8	30	34	76
Southampton	42	13	4	4	29	18	6	7	8	27	29	68
Chelsea	42	13	3	5	38	20	5	9	7	25	28	66
Arsenal	42	14	5	2	37	14	5	4	12	24	35	66
Sheffield W	42	12	7	2	39	21	5	7	9	19	24	65
Nottingham F	42	13	4	4	35	18	6	3	12	21	30	64
Aston Villa	42	10	7	4	34	20	5	4	12	26	40	56
Watford	42	10	5	6	48	30	4	8	9	33	41	55
WBA	42	11	4	6	36	23	5	3	13	22	39	55
Luton T	42	12	5	4	40	22	3	4	14	17	39	54
Newcastle U	42	11	4	6	33	26	2	9	10	22	44	52
Leicester C	42	10	4	7	39	25	5	2	14	26	48	51
West Ham U	42	7	8	6	27	23	6	4	11	24	45	51
Ipswich T	42	8	7	6	27	20	5	4	12	19	37	50
Coventry C	42	11	3	7	29	22	4	2	15	18	42	50
QPR	42	11	6	4	41	30	2	5	14	12	42	50
Norwich C	42	9	6	6	28	24	4	4	13	18	40	49
Sunderland	42	7	6	8	20	26	3	4	14	20	36	40
Stoke C	42	3	3	15	18	41	0	5	16	6	50	17

Gordon Cowans
— Villa's Midfield Artist

THERE were many stars when Aston Villa lifted the League championship and then the European Cup in the early 1980s. That Villa team was one of the finest in the club's history, from a rearguard that boasted the likes of Jimmy Rimmer, Ken McNaught, Allan Evans, Gary Williams, Colin Gibson and Kenny Swain to the strike force of Peter Withe, Gary Shaw and Tony Morley.

But it was perhaps in midfield where Villa held the key to their remarkable success, where Gordon Cowans, Des Bremner and Dennis Mortimer orchestrated the show week after week. And Cowans, in particular, was a player to catch the eye, a brilliant midfielder, so skilful and so enterprising in all he did. More than that even, Cowans recovered from a serious injury and, after a three-year break in Italy, returned to Villa Park and continued to serve the club well as yet another new decade dawned.

Born in County Durham in October 1958, Cowans first joined Villa as an apprentice in July 1974, turning full-time professional two years later. He had already broken into League football, making his debut as a substitute against Manchester City at Maine Road in a 2-1 defeat on 7 February 1976.

He established himself in the first team during the latter half of the 1976-77 season, so by the time Villa reached the League Cup Final against Everton, Cowans was in the side and played a big part in the extra-time replay victory at Old Trafford.

Cowans had already gained international recognition, playing for England Youth in a Monaco international tournament in 1976, and the Under-21s. In 1980-81, he was elevated to 'B' team status in what proved to be a memorable season. Villa's team was so settled and Cowans was one of the ever-presents, wearing the number-ten shirt all season and scoring five goals, four of them from the penalty spot.

The following year, when Villa were crowned as European champions, Cowans played in every game and, indeed, in the four seasons from 1979-80 to 1982-83 he did not miss a League or Cup game for Villa. In February 1983, he gained the first of nine full caps, when he lined up against Wales at Wembley.

Tragedy, though was just around the corner and in August 1983, playing in a pre-season game against FC America in Zarragoza, Spain, Cowans suffered a double fracture of his right leg. His remarkable run had come to an end and he missed a whole season before resuming his place on the opening day of 1984-85.

At the end of the season he was transferred to Bari, along with Paul Rideout, for £850,000, and spent three years in Italy — suffering another broken leg — before returning to Villa Park for £250,000 in July 1988. Villa had just returned to to the First Division and the following season, when they finished runners-up, Cowans missed only four games.

He took his overall appearances tally to over 500 before Kenny Dalglish paid £250,000 to take him to Blackburn in November 1991 and Cowans helped Rovers into the new FA Premier League via the play-offs.

With 500 games, Gordon Cowans stands third in the list of overall Villa appearances, behind Charlie Aitken (660) and Billy Walker (531). In the League alone, he played 403 times and altogether scored 59 goals.

Cowans was not the driving force behind that great Villa midfield on the early '80s — Dennis Mortimer was the real dynamo of that mdifield — but he supplied a great deal of imagination and he was so skilful. He was also one of the great servants in Aston Villa's history.

Action from the 1-0 defeat at the hands of Tottenham Hotspur in September 1984.

Steve McMahon forces his way past Leicester City's Kevin McDonald at Filbert Street in October 1984. Villa were hammered 5-0.

Steve McMahon, joined Villa from Everton and was later transferred to Liverpool after 91 appearances for the Midlanders.

season — and they went out of the Cups in the early stages, beaten 3-0 at Anfield in the third round of the FA Cup and 1-0 at Loftus Road in the second round of the Milk Cup after an aggregate win over Scunthorpe United.

Paul Rideout finished as Villa's leading League scorer with 14 goals — which included a hat-trick against Newcastle at Villa Park just before Christmas — followed by Peter Withe with 12 and Mark Walters with ten. The average attendance for League matches at Villa Park in 1984-85 had slumped dramatically, however, with a figure of 18,318. In the championship winning season it had been 33,641.

In June 1985, Aston Villa lost two of their biggest assets when Gordon Cowans and Paul Rideout moved to the Italian club, Bari, for a joint fee

DIVISION 1 1985-86											
	P	W	D	L	F	A	W	D	L	F	A	Pts
Liverpool	42	16	4	1	58	14	10	6	5	31	23	88
Everton	42	16	3	2	54	18	10	5	6	33	23	86
West Ham U	42	17	2	2	48	16	9	4	8	26	24	84
Manchester U	42	12	5	4	35	12	10	5	6	35	24	76
Sheffield W	42	13	6	2	36	23	8	4	9	27	31	73
Chelsea	42	12	4	5	32	27	8	7	6	25	29	71
Arsenal	42	13	5	3	29	15	7	4	10	20	32	69
Nottingham F	42	11	5	5	38	25	8	6	7	31	28	68
Luton T	42	12	6	3	37	15	6	6	9	24	29	66
Tottenham H	42	12	2	7	47	25	7	6	8	27	27	65
Newcastle U	42	12	5	4	46	31	5	7	9	21	41	63
Watford	42	11	6	4	40	22	5	5	11	29	40	59
QPR	42	12	3	6	33	20	3	4	14	20	44	52
Southampton	42	10	6	5	32	18	2	4	15	19	44	46
Manchester C	42	7	7	7	25	26	4	5	12	18	31	45
Aston Villa	42	7	6	8	27	28	3	8	10	24	39	44
Coventry C	42	6	5	10	31	35	5	5	11	17	36	43
Oxford U	42	7	7	7	34	27	3	5	13	28	53	42
Leicester C	42	7	8	6	35	35	3	4	14	19	41	42
Ipswich T	42	8	5	8	20	24	3	3	15	12	31	41
Birmingham C	42	5	2	14	13	25	3	3	15	17	48	29
WBA	42	3	8	10	21	36	1	4	16	14	53	24

of about £850,000, but the following month an old favourite returned when Andy Gray rejoined the club from Everton for £150,000.

Graham Turner was now more active in the transfer market and in

August he signed Steve Hodge, the Nottingham Forest midfielder, for £450,000. In September, striker Simon Stainrod came from Sheffield Wednesday for £250,000 and in December, Villa signed central defender Paul Elliott from Luton Town for £450,000. In the new year, Andy Blair and Steve Hunt returned to Villa Park, Hunt after a nine-year absence.

The Blair transfers cost Villa some big money. They had originally bought him from Coventry City for £300,000 and sold him to Sheffield Wednesday for £60,000 before buying him back from the Owls for £100,000. After a loan period with Northampton, Blair drifted into non-League football with Kidderminster Harriers, so his moves in and out of Villa Park hardly helped to balance the books.

Hunt had originally come to Villa from junior football before they sold him to Coventry for £40,000. He returned to the club via West Brom

Right: **Paul Rideout, moved to Bari with Gordon Cowans in July 1985.**

Steve Hodge, signed from Forest for £450,000 in August 1985.

for £90,000 plus former England youth player, Darren Bradley.

Besides the Cowans-Rideout transfer to Italy, Turner helped pay for some of his new acquisitions by selling Steve McMahon to Liverpool for £350,000 in September 1985, Colin Gibson to Manchester United for £275,000 in November and defender Brenden Ormsby, a former Villa apprentice, to Leeds United for £65,000 in February 1986.

Villa began the season badly, losing 4-0 at Old Trafford on the opening day, and they did not win a game until their fifth match, when they beat Luton Town 3-1 at Villa Park.

It was, indeed, a poor season. Twice Villa lost four matches on the trot and they eventually finished in 16th place in a bad year for the West Midlands as West Brom and Bir-

mingham City were relegated from Division One. Joint leading scorers were Walters and Stainrod with ten goals each and the average League attendance had slumped still further to 15,270.

Yet Villa were near to a Wembley appearance in 1985-86, when they reached the semi-finals of the Milk Cup. It was a long haul to get that far, for after beating Exeter City on

aggregate in the second round, and then dismissing Leeds, Villa had to battle through replays against West Brom and Arsenal before meeting Oxford United over two legs in the semi-final.

Birch and Stainrod earned them a 2-2 draw at Villa Park, but at the Manor Ground, Oxford took control and went through 2-1, Walters scoring for Villa.

Nigel Spink, the former West Ham schoolboy player who established himself with Villa and won an England cap against Australia in 1982-83.

The 1986-87 campaign was make or break time for Graham Turner and in an attempt to improve the club's fortunes he made pre-season signings in defender Martin Keown (from Arsenal for £200,000), striker Garry Thompson (from Sheffield Wednesday for £400,000) and defender or midfielder Neale Cooper (from Aberdeen for £300,000). Cooper was injured for most of his time at Villa Park and after making only 22 senior appearances, he returned to Scotland in the summer of 1988 and went on to win Premier League honours with Rangers in his first season at Ibrox.

The new blood could not help Villa's bid to stay in the First Division, however. They lost their opening game of the season, 3-0 at home to Tottenham Hotspur, and managed only one victory in their first eight games.

Turner could obviously not halt the slide and in September, with Villa already in the relegation zone, he was replaced by Billy McNeill, the former Celtic and Scotland star who left struggling Manchester City to try to do at Villa Park what he could not manage at Maine Road. Indeed, by the end of the season it was City who accompanied Villa (and Leicester City) into Division Two.

In December, McNeill sold Steve Hodge to Tottenham for £650,000 and two months later made his only big signing for Villa when he paid Everton some £300,000 for striker Warren Aspinall, who, as it turned out, was to be a key member of Villa's team which won back their First Division place.

In the Cups, Villa were knocked out by Chelsea in the third round of the FA Cup, after a replay, and by Southampton in the fourth round of the Littlewoods Cup, the League Cup's latest guise.

But all this was a sideshow to the main event, the battle against relegation. Villa rose only as high as 16th all season and had a dreadful run-in — only five points from their last eight matches and three consecutive defeats to end the season — to finish bottom of the table, three points behind Manchester City and six behind Leicester.

That goals were hard to come by was illustrated by the fact that three players — Evans, Stainrod and Thompson — shared the leading scorer's spot, with six goals apiece.

Inevitably, Aston Villa were looking for their 13th manager since World War Two.

DIVISION 1 1986-87	P	W	D	L	F	A	W	D	L	F	A	Pts
Everton	42	16	4	1	49	11	10	4	7	27	20	86
Liverpool	42	15	3	3	43	16	8	5	8	29	26	77
Tottenham H	42	14	3	4	40	14	7	5	9	28	29	71
Arsenal	42	12	5	4	31	12	8	5	8	27	23	70
Norwich C	42	9	10	2	27	20	8	7	6	26	31	68
Wimbledon	42	11	5	5	32	22	8	4	9	25	28	66
Luton T	42	14	5	2	29	13	4	7	10	18	32	66
Nottingham F	42	12	8	1	36	14	6	3	12	28	37	65
Watford	42	12	5	4	38	20	6	4	11	29	34	63
Coventry C	42	14	4	3	35	17	3	8	10	15	28	63
Manchester U	42	13	3	5	38	18	1	11	9	14	27	56
Southampton	42	11	5	5	44	24	3	5	13	25	44	52
Sheffield W	42	9	7	5	39	24	4	6	11	19	35	52
Chelsea	42	8	6	7	30	30	5	7	9	23	34	52
West Ham U	42	10	4	7	33	28	4	6	11	19	39	52
QPR	42	9	7	5	31	27	4	4	13	17	37	50
Newcastle U	42	10	4	7	33	29	2	7	12	14	36	47
Oxford U	42	8	8	5	30	25	3	5	13	14	44	46
Charlton A	42	7	7	7	26	22	4	4	13	19	33	44
Leicester C	42	9	7	5	39	24	2	2	17	15	52	42
Manchester C	42	8	6	7	28	24	0	9	12	8	33	39
Aston Villa	42	7	7	7	25	25	1	5	15	20	54	36

Taylor Made for Division One

STARTING their first season in the Second Division since 1975, Villa began the 1987-88 season with another new manager. Graham Taylor, the man who had won national fame by steering Elton John's Watford into Division One, took over at Villa Park and his first season was one of the most dramatic in the club's history, culminating in a nail-biting finale.

Taylor wasted no time in strengthening his squad. In came Wimbledon right-back Kevin Gage for £110,000, Steve Sims, a defender from Taylor's previous club, Watford, at a cost of £50,000, striker Alan McInally from Celtic for £225,000, and midfielder David Hunt, a free-transfer signing from Notts County.

On the way out of Villa Park were Gary Williams (to Leeds United for £230,000), Paul Elliott (to the Italian club, Pisa, for £400,000) and Tony Dorigo (to Chelsea for £475,000).

Yet Villa, under their new manager, had a poor start to the season, winning only once in their first seven games, a 2-0 victory at Leicester on 5 September. Some of the early setbacks were particularly painful — a 2-0 home defeat by arch-rivals Birmingham City and then a 1-0 home defeat by Middlesbrough, who were managed by their former player, Bruce Rioch.

By the middle of September, though, Villa scored a comforting 2-0 win at The Hawthorns and that set them up for a splendid run in which they lost only once — and that a 2-1 defeat against Millwall, the eventual champions — in 25 games to go shooting up the table despite continued indifferent home form.

At Villa Park they did not manage a win until the eighth League game of the season there and altogether they lost six times at home and drew

Graham Taylor, the former Watford boss who took over at Villa before the start of the 1987-88 season.

another seven. Away from home it was a different story. They lost only once in 15 trips up to the end of January and were beaten only four times on their travels all told, with only four games ending in draws. So they took 34 points from matches at Villa Park and 44 from their away games. It was a truly remarkable record.

In the Cups, Villa lost 2-0 at home

to Liverpool in the fourth round of the FA Cup before a bumper attendance of 46,324, and they went out of the Littlewoods Cup when Sheffield Wednesday won 2-1 at Villa Park in the fourth round.

This was all incidental, of course, to the main aim of a quick return to the First Division and as the season unfolded there was more activity on the transfer market.

Villa's David Hunt tries a shot against Leicester City at Filbert Street in September 1987.

A brave header by Garry Thompson finds the net against Birmingham City at St Andrew's in December 1987.

David Platt heads the only goal of the vital game against Bradford City in May 1988.

In September 1987, Taylor bought Mark Lillis, a forward or midfielder from Derby County, for £130,000. In October he sold veteran striker Andy Gray to West Brom for £25,000 and the following month signed another Andy Gray, this time the Crystal Palace striker for £150,000. If that wasn't confusing enough, Villa then signed Stuart Gray, a midfielder from Barnsley for £150,000.

In December, Simon Stainrod moved to Stoke City for £90,000 but the big transfer news that month concerned the exciting Mark Walters, who became the first black player to join Rangers when he was transferred to the Scottish Premier Division club for £600,000. Earlier in the season, Walters had been sent off against Shrewsbury Town.

The final signing of a busy season came in February when Villa paid Crewe Alexandra £200,000 for their hugely talented midfielder, David Platt.

It was 14 February before Villa lost their second away game of the season when fellow promotion contenders, Middlesbrough, beat them 2-1 at Ayresome Park. A crowd of 16,957 saw Tony Daley, a local Birmingham youngster who was developing into a devastatingly fast winger, give Villa the lead but 'Boro fought back with goals from Kernaghan and Mowbray. The Sunday afternoon game was the first Second Division match to be shown live on television.

The following week, Villa's promotion hopes suffered another setback when they went down 3-2 at Ewood Park to another promotion-chasing team in Blackburn Rovers.

Seven days on and Villa's drive to the top flight began to take shape again with a magnificent 5-2 victory over Plymouth Argyle at Villa Park.

A 2-1 win over Bournemouth followed, but there were still plenty of Easter jitters ahead and from 12 March to 9 April, Villa collected only four points out of a possible 18 and were knocked off the top of the table.

Again, though, Villa picked up the pieces and with two games to play, Millwall were already up, leaving Villa, Middlesbrough, Bradford City and Blackburn Rovers scrapping it out for the remaining automatic

DIVISION 2 1987-88											
	P	W	D	L	F	A	W	D	L	F	A	Pts
Millwall	44	15	3	4	45	23	10	4	8	27	29	82
Aston Villa	44	9	7	6	31	21	13	5	4	37	20	78
Middlesbrough	44	15	4	3	44	16	7	8	7	19	20	78
Bradford C	44	14	3	5	49	26	8	8	6	25	28	77
Blackburn R	44	12	8	2	38	22	9	6	7	30	30	77
Crystal P	44	16	3	3	50	21	6	6	10	36	38	75
Leeds U	44	14	4	4	37	18	5	8	9	24	33	69
Ipswich T	44	14	3	5	38	17	5	6	11	23	35	66
Manchester C	44	11	4	7	50	28	8	4	10	30	32	65
Oldham A	44	13	4	5	43	27	5	7	10	29	37	65
Stoke C	44	12	6	4	34	22	5	5	12	16	35	62
Swindon T	44	10	7	5	43	25	6	4	12	30	35	59
Leicester C	44	12	5	5	35	20	4	6	12	27	41	59
Barnsley	44	11	4	7	42	32	4	8	10	19	30	57
Hull C	44	10	8	4	32	22	4	7	11	22	38	57
Plymouth A	44	12	4	6	44	26	4	4	14	21	41	56
Bournemouth	44	7	7	8	36	30	6	3	13	20	38	49
Shrewsbury T	44	7	8	7	23	22	4	8	10	19	32	49
Birmingham C	44	7	9	6	20	24	4	6	12	21	42	48
WBA	44	8	7	7	29	26	4	4	14	21	43	47
Sheffield U	44	8	6	8	27	28	5	1	16	18	46	46
Reading	44	5	7	10	20	25	5	5	12	24	45	42
Huddersfield T	44	4	6	12	20	38	2	4	16	21	62	28

promotion place.

Villa's penultimate match, and their last home game, was against Bradford City and they went into it without key players Martin Keown and Paul Birch, who were both injured. It was vital that Villa took all three points from the Valley Parade club and the biggest Second Division attendance of the season, some 36,423 who included an estimated 6,000 Bradford fans, saw the vital goal scored by David Platt in the 23rd minute.

Celebrations in the Villa dressing-room at Swindon on the last day of the 1987-88 season after the Midlanders regained their First Division place as runners-up to Millwall.

Kevin Gage put over a perfect centre and there was Platt, running in to head past City goalkeeper Paul Tomlinson. The noise was deafening as the Villa fans saluted a magnificent goal.

At half-time, Villa learned that their fellow promotion rivals, Middlesbrough, were winning at Barnsley, whilst Blackburn Rovers were being held at home by lowly Reading.

It set up a tense second half but with Nigel Spink and Alan McInally in superb form, Villa held on to take the precious points. In the other games Middlesbrough had won 3-0 at Oakwell and Blackburn had drawn 1-1 at Ewood Park.

On the last Saturday of the season, Villa travelled to Swindon Town, Middlesbrough entertained Leicester City and Bradford City were at home to Ipswich Town. Middlesbrough needed a draw to go up, Bradford City had to win to stand any chance, whilst Villa needed to at least avoid defeat and then rely on their rival slipping up.

Villa held on for a goalless draw

and when news came through that both Middlesbrough and Bradford City had failed, they knew they were up. Although level on points with Middlesbrough — they had 78 each, Villa snatched the runners-up spot because they has scored more goals (68 to 'Boro's 63).

It was one of the closest promotion battles in the history of the Football League and Villa could look back to a club record 13 away wins for their success.

Two players, Nigel Spink and Kevin Gage, were ever-presents, Bernie Gallacher missed only one game and Martin Keown two. Warren Aspinall was joint top scorer with 11 League goals, the same number as Garry Thompson, who had played only since November because of injury. Mark Walters got seven in the League before his move to Rangers.

Before Villa resumed their place in the First Division, Graham Taylor again went into the transfer market. In June 1988 he bought full-back Chris Price (from Blackburn Rovers for £125,000) and defender Derek

Mountfield (from Everton for £450,000). And in July, Gordon Cowans returned from Bari for £650,000. Warren Aspinall, meanwhile, was sold to Portsmouth for £315,000. The other major figure to leave was Garry Thompson, who was transferred to Watford for £150,000 in October.

Although Villa did not taste defeat until their sixth game of the season, five of those games were drawn and they sailed uncomfortably close to relegation in 1988-89.

There was some early cheer when Birmingham City were beaten 2-0 and 5-0 in the Littlewoods Cup and 6-0 in the Simod Cup — a young apprentice called Ian Olney scored on his debut in the second leg of the Littlewoods tie against the Blues — but altogether this was a worrying campaign.

By the turn of the year, Villa were 13th in the table and defeat at Anfield on 3 January dropped them another three places. Morale was not improved when they lost to bogey side, Wimbledon, in the fourth round of the FA Cup and to West Ham in

Kevin Gage cannot prevent Peter Beardsley getting in his shot in the game against Liverpool at Villa Park in September 1988.

Tony Daley scores a superb goal against Everton at Villa Park in October 1988.

the quarter-finals of the Littlewoods Cup.

A run of eight games without a victory over February and March caused further concern and during this time there were further signings. Derby winger Nigel Callaghan, who had played under Taylor at Watford, came for £650,000 and Villa spent a similar amount on Bradford City's tall striker, Ian Ormondroyd.

Fortunately for Villa, relegation-threatened Newcastle, Middlesbrough and West Ham never improved and at the death, Villa finished in 17th place in a First Division now comprising only 20 clubs. Three went down and Villa ended only one point from the drop.

Leading scorer was Alan McInally with 14 League goals and David Platt, who had played so well all season, was the one ever-present.

Graham Taylor was to spend one more season at Villa Park before being called to higher things — and what a season it turned out to be.

Before 1989-90 got under way, Taylor was again busying himself in the transfer market.

David Platt scores Villa's second goal against Everton early in the 1988-89 season.

DIVISION 1 1988-89	P	W	D	L	F	A	W	D	L	F	A	Pts
Arsenal	38	10	6	3	35	19	12	4	3	38	17	76
Liverpool	38	11	5	3	33	11	11	5	3	32	17	76
Nottingham F	38	8	7	4	31	16	9	6	4	33	27	64
Norwich C	38	8	7	4	23	20	9	4	6	25	25	62
Derby Co	38	9	3	7	23	18	8	4	7	17	20	58
Tottenham H	38	8	6	5	31	24	7	6	6	29	22	57
Coventry C	38	9	4	6	28	23	5	9	5	19	19	55
Everton	38	10	7	2	33	18	4	5	10	17	27	54
QPR	38	9	5	5	23	16	5	6	8	20	21	53
Millwall	38	10	3	6	27	21	4	8	7	20	31	53
Manchester U	38	10	5	4	27	13	3	7	9	18	22	51
Wimbledon	38	10	3	6	30	19	4	6	9	20	27	51
Southampton	38	6	7	6	25	26	4	8	7	27	40	45
Charlton A	38	6	7	6	25	24	4	5	10	19	34	42
Sheffield W	38	6	6	7	21	25	4	6	9	13	26	42
Luton T	38	8	6	5	32	21	2	5	12	10	31	41
Aston Villa	**38**	**7**	**6**	**6**	**25**	**22**	**2**	**7**	**10**	**20**	**34**	**40**
Middlesbrough	38	6	7	6	28	30	3	5	11	16	31	39
West Ham U	38	3	6	10	19	30	7	2	10	18	32	38
Newcastle U	38	3	6	10	19	28	4	4	11	13	35	31

Kent Nielsen, the Danish centre-back from Brondby came in July 1989 for £500,000 and also in July, Taylor signed Manchester United's brave central defender or midfielder Paul McGrath, a Republic of Ireland international, for £450,000. McGrath, in particular, would have a big influence on Villa's bid for major honours.

Taylor was also raising money and in July he sold Alan McInally to Bayern Munich for £1 million, whilst Martin Keown moved to Everton for £750,000. In August, Andy Gray

Gordon Cowans, pictured on the day he made his 300th appearance for Aston Villa, at Coventry in November 1988.

Alan McInally is happy at Upton Park in September 1988, after scoring one of his two goals in the 2-2 draw. Villa's 'other' Andy Gray gives him a hug.

There is a bit of a fracas at the City Ground in January 1989, when Villa lost 4-0. Players (left to right) are Gordon Cowans, Nigel Clough, Stuart Pearce, Andy Gray, Kevin Gage and Terry Wilson.

In May 1989, Villa lost 2-1 at Derby. Here Dean Saunders, who scored the Rams' first goal and later to join Villa via Liverpool, challenges Steve Sims.

Top left: Garry Thompson, moved to Watford in October 1988 for £150,000. *Top right:* Kent Nielsen came from Brondby for £500,000 in July 1989. *Bottom left:* Nigel Callaghan, signed from Derby County for £650,000 in February 1989. *Bottom right:* Paul McGrath came from Manchester United for £450,000 in July 1989.

in the Littlewoods Cup did Villa disappoint. They chased Liverpool all the way in the First Division to finish runners-up, albeit nine points adrift of the champions, and reached the quarter-finals of the FA Cup and the Area Final of the Zenith Data Systems Cup, the latest title for the old Full Members' Cup. In the ZDS they eventually lost to Middlesbrough.

However, perhaps most pleasing of all was the emergence of several youngsters including Tony Daley, Dwight Yorke and Ian Olney. And David Platt was now elevated to star status with 19 goals in the League adding to his worth as a fine midfielder.

Villa had a modest enough start to the season, drawing their first three games and having to wait for their fifth to record a victory, when Olney's two goals defeated Tottenham.

There were two significant spells when Villa won five and seven games respectively on the trot. Everton were hammered 6-2 at Villa Park on Guy Fawkes Day and, altogether, these were great days for Villa fans. Even an early departure from the Littlewoods Cup, in a third-round replay at Upton Park, was more than compensated for by a run to the sixth round of the FA Cup, although once there, the 3-0 defeat at Boundary Park took some swallowing.

In March 1990, Taylor paid £1.5 million for the Millwall striker Tony Cascarino, who scored just twice in his ten League games to the end of the season. Both his goals came in 3-3 draws, at home to Norwich and at Goodison, right at the end of the season. Cascarino would be pleased enough with that, though, because his previous club were

			DIVISION 1		1989-90						
	P	W	D	L	F	A	W	D	L	F	A	Pts
Liverpool	38	13	5	1	38	15	10	5	4	40	22	79
Aston Villa	38	13	3	3	36	20	8	4	7	21	18	70
Tottenham H	38	12	1	6	35	24	7	5	7	24	23	63
Arsenal	38	14	3	2	38	11	4	5	10	16	27	62
Chelsea	38	8	7	4	31	24	8	5	6	27	26	60
Everton	38	14	3	2	40	16	3	5	11	17	30	59
Southampton	38	10	5	4	40	27	5	5	9	31	36	55
Wimbledon	38	5	8	6	22	23	8	8	3	25	17	55
Nottingham F	38	9	4	6	31	21	6	5	8	24	26	54
Norwich C	38	7	10	2	24	14	6	4	9	20	28	53
QPR	38	9	4	6	27	22	4	7	8	18	22	50
Coventry C	38	11	2	6	24	25	3	5	11	15	34	49
Manchester U	38	8	6	5	26	14	5	3	11	20	33	48
Manchester C	38	9	4	6	26	21	3	8	8	17	31	48
Crystal P	38	8	7	4	27	23	5	2	12	15	43	48
Derby Co	38	9	1	9	29	21	4	6	9	14	19	46
Luton T	38	8	8	3	24	18	2	5	12	19	39	43
Sheffield W	38	8	6	5	21	17	3	4	12	14	34	43
Charlton A	38	4	6	9	18	25	3	3	13	13	32	30
Millwall	38	4	6	9	23	25	1	5	13	16	40	26

moved back to Crystal Palace and Allan Evans went to Leicester City on a free transfer. A month later, Mark Lillis dropped down to the

Fourth Division with Scunthorpe, who paid £40,000 for his signature.

All was set, then, for a major assault on all the honours and only

Jubilant Tony Daley after a dazzling run and goal against West Bromwich Albion in the 1989-90 FA Cup. Villa won 2-0 but went out 3-0 to Oldham in the quarter-finals.

relegated after finishing bottom of the table.

Platt's performances had put him in the £2 million bracket at least and that estimate was to double by the time he returned from the World Cup finals in Italy, where he had been one of the stars of England's progress to the semi-finals.

Italia 90 also saw the end of Bobby Robson's term as England manager and it was one of the worst-kept secrets in football that Villa's Graham Taylor would succeed him. So for 1990-91, the club were under the managership of yet another new face.

It was an imaginative appointment, that of Jozef Venglos, a 54-year-old Czechoslovakian who had managed the Australian national team, Slovan Bratislava, the Czech national side, Sporting Lisbon, Kuala Lumpur, the Malaysian national team and then went back to manage Czechoslovakia, who he took to a 1990 World Cup quarter-final, where they were beaten 1-0 by West Germany, the eventual winners.

Venglos could speak four languages and graduated as a PhD from university in Bratsilava. The Football League had never seen a manager quite like him.

Perhaps not unnaturally, Venglos decided to work with the players he had inherited and, unlike the transfer deals of previous seasons, it was well into the new year before Villa were active in the market.

Runners-up spot in the First Division the previous season had given Villa a place in the UEFA Cup and the prospect of a return of European football caused quite a stir around Villa Park.

In the first round of the UEFA

Peter Shilton looks back as Ian Ormondroyd scores the only goal of the game against Derby County at Villa Park in March 1990. Ormondroyd later joined the Rams.

Graham Taylor, who has just been appointed England manager, greets his successor Dr Jozef Venglos, an imaginative appointment which, alas, did not work out.

David Platt
— Goals from Midfield

IT'S a long way from Crewe Alexandra's homely but basic Gresty Road ground to the heady atmosphere of the World Cup finals in Italy, but that was the leap which David Platt made to establish himself as an international-class who brought a remarkable £5.5 million into Aston Villa's coffers after Italia 90.

Platt, the man released by Manchester United when Ron Atkinson was manager at Old Trafford, had established himself as one of the games's leading midfield players after his performances for England as they reached the World Cup semi-finals. And it was in the Stadio Dall'Ara in Bologna that Platt became a national hero when his brilliant goal against Belgium, 30 seconds from the end of extra-time, earned England a victory which clinched their place in the last eight.

Platt's value was increased by that flair for goals which made him a very special commodity indeed — a midfielder who could find the net. His strike-rate for Villa was certainly impressive — 68 goals in only 155 senior appearances — and persuaded Bari to pay £5.5 million to take Platt into the Italian Serie A in August 1991.

He could hardly have imagined such a move when he started out in the game. Platt was born in Oldham in June 1966, just before England won the World Cup for the only time, and after playing briefly with the local Chadderton club, he signed professional forms for Manchester United in July 1984.

But he never made the first team at Old Trafford and in January 1985 he was released on a free transfer to Dario Gradi's Crewe Alexandra. At Gresty Road, Platt soon forced his way into the first team and developed quickly in the lower reaches of the League. After 61 goals in 152 League and Cup games for Crewe, he was transferred to Villa for £200,000 in January 1988.

Villa had been relegated the previous season and were now fighting their way back to the top flight. Platt came into the side for a game at Ewood Park and scored on his debut, although Villa went down 3-2 to Blackburn that day. He scored again in the next match, a 5-2 romp over Plymouth, and in the next, a 2-1 win at Bournemouth. Villa's promotion challenge wavered but they picked themselves up to finish runner-up. Platt's contribution was five goals in 11 appearances.

The following season, when Villa finished 17th in the First Division, the highlight of their campaign was a run to the quarter-finals of the Littlewoods Cup. Platt will have special memories of that because in the fourth round against Ipswich Town, he scored four times in a 6-2 win. That season he was ever-present

and the following season he missed only one League game as Villa finished runners-up.

Platt's full England debut came as a substitute against Italy at Wembley in November 1989, when he replaced Peter Beardsley, and by the time he left Villa, he had played 23 times for his country.

In 1990-91, his last season with Villa, Platt scored 19 League goals in 35 matches, including a hat-trick when Tottenham were beaten 3-2 at Villa Park in March.

After the World Cup finals, he had been the target of several European clubs but had decided to stay with Villa for one more season. Eventually, the pull of a multi-million pound move to what has been described as the most compeitive league in the world was too much for an ambitious young man.

Alas, Platt had a disappointing first season and Bari were relegated, transferring the Englishman to Juventus in 1992, where again his career in Italian football did not really take off. Yet there was no denying his tremendous skill, a player who loves to drive forward from midfield, a skilful footballer with great stamina and the ability to turn a game instantly.

New boss Jozef Venglos shows his players an exercise before the start of 1990-91.

Above: Derek Mountfield scores Villa's equaliser in the UEFA Cup first-round second-leg match against Banik Ostrava in Czechoslovakia in October 1990. *Below:* Derek Mountfield (5) and Chris Price celebrate Mountfield's strike in the home leg.

Chris Price, joined Villa from Blackburn Rovers for £125,000 in June 1988.

Cup, Villa beat Banik Ostrava of Czechoslovakia and were rewarded with a plum tie against the Italians, Inter-Milan. A crowd of 36,461 were in Villa Park to see the first leg with millions more watching the match live on television. They witnessed a superb Villa performance.

After 15 minutes, Villa took the lead when goalkeeper Walter Zenga blocked Platt's effort, only to watch helplessly as Kent Nielsen hammered the ball back past him from 30 yards. In the 68th minute, Villa went 2-0 ahead when Platt scored a fine goal from Cowans' measured pass.

It was a great Villa victory and Platt had been quite superb. The only pity was that Villa could not have extended their lead, for they had the chances to do so. Two goals was perhaps not enough to take to the San Siro Stadium and so it proved, for Villa were beaten 3-0, their European dream shattered.

Villa were lying ninth in Division One at this stage, handily placed for an assault on the title, but after more Cup defeats, against Wimbledon in the FA Cup and Leeds United in the Rumbelows Cup (the latest name for the League Cup), their season fell apart.

In February, Venglos at last moved into the transfer market, selling Paul Birch to Wolves for £400,000 and spending £400,000 on Scunthorpe's Neil Cox (who had to wait for the following season for his debut) and Watford striker Gary Penrice arrived in early March for £800,000.

Penrice was signed to improve

Villa's Kent Nielsen fires home their first goal in the UEFA Cup second-round first-leg game against Inter-Milan at Villa Park in October 1990.

David Platt celebrates his goal – Villa's second – against Inter-Milan at Villa Park.

Inter-Milan's Nicola Berti tips the ball away from David Platt in the return leg. Villa went down 3-0 in Italy to lose 3-2 on aggregate.

Villa's scoring rate but he did not really fit the bill and when the side won only five of their last 19 games of the season, it pushed them down into 17th place.

The great success had been David Platt, leading scorer again, this time with 24 goals in all games including 19 in the League, and that sort of form meant that he was on the verge of a multi-million transfer out of British football.

DIVISION 1   1990-91

	P	W	D	L	F	A	W	D	L	F	A	Pts
Arsenal	38	15	4	0	51	10	9	9	1	23	8*	83
Liverpool	38	14	3	2	42	13	9	4	6	35	27	76
Crystal P	38	11	6	2	26	17	9	3	7	24	24	69
Leeds U	38	12	2	5	46	23	7	5	7	19	24	64
Manchester C	38	12	3	4	35	25	5	8	6	29	28	62
Manchester U	38	11	4	4	34	17	5	8	6	24	28†	59
Wimbledon	38	8	6	5	28	22	6	8	5	25	24	56
Nottingham F	38	11	4	4	42	21	3	8	8	23	29	54
Everton	38	9	5	5	26	15	4	7	8	24	31	51
Tottenham H	38	8	9	2	35	22	3	7	9	16	28	49
Chelsea	38	10	6	3	33	25	3	4	12	25	44	49
QPR	38	8	5	6	27	22	4	5	10	17	31	46
Sheffield U	38	9	3	7	23	23	4	4	11	13	32	46
Southampton	38	9	6	4	33	22	3	3	13	25	47	45
Norwich C	38	9	3	7	27	32	4	3	12	14	32	45
Coventry C	38	10	6	3	30	16	1	5	13	12	33	44
Aston Villa	38	7	9	3	29	25	2	5	12	17	33	41
Luton T	38	7	5	7	22	18	3	2	14	20	43	37
Sunderland	38	6	6	7	15	16	2	4	13	23	44	34
Derby Co	38	3	8	8	25	36	2	1	16	12	39	24

*Arsenal had two points deducted for disciplinary reasons.
†Manchester United had one point deducted for disciplinary reasons.

Far left: Gary Penrice had only a brief career at Villa Park after coming from Watford. After only 14 full appearances he was transferred to QPR. *Left:* Andy Comyn.

Platt scores the first goal of his hat-trick against Tottenham Hotspur at Villa Park in March 1991. Villa won 3-2.

Lee Sharpe scores Manchester United's equalising goal in their 5-1 win at Villa Park in April 1991.

Other players already on their way were Tony Cascarino (to Celtic), young central defender Andy Comyn (to Derby County) and reserve goalkeeper Lee Butler (to Barnsley).

Jozef Venglos also left, returning to Czechoslovakia after failing to build on the situation that Graham Taylor had left him. His successor would be a very different figure from the studious Eastern European.

David Platt with the ball with which he scored his hat-trick against Tottenham. The goals took Platt's total of League goals from 97 to 100.

So Near And Yet . . .

IN JULY 1991, Aston Villa announced that Ron Atkinson, the former Manchester United boss, was to be their new manager is succession to Jozef Venglos. It was a controversial appointment because Atkinson had just led Sheffield Wednesday to a Rumbelows Cup victory at Wembley, having previously taken them back to Division One, and had publicly pledged himself to the Owls for another season.

But the chance of managing Aston Villa was too great a temptation for a man who had been a part-timer with Villa in the 1950s and who still lived in the Birmingham area, commuting each day to Hillsborough.

Atkinson had a flamboyant image — big cigars, champagne and gold jewellery appeared to be his trade marks — and he soon set about spending big sums of money, buying £5 million-worth of playing talent for Villa, but at the same time making the club a handsome profit by raising some £9 million in sales.

The biggest outgoing transfer was that of David Platt. It was obvious after Italia 90 that Villa would find it impossible to hold on to an ambitious player of his talent and in August 1991, Platt moved to Bari, the Italian Serie A club, for a staggering £5.5 million.

Others who went during the season included Gareth Williams (to Barnsley for £200,000 in August) and Stuart Gray (to Southampton for £200,000 in September), whilst Ian Ormondroyd went on loan to hard-up Derby until they could afford to pay for him in December, when Villa reaped £350,000.

Gary Penrice's career at Villa Park had been a short one and he was transferred to QPR in October for

Cheers! Chairman Doug Ellis and new manager Ron Atkinson toast the future at Villa Park in July 1991.

Above: Cyrille Regis gets in a header against Wimbledon at Villa Park in October 1991. *Far left:* Kevin Gage, signed from Wimbledon in July 1987 and moved to Sheffield United in November 1991. *Left:* Ian Ormondroyd joined Villa in 1989 and moved to Derby in September 1991.

£625,000 after one goal in 20 games for Villa, six of those appearances coming as a substitute. The same month winger Paul Mortimer, who had been bought from Charlton for £350,000 only three months earlier moved to Palace for £500,000 and in November, ambitious Blackburn paid £200,000 for Gordon Cowans. After the turn of the year, Kevin Gage was sold to Sheffield United for £150,000, Derek Mountfield, after a lengthy loan spell at Molineux, moved to Wolves for a similar figure and Chris Price joined Cowans at Ewood Park, for £150,000.

Atkinson's incoming players included Shaun Teale (from Bournemouth for £300,000 in July), and the August signings of former Sheffield Wednesday striker Dalian Atkinson (from Real Sociedad for £1.6 million), midfielder Kevin Richardson (from the same Spanish club, for £400,000) and Republic of Ireland full-back

Derek Mountfield, joined Wolves in March 1992 for £150,000 after a spell on loan at Molineux.

Dwight Yorke scores for Villa against Notts County at Villa Park in November 1991. It was the only goal of the game.

Paul McGrath is first to the ball as Leeds United's Rodney Wallace challenges him at Villa Park later that month. Yorke scored again but this time Villa went down 4-1.

Steve Staunton (from Liverpool for £1.4 million).

At the other end of the scale, Cyrille Regis was allowed a free-transfer move from Coventry and goalkeeper Les Sealey was also a free-transfer signing from Manchester United. Sealey came as cover for Nigel Spink but from October to February he found himself first choice and helped Villa into the quarter-finals of the FA Cup before being allowed to go to Coventry City, on loan following a four-game suspension and a £2,000 fine after an incident involving the referee of a match against Sheffield Wednesday.

In November, Villa signed Nottingham Forest's midfielder Garry Parker for £650,000 and in February 1992, Oldham's England international central defender Earl Barrett moved to Villa Park for £1.7 million. The Polish international right-back Dariusz Kubicki, signed from Legia Warsaw at the start of the season, was introduced into the side at the end of August but eventually lost his place when Barrett came from Boundary Park.

Ironically, the Football League fixtures computer sent Villa to Atkinson's former club, Sheffield Wednesday, on the opening day of the season and three newcomers — Dalian Atkinson, Regis and Staunton — all scored on their debut as Villa won 3-1 before a near-37,000 crowd.

The first home game was against another of Atkinson's former clubs,

Villa goalkeeper Les Sealey looks typically angry after Paul McGrath (5) is felled during the FA Cup fifth-round tie against Swindon Town at the County Ground in February 1992. Villa won 2-1 but lost 1-0 to Liverpool in the quarter-final.

Left: Les Sealey, ousted Nigel Spink. *Right:* Dariusz Kubicki, signed from Legia Warsaw.

Manchester United, but this time Villa went down, losing 1-0 to a Steve Bruce penalty. Then came a magnificent 3-1 victory over champions Arsenal and after a wobble which brought only one victory in eight games, Villa strung together five consecutive League wins. By mid-November, Villa had climbed to fourth place in the table.

The shape of the team was gradually changing and with Atkinson suffering from injury, Ian Olney was now partnering Regis up front. Tony Daley had now won full England honours but he, too, was plagued by injury and yet when he was available he gave full value, none more so than his brilliant goal against Manchester City at Villa Park in early December when he hit a stunning volley in Villa's 3-1 win.

By now, Garry Parker had replaced Cowans in midfield and into the new year, Villa were still chasing two major competitions. They had been knocked out of the League Cup, on aggregate against Grimsby Town at the first hurdle, but the FA Cup brought a 1-0 replay win over Tot-

Berliners Matthias Breitkreutz (left) and Stefan Beinlich, (right) who both joined Villa from East German League club Bergmann Borsig in October 1991 for a combined fee of £200,000. Both made a contribution at Villa Park.

tenham before a sensational night at Derby's Baseball Ground where Villa eventually emerged 4-3 winners after a breathtaking Cup tie. Dwight Yorke scored a hat-trick, despite missing two penalties. Peter Shilton saved them both, although Yorke managed to hit one rebound into the net.

Villa beat Swindon 2-1 in the next round before losing 1-0 at Anfield in the quarter-finals.

That Cup defeat effectively signalled the end of Villa's season. Thereafter they fell away badly and scoring goals became a major problem. Indeed, in 14 League games up to early April, Villa managed to find the net only four times and in two separate five-match sequences they failed to score.

It was quite remarkable, then, that on 4 April, Villa managed to rattle in five against Tottenham at White Hart Lane. The goals did not flow again quite so impressively after that, but Villa did manage a 1-0 victory over Liverpool before a crowd of 35,755 at Villa Park.

DIVISION 1 1991-92											
	P	W	D	L	F	A	W	D	L	F	A	Pts
Leeds U	42	13	8	0	38	13	9	8	4	36	24	82
Manchester U	42	12	7	2	34	13	9	8	4	29	20	78
Sheffield W	42	13	5	3	39	24	8	7	6	23	25	75
Arsenal	42	12	7	2	51	22	7	8	6	30	24	72
Manchester C	42	13	4	4	32	14	7	6	8	29	34	70
Liverpool	42	13	5	3	34	17	3	11	7	13	23	64
Aston Villa	42	13	3	5	31	16	4	6	11	17	28	60
Nottingham F	42	10	7	4	36	27	6	4	11	24	31	59
Sheffield U	42	9	6	6	29	23	7	3	11	36	40	57
Crystal P	42	7	8	6	24	25	7	7	7	29	36	57
QPR	42	6	10	5	25	21	6	8	7	23	26	54
Everton	42	8	8	5	28	19	5	6	10	24	32	53
Wimbledon	42	10	5	6	32	20	3	9	9	21	33	53
Chelsea	42	7	8	6	31	30	6	6	9	19	30	53
Tottenham H	42	7	3	11	33	35	8	4	9	25	28	52
Southampton	42	7	5	9	17	28	7	5	9	22	27	52
Oldham A	42	11	5	5	46	36	3	4	14	17	31	51
Norwich C	42	8	6	7	29	28	3	6	12	18	35	45
Coventry C	42	6	7	8	18	15	5	4	12	17	29	44
Luton T	42	10	7	4	25	17	0	5	16	13	54	42
Notts Co	42	7	5	9	24	29	3	5	13	16	33	40
West Ham U	42	6	6	9	22	24	3	5	13	15	35	38

In the penultimate game, a 2-0 defeat at Luton, Ron Atkinson gave a League debut to young Australian goalkeeper Mark Bosnich, who had been signed on the transfer deadline after paying up the remaining six months of his contract with Sydney Croatia so that he could try his luck in English football for a second time. Bosnich had earlier been with Manchester United.

Villa ended the season with a 2-0 win over Coventry City, which

pushed them into a final position of seventh in the First Division, and then looked towards a 'new age' of football as they prepared for the new FA Premier League in 1992-93.

Yet when the curtain came down on the first-ever Premier League season, it was a case of so near and yet so far for Aston Villa. Finishing runners-up to Manchester United was certainly a very commendable performance for Ron Atkinson's side. But it could have been so much better — the championship trophy itself was there for the taking at one stage towards the end of the campaign.

On 4 April, after beating Nottingham Forest 1-0 away, Villa took over again at the top — they had held the lead before, in February and in March — but this time they were in form and games were fast running out.

Alas, a goalless home draw with Coventry was not the result Villa wanted and the same day they were toppled by Manchester United, who held pole position right through to the end.

Far left: Ian Olney, moved to Oldham at the start of 1992-93. *Left:* Mark Blake, loaned to Wolves in January 1991 but returned to Villa Park.

On reflection the season had been a very good one for Aston Villa, the country's fourth biggest-spending club behind Blackburn, Derby County and Liverpool.

And if someone had told manager Ron Atkinson around early September that Villa will qualify for Europe in 1993-94, he would have been a delighted man, of course. But after coming so close to glory, he left the dug-out at Loftus Road on the last day of the season, somewhat disappointed. For he knew that Villa had come so close to taking the star prize in English football.

For Villa fans there was also the worry that Atkinson was being linked with the Liverpool job. Although

Garry Parker celebrates his goal against Liverpool in September 1992.

Above: Dean Saunders, recently transferred from Liverpool, scores his second goal against the Merseysiders at Villa Park in September 1992. **Below:** Saunders congratulates Dalian Atkinson on his goal against Liverpool.

that wasn't vacant, the Merseysiders' failures in 1992-93 had brought Graeme Souness' position at Anfield into question. And it was inevitable that a man of Atkinson's stature would be mentioned as a replacement.

Villa, in fact, had not begun the season too well, drawing three and losing one of their opening four League games.

Their first win came on 29 August — 2-0 at Sheffield United — but at this juncture goalscoring was causing concern. Enter Dean Saunders — signed from Liverpool for £2.2m in September — and what a start the Welsh international striker made with his new club.

He scored twice on his debut — against his previous club — and his presence alongside Dalian Atkinson in the front line, triggered off a terrific run of results, Villa increasing their run to 13 League and Cup games without defeat and moving up to fourth in the table.

A 3-2 home lapse against Norwich

Paul McGrath
— The Ultimate Battler

AFTER Paul McGrath joined Aston Villa from Manchester United in August 1989, for £400,000, he became an instant success with the club, where his utter commitment to the Villa cause was appreciated by the fans, whether he performed in the centre of defence or midfield.

Born in Ealing in December 1959, McGrath went to Dublin as a youngster and established himself as a leading schoolboy player in the Republic before joining League of Ireland club, St Patrick's Athletic. Manchester United's Irish scouting network is well known and in March 1982, McGrath joined the Old Trafford staff for what turned out to be a bargain fee of £30,000.

McGrath repaid the fee many times over. He won his first full Republic of Ireland caps whilst with Manchester United and in 1985 he was one of the United stars in the FA Cup Final defeat of Everton.

McGrath had battled hard for a first-team place with United, a strong player who was totally committed to the cause. He made his first appearance in the Reds' senior side before the start of the 1982-83 season, in a South Atlantic Fund match against Aldershot, but had to wait until November that season for his League debut, when he took over from Kevin Moran for a 1-0 win at home to Spurs, having been given his first competitive run-out three days earlier in a Milk Cup tie against Bradford City.

In his early days he was held back by a series of niggling injuries but after regaining his place midway through 1984-85 he held on to take an FA Cup winners's medal and went on to make 198 League and Cup appearances, scoring 16 goals, before Graham Taylor took him to Villa Park for the start of the 1989-90 season.

By then McGrath was a full-fledged Republic of Ireland international, having made his debut as a substitute against Italy in 1985, and he also represented the Football League against the Rest of the World XI in the League's centenary match at Wembley in 1987.

He had appeared 31 times for the Irish and at the end of his first season with Villa went to Italy for the World Cup finals. McGrath was one of his country's stars as they reached the quarter-finals before losing 1-0 to Italy.

In that first season with Villa, McGrath had missed only three games, helping the club to runners-up spot in the First Division. He scored only once but it was a vital goal, coming in the 3-3 draw against Norwich City in the penultimate game of the season. He also helped Villa to the FA Cup quarter-finals.

In 1990-91, when Villa slipped to 17th place, McGrath again missed only three games and the following season he was absent from only one game as they climbed back to seventh and again reached the last eight of the FA Cup. During the season he took his overall tally of appearances past 300 and also took his full international caps well past the 50 mark.

When Villa chased the League championship in 1992-93, McGrath was again a linchpin. Besides his fierce competitive nature and skill, he was one of the coolest heads in the Villa side, especially vital when the pressure began to build up towards the dramatic run-in to the season. It did not go unnoticed by his fellow professionals, who voted him PFA Player of the Year.

Dalian Atkinson celebrates another goal, this time against Ipswich Town in the Coca-Cola Cup in December 1992.

Neil Cox (diving, centre) scores against Bristol Rovers in the FA Cup at Villa Park in January 1993.

Paul McGrath is happy. He has just scored the only goal of the game against Nottingham Forest at the City Ground in March 1993.

Former Villa junior Steve Froggatt, playing well until he was injured.

Dwight Yorke wheels away after scoring the winner against Wimbledon at Villa Park in February 1992.

City disrupted progress briefly before the show got back on the road again.

An exit from the Rumbelows League Cup, at Ipswich, and a 3-0 reverse in the League at Coventry were only minor blemishes on a sequence of outstanding displays which saw Villa produce some exciting, all-action football. Middlesbrough (5-1), Liverpool (2-1 at Anfield), Sheffield United (3-1) and Bristol Rovers (3-0 in the FA Cup) were brushed aside, although occasionally a mediocre performance crept in. Wimbledon knocked Villa out of the FA Cup (winning a replay on penalties) and both Southampton and Crystal Palace took the honours in away League games.

But generally it was Villa who called the tune and another unbeaten run, this time spanning six matches, four of which were won, pushed them into top spot with eight games remaining. A 1-0 lapse at Carrow Road against Norwich allowed Manchester United to close the gap and indeed, the Canaries took over the number one place.

But Paul McGrath's powerful header brought victory at the City

Steve Staunton scores a spectacular goal at Old Trafford in March 1993, when Villa earned a 1-1 draw against their League championship rivals.

Ground and it was all to play for as the pace hotted up with Villa again League leaders.

The biggest crowd of the season — 38,543 — witnessed the 0-0 home draw with Coventry City on Easter Saturday — but the two points dropped saw Villa replaced at the top by Manchester United — and that is how it stayed until the end of an exhilarating season in which Aston Villa matched — and often bettered — the top sides in the land. In the end, though, they had to settle for second place in arguably the

world's toughest football league competition and United were confirmed as champions over the May Bank Holiday weekend, when Villa lost at home to Oldham, who were fighting against relegation.

Paul McGrath had a magnificent season, being voted the PFA Footballer of the Year. His fellow defender Shaun Teale was also outstanding along with left-back Steve Staunton and Earl Barrett. In midfield, Ray Houghton — a £900,000 buy from Liverpool in July 1992 — skipper Kevin Richardson and Garry Parker

FA PREMIER LEAGUE 1992-93											
	P	W	D	L	F	A	W	D	L	F	A	Pts
Manchester U	42	14	5	2	39	14	10	7	4	28	17	84
Aston Villa	42	13	5	3	36	16	8	6	7	21	24	74
Norwich C	42	13	6	2	31	19	8	3	10	30	46	72
Blackburn R	42	13	4	4	38	18	7	7	7	30	28	71
QPR	42	11	5	5	41	32	6	7	8	22	23	63
Liverpool	42	13	4	4	41	18	3	7	11	21	37	59
Sheffield W	42	9	8	4	34	26	6	6	9	21	25	59
Tottenham H	42	11	5	5	40	25	5	6	10	20	41	59
Manchester C	42	7	8	6	30	25	8	4	9	26	26	57
Arsenal	42	8	6	7	25	20	7	5	9	15	18	56
Chelsea	42	9	7	5	29	22	5	7	9	22	32	56
Wimbledon	42	9	4	8	32	23	5	8	8	24	32	54
Everton	42	7	6	8	26	27	8	2	11	27	28	53
Sheffield U	42	10	6	5	33	19	4	4	13	21	34	52
Coventry C	42	7	4	10	29	28	6	9	6	23	29	52
Ipswich T	42	8	9	4	29	22	4	7	10	21	33	52
Leeds U	42	12	8	1	40	17	0	7	14	17	45	51
Southampton	42	10	6	5	30	21	3	5	13	24	40	50
Oldham A	42	10	6	5	43	30	3	4	14	20	44	49
Crystal P	42	6	9	6	27	25	5	7	9	21	36	49
Middlesbrough	42	8	5	8	33	27	3	6	12	21	48	44
Nottingham F	42	6	4	11	17	25	4	6	11	24	37	40

The vital game against Manchester City in April 1993. *Above:* Good luck wishes from United's greatest rivals. *Right (top):* Dalian Atkinson congratulates Dean Saunders on his goal. *Right (bottom):* Garry Parker has just scored against City. *Below:* Earl Barrett, outstanding for Villa.

were as good as any trio in the country while up front Saunders was Villa's leading scorer, his move from Liverpool fully justified.

It was unfortunate that Dalian Atkinson suffered injury for long periods, but he too put in some sterling work as did Dwight Yorke, Cyrille Regis and Tony Daley, who came back towards the end of the campaign after being out for quite some time.

In goal Villa initially used Nigel Spink but ended up with the Australian international Mark Bosnich,

Above: Relegation battlers Oldham Athletic proved too determined a hurdle for Villa and when Nicky Henry scored the only goal of the game (pictured here) it meant the end of Villa's League championship hopes. *Right:* Manager Ron Atkinson urges on his team but the title is slipping from Aston Villa's grasp. Oldham eventually survived and Villa, of course, had to be content with runners-up spot, but with all to play for in 1993-94.

who put in some grand performances, although some controversy now surrounded his signing.

Others who grafted hard and admirably in 1992-93 were defenders Ugo Ehiogu and Bryan Small, midfielder Neil Cox and winger Stephen Froggatt, all of whom won England Under-21 caps, with Ehiogu skippering his country against Holland at Portsmouth. The two Germans, Matthias Breitkreutz and Stefan Beinlich, also did well when called upon.

Aston Villa had a superb season and everyone associated with this famous Midlands club is now looking forward to 1993-94 with great optimism and confidence, with another European adventure in store.

Thanks for your support – we'll be back: Dean Saunders, Villa's leading scorer in 1992-93, salutes the magnificent fans after the defeat by Oldham ended their League championship dreams.

Villa's Thrillers of '93

Nigel Spink
He regained his place and took his appearances tally to well over 400 in 1992-93 before missing the end of the season.

Mark Bosnich
The Australian took over from Spink and established himself as one of the leading 'keepers in the country. He had previously been with Manchester United.

Earl Barrett
The former Oldham defender and England international added such stability to Villa's battle for the title after joining them for a seven-figure fee.

Steve Staunton
The Republic of Ireland international joined Aston Villa from Liverpool and found himself in a championship-chasing side once more.

Shaun Teale
The former Everton apprentice who joined Aston Villa from Bournemouth and was so outstanding alongside Paul McGrath in Villa's defence.

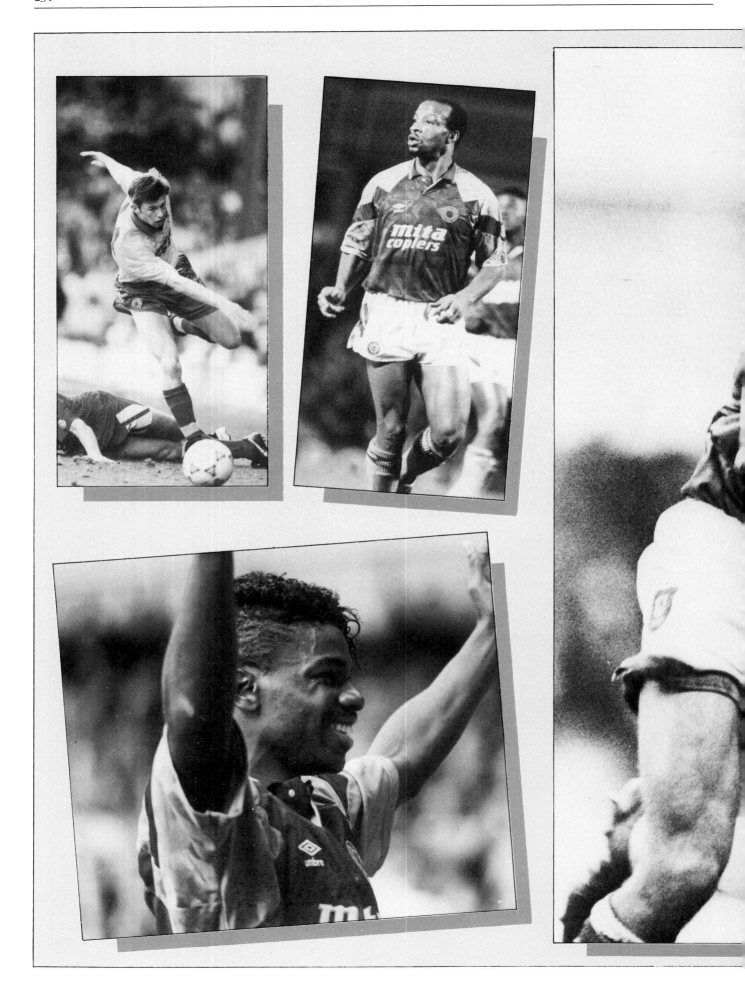

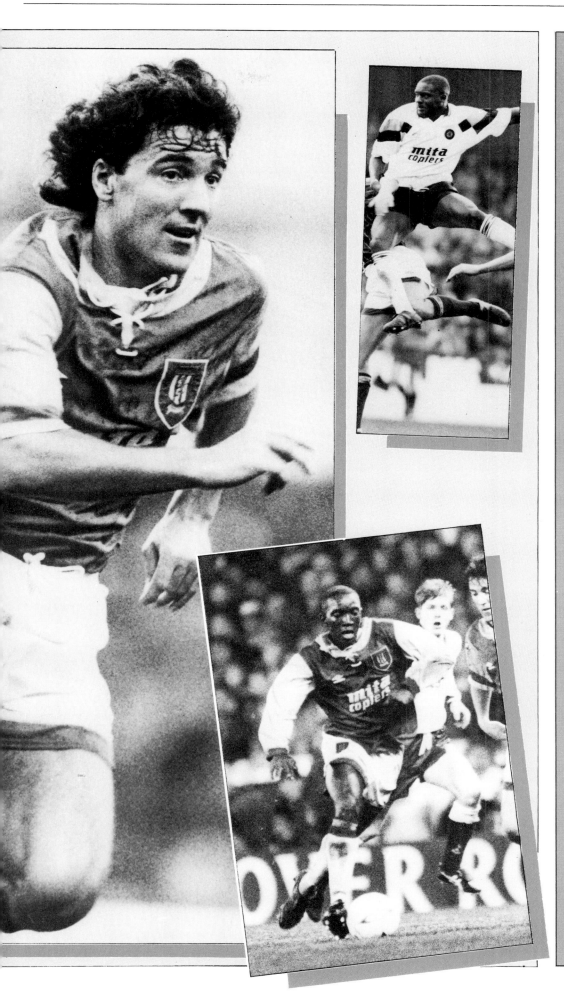

Ugochuko Ehiogu
Signed for a tribunal-fixed bargain fee from West Bromwich Albion, he became the first black player to captain an England team when he led the Under-21s against Holland at Fratton Park.

Neil Cox
He signed from Scunthorpe United and made useful contributions as a substitute in Villa's title-chasing campaign after they had paid £400,000 for a player with only six months' League experience.

Paul McGrath
The former Manchester United defender was voted PFA Player of the Year in 1993 as he proved such a great inspiration to Villa in their quest for the first FA Premier League title.

Kevin Richardson
The former Everton, Watford and Arsenal midfielder who joined Aston Villa from Real Sociedad and played with such distinction in seasons 1991-92 and 1992-93.

Garry Parker
The former Nottingham Forest midfielder who proved a fine striker of the ball, scoring some splendid goals after joining Villa.

Ray Houghton
Another Republic of Ireland international and another former Liverpool player who chased new honours with Aston Villa.

Steve Froggatt
The Lincoln-born junior who scored a spectacular goal in the FA Cup at Swindon and the following season of 1992-93 continued to show some exciting touches when given the chance.

Cyrille Regis
The big striker still enjoying some top-flight football with Aston Villa in 1993 after starting out with West Brom some 16 years earlier.

Tony Daley
The pacey winger who created such havoc in oppposing defences before being injured. He returned towards the end of the season, hitting the winner at Highbury.

Dean Saunders
He joined Aston Villa from Liverpool, soon netted twice against his old club and ended the season as Villa's leading scorer.

Dalian Atkinson
Signed by Ron Atkinson, his former manager at Hillsborough, he suffered injury in his first season at Villa Park but recovered to score some vital goals in 1992-93.

Dwight Yorke
Another exciting forward who joined Villa as a junior. He also contributed some fine goals in 1992-93 and throughout his period at Villa Park has scored some brilliant individual efforts.

Above and below Villa Park has always been a fine stadium. It is pictured here some years ago, before further development. As 1994 approached, the ground took on an even more impressive look.

Artist's impression of the new £5 million double-decker cantilever stand scheduled to be open ready for the kick-off to the 1993-94 season.

New Witton Stand

WHEN Aston Villa ended the 1992-93 campaign, their supporters had a great deal to look forward to as the new season was only three months away. Not least, of course, was the prospect of their exciting team going one better and lifting the FA Premier League championship in 1994.

But a further reason to view the new season with great anticipation was yet another development which promised to make Villa Park, already one of the truly great football stadiums of the world, into an even more impressive arena.

In the programme for the home game against Manchester City on 18 April 1993, the club updated supporters about the new Witton Lane Stand, due to open the following August.

It was estimated that the stand — a double-decker cantilever construction which would double the capacity there from 5,000 to 10,000 — would cost around £5 million and at the same time meet all the requirements of Justice Taylor's Report into sports ground safety following the Hillsborough disaster.

Supporters were told: 'The futuristic Witton development will contain catering and comfort facilities for the public's enjoyment and convenience up to the high specifications admired elsewhere in the ground.

'But where the project is believed to be pioneering and unique in football is that the entire exercise is being carried out under in-house supervision rather than through a major construction company.

'For some ten years, Aston Villa have been, in effect, their own building company by using club expertise and labour or sub-contracting where necessary.

'Now Villa are the first club to undertake a full stand construction in this way. And it reduces the outlay by at least half-a-million pounds, in addition to controlling cash flow.'

Attendance Facts & Figures

Progressive Home Attendance Records for Villa League Games

10,000	v West Bromwich A	19 January 1888
12,000	v Preston North End	9 February 1889
12,100	v West Bromwich A	27 September 1890
14,000	v Everton	28 December 1891
16,000	v Sunderland	17 September 1892
18,000	v Blackburn R	24 March 1894
20,000	v Small Heath	1 September 1894
35,000	v Wolverhampton W	19 April 1897
42,000	v Sheffield U	15 January 1898
50,000	v Sheffield U	3 March 1900
50,885	v Manchester U	22 April 1911
55,064	v West Bromwich A	21 September 1912
59,740	v Sunderland	23 April 1913
66,094	v West Bromwich A	6 November 1920
68,029	v Coventry C	30 October 1937
68,099	v Wolverhampton W	26 December 1947
68,354	v Manchester U	19 February 1949
69,492	v Wolverhampton W	27 December 1949

Progressive Home Attendance Records for Villa FA Cup Games

4,000	v Stafford Road	24 January 1880
5,000	v Stafford Road	19 February 1881
6,000	v Nottingham Forest	5 November 1881
7,000	v Notts County	31 December 1881
12,000	v Notts County	14 Janaury 1882
22,088	v West Bromwich A	3 January 1885
26,849	v Preston North End	7 January 1888
40,000	v Nottingham Forest	23 February 1901
47,000	v Sunderland	7 February 1903
49,734	v Bristol C	8 January 1921
50,627	v Huddersfield T	19 February 1921
54,000	v Luton T	28 January 1922
60,015	v West Bromwich A	25 February 1925
71,446	v Arsenal	20 February 1926
73,686	v Arsenal	2 March 1929
74,626	v Walsall	25 January 1930
75,540	v Manchester C	5 March 1938
76,588	v Derby County	2 March 1946

Highest Attendances for Villa Games

121,919	v Sunderland, FA Cup Final, The Crystal Palace	19 April 1913
110,000	v German Select XI, Friendly, Reichssportfield, Berlin	15 May 1937
101,117	v Newcastle United, FA Cup Final, The Crystal Palace	15 April 1905
99,225	v Manchester United, FA Cup Final, Wembley	4 May 1957
97,024	v Tottenham Hotspur, League Cup Final, Wembley	27 February 1971
96,223	v Everton, League Cup Final, Wembley	12 March 1977
95,946	v Norwich City, League Cup Final, Wembley	1 March 1975
92,445	v Tottenham Hotspur, FA Charity Shield, Wembley	22 August 1981
91,645	v Newcastle United, FA Cup Final, Wembley	26 April 1924

Lowest Attendances at Villa Park
(For competitive games involving Villa's first team)

2,900	v Bradford City, Division One	13 February 1915
3,000	v Derby County, Division One	6 September 1902
4,000	v Nottingham Forest, Division One	30 April 1898
4,000	v Notts County, Division One	21 April 1906
4,217	v Bradford City, Simod Cup	11 November 1987
4,500	v Nottingham Forest, Division One	16 April 1904
4,500	v Everton, Division One	10 February 1915
4,850	v Sheffield Wednesday, Division One	28 April 1913
5,000	v Sheffield Wednesday, Division One	30 March 1901
5,000	v Everton, Division One	12 September 1904
5,124	v Derby County, Full Members' Cup	12 November 1986
6,000	v Derby County, Division One	3 February 1900

Above does not take into account the European Cup match against Beşiktaş, played behind closed doors at Villa Park on 15 September 1982.

The three Football League Cup Finals (the original game plus two replays) between Aston Villa and Everton in 1977 saw an aggregate attendance of 205,812.

A record Central League crowd of 23,667 saw Tom 'Pongo' Waring make his debut in an Aston Villa shirt, against Birmingham Reserves at Villa Park in February 1928.

FA Cup
Villa's lowest home FA Cup attendance at Villa Park is 12,205 v Millwall, 25 January 1986.

League Cup
Villa Park's lowest 'gate' for a League Cup match is 7,678 v Exeter City, 9 October 1985.

Charlton Athletic's former home at The Valley had an attendance record of 75,031, set against Aston Villa for an FA Cup match on 12 March 1938.

Plymouth Argyle's record attendance for Home Park is 43,686, set when Villa drew 2-2 in a Second Division match there on 10 October 1936.

A record crowd of 48,745 at Vale Park saw an FA Cup match between Port Vale and Villa on 20 February 1960.

Villa chairman Doug Ellis, guiding through plans to take Villa Park into the 21st century as one of the truly great football stadiums.

Subscribers

1 Aston Villa FC
2 The Football Association
3 Douglas Ellis Esq
4 Steven Stride Esq
5 Ron Atkinson Esq
6 J A Harris
7 Andrew Clayton
8 Hannah Mary Kirby
9 Craig Wilson
10 Steven Wilson
11 Neil Strevens
12 James Alexander Curry
13 Terry Williams (Bedford)
14 K W Powell
15 Ron Jenkins
16 Mr John A Gould
17 R A Clarkson
18 Robert Panting
19 Kevin David Roberts
20 John Treadwell
21 Bobby Mendonca
22 Jason Hateley
23 Richard & Dan Ford
24 K J Knowles
25 Philip Lofthouse
26 Richard Andrew French
27 Ashley G Bowerman
28 John K Mackin
29 Stuart Murray (Bedford)
30 Paul Joiner
31 Mr S M Legge
32 Robert James Upton
33 Carl Priest
34 Neil Witcomb
35 Edward Thomas Foster
36 Mr A Nicholls
37 David, Robert & Lucy
    Turner
38 Philip O'Toole
39 Mr Stephen Sparks
40 Miss Jennifer Lowe
41 William John Bailey
42 Philip Gray
43 Phil Hawthorne
44 Robert A C Smith MA
45 Joel Sean Smith
46 Ray Pearson
47 David R Howarth
48 Gary James
49 Rob Hale
50 Anthony Lavelle
51 Anthony Woolley
52 Mick Brown
53 Stuart T Swann
54 Stephen David Garner
55 Elizabeth Dunbar
56 Michael Dolby
57 Steve Ewer
58 Antony Richard Joyner
59 Jane Amanda Boyce

60 Mr Nigel Iwanski
61 Robert Gough
62 Mr Michael Murphy
63 Christopher Deakin
64 H John Desaulles
65 Sue & Mick Tilt
66 Penny Willits
67 P S Patterson
68 Adrian Thorne
69 S J Humpherson
70 Carl Yates
71 Barry Curtis
72 Mark 'H' Homer
73 Mr E C Ashenford
74 David Foster
75 Sarah L Kennedy
76 Susan Pudge
77 Mark Preston
78 John Hall
79 Mr J R Onyon
80 Kevin Portley
81 Mr R J Bunn
82 Brian Hartley
83 Derek T Hough
84 Brian J Maybury
85 Gary D Sewell
86 Alan Robert Wilkinson
87 Brian C Seadon
88 Oliver Eagle
89 Gary Walden
90 D J Hodges
91 A L Brusch
92 Richard R Carter
93 Steve Knott
94 Simon Foxall
95 C R Brown
96 David Warman
97 Jack Pinnock
98 Paul Dann
99 Mr John Oates
100 Rob Rodway
101 Christine & Ian Rossiter
102 Peter Harrold
103 Phil Gautrey
104 Alan Gautrey
105 David John Edward Clayton
106 Adrian Chamberlain
107 Mr Adam Small
108 Gregory Upton BSc ACA
109 Mr R G Luckhurst
110 Matthew Stephen Allen
111 Andy Congrave
112 Andrew John Pitt
113 Norman Hughes
114 Malcolm Taylor
115 Patrick Gerard Healy
116 James Sinfield
117 Mark Hodges
118 Tim Evans
119 R Hemus

120 Stuart Sturmey
121 Brian Callaghan
122 Martin Lane
123 Ian R Lane
124 Colin R Walster
125 James Michael Deeley
126 Neil Wilson
127 Gareth C Jones
128 Richard Whitehead
129 Paul Biddlestone
130 Mark Alexander Smith
131 Kevin Gledhill
132 Peter Gledhill
133 Robert Coomber
134 Mathew Chapman
135 Mr Scott A Rumsey
136 David F Cox
137 Ralf Schulz
138 Damian Barrow
139 Stephen J Ellis
140 David John Elliman
141 Brian Thomas Berry
142 Helen Garfield
143 John Lacey
144 Robin Peck
145 Keith Harris
146 R L Davies
147 Kenny Hall
148 Martyn Harris
149 Ian David Sturgess
150 Michael J Daniels
151 Vera Ellen Ragsdale
152 Keith Feaver
153 Robert Hughes
154 Desmond O'Donoghue
155 Graham & Keith Rickett
156 Kevin Whittick
157 Kevin Whittick
158 David Cornforth
159 Graham & Neil Jinks
160 Paul Williams
161 Silvestre A Tangalan Jr
162 Arthur A Bent
163 Dr Robert Tighe
164 David Bridgewater
165 Pamela Bridgewater
166 Alfred Hoe
167 Simon Protheroe
168 David W Goodyear
169 Simon D Goodyear
170 Robert W Brooke
171 Sidney Eric Ablewhite
172 Abdul Rashid
173 Dennis Rye
174 J Ringrose
175 S Emms
176 Mr G M Briggs
177 Mike Young
178 Gerald Hill
179 David Keats